Bicycle Vacation Guide

Minnesota   Wisconsin
by Doug Shidell and Vicky Vogels
Little Transport Press   Minneapolis

Copyright Page

Cover art and design by Mike Wohnoutka
Interior production and design Shannon Brady and Mori Studio
Trail information Doug Shidell
Vacation information Vicky Vogels and Marie VanValkenberg
Maps Doug Shidell

08 07 06 05 04 03 02 01   10 9 8 7 6 5 4 3 2 1

Little Transport Press
P.O. Box 8123
Minneapolis, MN 55408

ISBN 0-9641238-7-8

Disclaimer: No road can be guaranteed safe. No trail is without hazards. Road and trail conditions can change without notice, and traffic conditions can change unexpectedly. The maps and descriptions are intended to aid in the selection of routes, but do not guarantee safety while riding. Use your best judgement. Ride at your own risk.

Acknowledgements

Special thanks to our researcher, Marie VanValkenberg, for making the phone calls and researching the tourist and travel information so critical to the development of Bicycle Vacation Guide. Special thanks also to Dave Olson for his critical looks at the maps for readability and accuracy.

Thanks to the Minnesota and Wisconsin Departments of Transportation and Departments of Natural Resources. Thanks also to Hennepin Parks, to Tom Lutz of Cass County and to William Johnson and Buz Swerkstrom for their help on the Gandy Dancer Trail. Mr. Johnson was instrumental in getting the Gandy Dancer Trail opened to bicyclists. Thanks to Thom Peterson for road route information along the Heartland Trail and Mike Anderson for route information near Eau Claire and the Chippewa Valley Trail.

Preface

New bicycle trails don't just happen. They are the result of strong citizen support, a well organized campaign and money. We at Little Transport Press are pleased to introduce you to the non-profit group most responsible for growing and protecting hundreds of miles of state trails in Minnesota. The Parks & Trails Council of Minnesota, in coordination with local advocacy groups, has played an essential role in creating the Gateway Trail, the Cannon Valley Trail, the Paul Bunyan Trail and many more trails in Minnesota.

Since 1954, the Parks & Trails Council has been in the business of saving special places across Minnesota. In the early days, with a small membership, the group was responsible for creating Afton, Fort Snelling and Grand Portage State Parks. In more recent years, they have added almost a mile of spectacular rocky shoreline to Split Rock Lighthouse State Park and helped fund the extension of the Root River Trail in southeastern Minnesota. During the decade from 1990 to 2000, the Parks & Trails Council purchased land valued at several million dollars throughout Minnesota for eventual use as parkland and trail corridors.

The Parks & Trails Council has made this second edition of *Bicycle Vacation Guide* possible, and essential. Because of their efforts and those of local trail advocacy groups, Minnesota has one of the highest number of trail miles in the country and more miles are being added each year. We don't mind. Researching new trails and updating existing trails is a joy for both of us.

We joined the Parks & Trails Council, and donated hundreds of our map sets for them to use as incentives for others to join, because we see their impact each time we update our guide. Today the Council feels the urgent need to grow to bring strength to its message at the State Capitol and to keep up with the growing number of important projects that it is asked to support. We urge you to join us in supporting the Parks & Trails Council of Minnesota. To learn more, visit their website at www.mnptc.org or call 651-281-0508. With your help, the Parks & Trails Council of Minnesota will be able to preserve more trails and parkland for our generation and that of many generations to come.

Sincerely,

Doug Shidell and Vicky Vogels

Little Transport Press

Table of Contents
(Legend for Maps on page M2)

Vital Information:

Trail Distance: 39 miles

Trail Surface: asphalt

Access Points: Grand Rapids, Coleraine, Bovey, Taconite, Hibbing, Chisholm, Buhl, Kinney, Mt Iron, Virginia, Gilbert

Fees and Passes: $5 per week $10 annual

Trail Website: www.irontrail.org

See Trail Map on page M3

ABOUT THE TRAIL

From Grand Rapids to Gilbert, the trail dips, rolls and twists its way from mining town to open pit. It skirts the edge of active mines and 300 foot deep pit lakes. It wanders down the back streets of small towns, hooks up with abandoned roads, and runs next to old rail lines with aspens sprouting between the rail ties. The Iron Range is full of history and everything from museums and mine views to the long hills of mine tailings reflects its active industrial past. The Mesabi Trail never wanders far from that history. The trail is being developed in sections. The 40 mile stretch from Grand Rapids to Kinney is finished in all but one 8 mile segment. The next largest section, from Mt. Iron to Gilbert, covers 11 miles. Eventually the trail will to be completed to Ely, for a total distance of 130 miles. This is an ideal trail for anyone who likes a few hills and a lot of history.

TRAIL HIGHLIGHTS

The 11 mile stretch from Mt Iron to Gilbert is the most charming, with the prettiest stretch between Gilbert and Virginia. In Virginia, follow Veteran's Drive through Olcott Park. Allow some time in the park to explore the greenhouse, relax near the fountain and enjoy the flower gardens. The Hibbing section is the richest in Iron Range history. The Greyhound Bus Origin Museum and Hull Rust Mahoning Mine View are both within blocks of the Hibbing Trailhead. The Trailhead in Grand Rapids starts from the north end of the fairgrounds, then skirts the edge of a pit lake where a huge

wedge of mine tailings juts into it like the prow of a ship in harbor. Later it crosses the Prairie River and works its way to the sleepy town of Taconite. If you have time, take the spur trail to Gunn Park, a donation from the Blandin Foundation.

ABOUT THE ROADS

Paved roads are limited in the area and the through routes usually carry a lot of traffic. It's possible to take short out and back trips from some of the towns but if you want to make loops on low traffic roads, expect to ride long sections of gravel.

ROAD ROUTE HIGHLIGHTS

None

HOW TO GET THERE

Highway 169 goes straight north from the Twin Cities to Grand Rapids, then connects the Range Cities along the trail. Turn south on Highways 53/135, near Virginia, and follow Highway 135 to the Gilbert trailhead. Highway 53 from Duluth runs due north to Virginia near the eastern end of the trail. Travel distance from the Twin Cities to the Range Cities is approximately 200 miles, depending on your destination.

Information Mesabi Trail

TOURIST INFORMATION

City of Gilbert City Hall
Phone (218) 741-9443
Fax (218) 741-9456
Email clerk@gilbertmn.org
Web www.gilbertmn.org

Grand Rapids Area Information Center
Toll Free (800) 472-6366
Phone (218) 326-6619
Email answers@visitgrandrapids.com
Web www.visitgrandrapids.com

City of Mountain Iron
Phone (218) 735-8890

Hibbing Tourist Information Center
Phone (218) 262-4166

Hibbing Area Chamber of Commerce
Toll Free (800) 444-2246
Phone (218) 262-3895
Email hibbcofc@hibbing.org
Web www.hibbing.org

Chisholm Area Chamber of Commerce
Toll Free (800) 422-0806
Phone (218) 254-7930
Email chisc@the-bridge.net
Web www.chisholmmnchamber.com

Virginia/Mt Iron Area Chamber
Phone (218) 741-2717
Email vchamber@virginiamn.com
Web www.mtiron.com,
www.virginiamn.com

Iron Trail Visitors Center
Toll Free (800) 777-8497
Phone (218) 749-8161
Web www.irontrail.org

LODGING

Motels/Resorts

Chisholm
Country Inn & Suites
Highway 169
Zip Code 55719
Toll Free (800) 456-4000
Phone (218) 254-2000

Grand Rapids
Forest Lake Motel
West Highway 2
Zip Code 55744
Toll Free (800) 622-3590
Phone (218) 326-6609

Best Western Rainbow Inn
1300 East Highway 169
Zip Code 55744
Toll Free (800) 528-1234
Phone (218) 326-9655

Country Inn
2601 South Highway 169
Zip Code 55744
Toll Free (800) 456-4000
Phone (218) 327-4960

Sawmill Inn
2301 Pokegama Ave South
Zip Code 55744
Toll Free (800) 804-8006
Phone (218) 326-8501

Super 8 Motel
Box 335 Highway 169 South
Zip Code 55744
Toll Free (800) 800-8000
Phone (218) 327-1108

AmericInn
1812 South Pokegama Ave
PO Box 435
Zip Code 55744
Toll Free (800) 634-3444
Phone (218) 326-8999
Fax (218) 326-9190

Itascan Motel
610 South Pokegama Ave
Zip Code 55744
Toll Free (800) 842-7733
Phone (218) 326-3489
Web www.itascan.com

Hibbing
Hibbing Park Hotel
Highway 169 & Howard St
Zip Code 55746
Toll Free (800) 262-3481
Phone (218) 262-3481

Arrowhead Motel
3701 West 2nd Ave
Zip Code 55746
Phone (218) 262-3477

Star Motel
3901 1st Ave
Zip Code 55746
Phone (218) 262-5728

Super 8 Motel
1411 40th St
Zip Code 55746
Toll Free (800) 800-8000
Phone (218) 263-8982

Mountain Iron/Virginia
AmericInn Motel & Suites
Highway 13
Zip Code 55768
Toll Free (800) 634-3444
Phone (218) 741-7839
Fax (218) 741-9050

Virginia
Ski View Motel
903 North 17th St
Zip Code 55792
Toll Free (800) 255-7106
Phone (218) 741-8918

Park Inn International
502 Chestnut St
Zip Code 55792
Toll Free (800) 777-4699
Phone (218) 749-1000

Voyageur North Motel
Highway 53 & 13th St South
Zip Code 55792
Toll Free (800) 235-3524
Phone (218) 741-9235

LODGING cont'd

Lakeshor Motor Inn Downtown
404 North 6th Ave
Zip Code 55792
Toll Free (800) 569-8131
Phone (218) 741-3360

Midway Motel
Highway 53 & Midway Rd
Zip Code 55792
Toll Free (800) 777-7956
Phone (218) 741-6145

Northern Motel
1705 North 9th Ave
Zip Code 55792
Phone (218) 741-8687

Super 8 Motel
Highway 53
Zip Code 55792
Toll Free (800) 800-8000
Phone (218) 744-1661

Bed and Breakfast

Hibbing
Adams House
201 East 23rd St
Zip Code 55746
Toll Free (888) 891-9742
Phone (218) 263-9742

Northland B & B
4859 First Ave
Zip Code 55746
Phone (218) 263-7864
Fax (218) 263-5642
Email radiator@uslink.net
Web www.innkeepersonly.com

Camping

Coleraine
Greenway Lions
PO Box 696
Zip Code 55722
Phone (218) 245-3382

Gilbert
Sherwood Forest Campground
Lake Ore-Be-Gone
Wisconsin Ave E
Zip Code 55741
Phone (218) 749-0703

Grand Rapids
Prairie Lake Campground & RV Park
30730 Wabana Rd
Zip Code 55744
Phone (218) 326-8486

Itasca County Fairgrounds
1336 Northeast 3rd Ave
Zip Code 55744
Phone (218) 326-6470

Hibbing
Button Box Lake State Forest
Campground
1208 East Howard St
Zip Code 55746
Phone (218) 262-6760

Bear Lake State Forest Campground
1208 East Howard St
Zip Code 55746
Phone (218) 262-6760

Forest Heights Campground
Zip Code 55746
Phone (218) 263-5782

Mountain Iron
West Two Rivers Campground
Recreation Area
Campground Rd
Zip Code 55768
Phone (218) 735-8831

RESTAURANTS

Biwabik
Vi's Pizza
Phone (218) 865-9983

Chisholm
Valentini's
Phone (218) 254-2607

Tom & Jerry's Bar & Lounge
Phone (218) 254-9980

Ethnic Restaurant–Ironworld
Discovery Center
Toll Free (800) 372-6437
Phone (218) 254-3321
Web www.ironworld.com

Grand Rapids
La Rosa's Mexican Restaurant
Phone (218) 327-4000

Forest Lake Restaurant & Lounge
Phone (218) 326-3423

Bridgeside Restaurant & Sports Bar
Phone (218) 326-0235

Negron's Bakery
Phone (218) 326-0801

Hong Kong Restaurant
Phone (218) 327-1131

New China Buffet
Phone (218) 327-1455

Home Town Cafe
Phone (218) 326-8646

Mad Dog's Pizza
Phone (218) 326-1774

Hibbing
Atrium Restaurant
Phone (218) 262-6145

Grandma's in the Park Bar & Grill
Toll Free (800) 262-3481

Hibbing Park Hotel
Toll Free (800) 262-3481
Phone (218) 262-3481

Virginia
Lynda's 4 Seasons Restaurant
Phone (218) 741-4200

Information Mesabi Trail

RESTAURANTS cont'd

Italian Bakery
Phone (218) 741-3464

Lakeshor Motor Inn
Toll Free (800) 569-8131
Phone (218) 741-3360

5th Avenue–Park Inn International
Phone (218) 749-1000

Scorecard Restaurant & Lounge
Phone (218) 749-2072

DeDe's Rainy Lake Saloon & Deli
Phone (218) 741-6247

GROCERIES

Chisholm
IGA
(218) 254-5723

Gilbert
IGA
(218) 749-6590

Grand Rapids
Gordy's Econo Foods
(218) 326-9695

Hibbing
Super One Foods
(218) 262-5275

Mt. Iron
IGA
(218) 735-8778

Virginia
Natural Harvest Food Coop
(218) 741-4663

Festival Foods
(218) 741-3229

BIKE REPAIR

Grand Rapids
Itasca Bike Ski and Fitness
Phone (218) 326-1716

Hibbing
Bikes on Howard
Phone (218) 262-0899
Fax (218) 262-0899
Email bikesonh@uslink.com

FESTIVALS AND EVENTS

Bovey
September
Bovey Farmers Day
Crafts fair, First Weekend

Chisholm
June
International Polka Fest
At Ironworld, non-stop polka music by
35 polka bands performing on 4 stages,
daily dance contest, Polka Hall of Fame
inductions, polka mass, ethnic food,
Fourth Weekend
Toll Free (800) 372-6437
Phone (218) 254-7959

Blues on the Range
At Ironworld, presented by Bayfront
Blues, showcases local and national
talent, Second Weekend
Phone (715) 394-6831

July
Festival Finlandia
At Ironworld, highlights Finnish history
of the area, includes Scandinavian
holiday, games, youth talent show,
Finnish market place, live music and
dance, food, language classes, Third
Weekend
Toll Free (800) 372-6437
Phone (218) 254-7959

August
St Louis County Fair
Exhibits, food, entertainment, midway,
at Ironworld, First Weekend
Toll Free (800) 372-6437
Phone (218) 254-7959

September
Chisholm Fire Days
Kiddie parade, softball tourney, city-
wide garage sales, food vendors,
street dance, Second Weekend
Toll Free (800) 422-0806
Phone (218) 254-7930

Gilbert
July
4th of July Celebration
Huge parade, street dance, and fireworks July 3rd, kiddie parade and
games July 4th
Phone (218) 741-9443

Sherwood Forest Days
Softball and volleyball tourneys, fishing
contest, kids' games, food vendors,
Third Weekend
Phone (218) 749-3837

Grand Rapids
July
Wood Craft Festival
Forest History Center, Third Weekend

August
Itasca County Fair
Itasca County Fairgrounds, Third
Weekend

FESTIVALS AND EVENTS cont'd

Hibbing
July
Mines and Pines Jubilee
Ten day celebration, parade, street dance, arts and crafts displays and sales, fly-in breakfast, golf tourney, radio flyer show, flea market, fireworks, ice-cream social, children's day events, Second Weekend
Toll Free (800) 444-2246
Phone (218) 262-3895

Mountain Iron
July
4th of July Celebration
Old-fashioned celebration, sports tourneys, polka bands, watermelon eating contest, five minute parade, First Weekend
Phone (218) 748-7570

August
Merritt Days
Commemorating the discovery of iron ore in the area, street dance, parade, pet show, live music, food vendors Second Weekend
Phone (218) 748-7570

Virginia
June
Land of the Loon Festival
At Olcott Park and downtown, parade, jugglers, food vendors, arts and crafts, music, Third Weekend
Phone (218) 749-5555

ALTERNATE ACTIVITIES

Biwabik
Giants Ridge
Over 75 miles of mountain biking trails, hiking trails, disc golf, 18 hole championship golf course

Toll Free (800) 688-7669
Phone (218) 865-4143
Fax (218) 865-4733
Email info@giantsridge.com
Web www.giantsridge.com

Chisholm
Ironworld Discovery Center
Tours, exhibits and climb-on equipment displays, electric trolley, concerts, living history exhibits, ethnic restaurant. Accessible via spur trail from the Mesabi Trail.
Toll Free (800) 372-6437
Phone (218) 254-3321
Web www.ironworld.com

Minnesota Museum of Mining
Mining trucks, steam locomotive, 1910 Atlantic steam shovel, early diamond drills, replica underground mine and mining town, open daily end of May to mid-Sept
Phone (218) 254-5543

Eveleth
Veteran's Lake Park
Swimming beach, picnic area
Phone (218) 744-1940

US Hockey Hall of Fame
Displays of enshrined players, exhibit and film library, shooting rink, Zamboni display, theater and gift shop, open year 'round
Toll Free (800) 443-7825
Phone (218) 744-5167

Gilbert
Iron Range Historical Museum
Includes sleds used by the Will Steger North Pole Expedition, mining exhibit and research library, open Mon–Wed & Sat May–Sept
Phone (218) 749-3150

Iron Range Historical Society
Photographs, artifacts, and memorablilia reflecting the area's heritage
Phone (218) 749-3150

Grand Rapids
Old Central School, turn of the century schoolhouse converted into marketplace, specialty shops, restaurant, Itasca County Historical Society Museum
Toll Free (800) 472-6366
Web www.grandmn.com

Forest History Center
Open air living history center operated by the Minnesota Historical Society, with full sized 1900 logging camp, costumed interpreters. Open 7 days a week, June 1–Oct 15.
Phone (218) 327-4482
Fax (218) 327-4483
Email foresthistory@mnhs.org

Mississippi Melody Showboat
Outdoor theater on the banks of the Mississippi, last three weekends of July
Phone (218) 326-4654

Judy Garland Birthplace
Restored childhood home, including Judy Garland memorabilia and the carriage from the Wizard of Oz, educational hands-on exhibits in the museum
Toll Free (866) 236-5437
Phone (218) 327-9276
Fax (218) 326-1934
Email education@cdmkids.org
Web www.judygarlandmuseum.com

K&K Stables
27734 Scenic Dr
Phone (218) 245-3814

Information Mesabi Trail

ALTERNATE ACTIVITIES cont'd

Hibbing

Palucci Space Theater
70mm wide-screen movies on various topics, multimedia presentations, gift shop, open year 'round, call for hours
Phone (218) 262-6720

Hibbing High School
National Register of Historic Places, hand painted murals, cut glass chandeliers, 1800 seat auditorium and more, open Mon-Sat (summers), by appointment during school year
Phone (218) 263-3675

Hull Rust Mahoning Mine
National Historic Place. World's largest open pit mine. Mine exhibits, scenic views, walking trail, at the Hibbing Trailhead, open daily mid-May–Sept
Phone (218) 262-4900

Greyhound Bus Origin Museum
Vintage buses, models and artifacts from the 1900s, open Mon-Sat 9am-5pm mid-May-Sept. Located at the Hibbing Trailhead.
Phone (218) 263-6485

Ore

Vince Shute Wildlife Sanctuary
View wildlife black bears in a natural setting from an elevated observation deck, open 5 until dusk summer evenings. about 20 miles north of Virginia.
Toll Free (800) 749-5555
Phone (218) 757-0172
Web www.americanbear.org

Virginia

Olcott Park Greenhouse
Profusion of flowers and plants, some exotic, some common household plants, Located in Olcott Park near the heart of Virginia, open daily June–Labor Day, weekdays rest of the year
Phone (218) 741-2149

Mineview in the Sky
Overlooks the Rouchleau Mine Group, the area's deepest mine. Accessible directly from the Trail via a steep driveway. Open daily May-Sept, 8 am–7 pm
Phone (218) 741-2344

Heritage Museum
Maintained by the Virginia Area Historical Society. Permanent exhibits housed in historical cabins and former park superintendent's residence.
Phone (218) 741-1136
Web www.virginia-mn.com

Vital Information:

Trail Distance: 28 miles

Trail Surface: asphalt

Access Points: Park Rapids, Dorset, Nevis, Akeley, Walker

Fees and Passes: none

See Trail Map on page M7

ABOUT THE TRAIL

From Park Rapids to Akeley, the land is quite flat with a mix of pine wood-lots, farmland and lakes. The trail passes through a glacial moraine between Akeley and Walker and the surrounding land becomes hilly and pine forested. The eleven Crow Wing Lakes along Highway 33 are examples of "kettles" formed when large blocks of ice from the retreating glacier were buried in dirt. Eventually the ice melted, leaving deep depressions, or "kettles" that filled with water.

TRAIL HIGHLIGHTS

Look for the fire tower on the south side of the trail, about 4 miles east of Park Rapids, then take the hard pack road to its base. The tower is climbable, but not for children or the faint of heart. Very few safety features and some missing steps make this a dangerous climb. Heartland Park in Park Rapids is a better place to start than the official trailhead on the south side of Highway 34. See city map. This is Paul Bunyan Country. The theme is overdone, but indulge in a little kitsch and sit in the hand of Paul. He's on one knee for you in the town of Akeley. Akeley also has the Woodtick Theater, featuring Country Music and other talent from within 100 miles of town. Stop for food in Dorset. This little town barely merits a wide spot in the road, but has Mexican Food, Italian Food, antique stores, etc.

ABOUT THE ROADS

The two routes between Park Rapids and Nevis feature medium sized rolling hills and a mosaic of lakes, woods and farmland. Watch and listen for Loons on the lakes and check out the moneyed homes along the eastern edge of Fish Hook Lake.

ROAD ROUTE HIGHLIGHTS

Highways 12 and 6 between Akeley and Hackensack offer a connector between the Heartland and Paul Bunyan Trails. These are great roads even if you just go out and come back. Highway 12 out of Walker is paved, low traffic and has a shoulder, then turns to gravel at the Hubbard County Line. It's a good 10 mile out and back route. There is a gravel road connector between Highway 12 and the trail, but the surface is loose, recommended for wide tired bikes only. Itasca State Park, not shown, is about 20 miles north of Park Rapids on Highway 71. Source of the Mississippi River, it is a beautiful, although heavily used, state park with a bike path through the populated eastern edge of the park and the wonderful, narrow, twisting Wilderness Drive. Some traffic along Wilderness Drive, but well worth the ride. Stop along the Drive to see the Minnesota Record Red Pine, hike the Big Pine Trail, and climb the observation tower.

HOW TO GET THERE

From the Twin Cities, take Interstate 94 west to Sauk Centre. Go north on Highway 71 to Park Rapids. Take Highway 34 east from Park Rapids to get to access points along the trail. Park Rapids is about 5 hours from the Twin Cities. From Duluth, take Highway 2 west to Cass Lake. Take Highway 371 south to Walker on the eastern edge of the trail. Take Highway 34 west from Walker for access points along the trail.

Information Heartland Trail

Nevis Civic & Commerce Association
Phone (218) 652-3474

Akeley Civic & Commerce Association
Phone (218) 652-2600
Web www.akeleyminnesota.com

Leech Lake Chamber of Commerce
Toll Free (800) 833-1118
Phone (218) 547-1313
Web www.leech-lake.com

DNR Trails and Waterways, Nevis
Phone (218) 652-4054

Park Rapids Chamber of Commerce
Toll Free (800) 247-0054
Phone (218) 732-4111
Web www.parkrapids.com

LODGING

Hotels/Resorts

Akeley
Crow Wing Crest Lodge
11th Crow Wing Lake
RR2, Box 33
Zip Code 56433
Toll Free (800) 279-2754
Phone (218) 652-3111
Web www.crowwing.com

Nevis
Pine Beach Resort
Rt 1
Zip Code 56467
Phone (218) 652-3985
Web www.pine-beach.com

Belle Shores Resort
22307 - 200th St
Zip Code 56467
Toll Free (800) 864-3750
Phone (218) 652-3197
Email wjohnson@eot.com
Web www. Belleshoresresort.com

Island View Resort
22492 County 80
Zip Code 56467
Toll Free (800) 429-1388
Phone (218) 652-3692
Email jmlarson@eot.com
Web www.islandviewresort.net

Nevis Welcome Inn Motel & RV Park
117 Highway 34
PO Box 485
Zip Code 56467
Phone (218) 652-3600

Paradise Cove Resort
21428 County 80
Zip Code 56467
Toll Free (800) 765-2682
Phone (218) 732-3779
Fax (218) 732-3779
Email view@visitparadisecove.com
Web www.visitparadisecove.com

Resort Content
24519 Fairwood Lane
Zip Code 56467
Toll Free (877) 726-7716
Phone (218) 652-3437
Fax (218) 652-4380
Email resortcontent@unitelc.com
Web www.resortcontent.com

Park Rapids
AmericInn Motel
Highway 34 East
Zip Code 56470
Toll Free (800) 634-3444
Phone (218) 732-1234

Super 8 Motel
1020 East 1st St
Zip Code 56470
Toll Free (800) 800-8000
Phone (218) 732-9704
Fax (218) 732-9704

Lee's Riverside Resort Motel
700 North Park
Zip Code 56470
Toll Free (800) 733-9711
Phone (218) 732-9711
Fax (218) 732-9711
Web www.leesriverside.com

King's Cottages Resort/Motel
609 North Park
Zip Code 56470
Toll Free (800) 769-4526
Phone (218) 732-4526

Gramma's Cabins
900 North Park Ave
Zip Code 56470
Toll Free (888) 272-1240
Phone (218) 732-0987
Email grammasbb@unitelc.com
Web www.customer.initelc.com/
grammasbb/

Terrace View Motor Lodge
716 North Park
Zip Code 56470
Toll Free (800) 731-1213
Phone (218) 732-1213
Fax (218) 732-1252

Walker
Lakeview Inn
PO Box 1359
Zip Code 56484
Toll Free (800) 252-5073
Phone (218) 547-1212
Web www.wlkermn.com/lakeviewinn

AmericInn
Highway 371 Box 843
Zip Code 56484
Toll Free (800) 634-3444
Phone (218) 547-2200

Forest Inn Motel
6615 State Highway 371 NW
Zip Code 56484
Phone (218) 547-2400

City Dock Cottages
#1 City Dock
PO Box 544
Zip Code 56484
Phone (218) 547-1662
Fax (218) 547-6141

Chase Motor Inn and Cottages
5th & Leech Lake
Zip Code 56484
Toll Free (800) 772-6769
Phone (218) 547-2882

Bed and Breakfast
Nevis
The Park Street Inn
554 Park St
Zip Code 56467
Toll Free (800) 797-1778
Phone (218) 652-4500

Heartland Trail B&B
Rt 3, Box 39
Zip Code 56470
Phone (218) 732-3252
Email corbidpj@aol.com
Web www.heartlandbb.com

Red Bridge Inn B&B
Zip Code 56470
Phone (218) 732-0481

Gateway Guest House
203 Park Ave N
Zip Code 56470
Phone (218) 732-1933

Dickson Viking House
202 East 4th St
Zip Code 56470
Toll Free (888) 899-7292
Phone (218) 732-8089
Fax (218) 732-2927
Email iaia@wcta.net
Web www.itascaarea.net

Walker
Peacecliff
7361 Breezy Point Rd NW
Zip Code 56484
Phone (218) 547-2832

Camping
Lake Itasca
Itasca State Park Campground
HC05, Box 4
Zip Code 56470
Toll Free (800) 246-2267
Phone (218) 266-2114
Web
www.itasca.park@dnr.state.mn.us

Park Rapids
Vagabond Village
HCO 6, Box 381-A
Zip Code 56470
Phone (218) 732-5234
Web www.vagabondvillage.com

Spruce Hill Campground
Rt 4, Box 449
Zip Code 56470
Phone (218) 732-3292
Email sprucehill@wcta.net

Big Pines Tent & RV Park
501 South Central Ave
Zip Code 56470
Toll Free (800) 245-5360
Phone (218) 732-4483

Mantrap Lake State Forest
Campground
607 West 1st St, Highway 34
Zip Code 56470
Phone (218) 732-3309

Walker
Waters Edge RV Park
HCR 73, Box 327
Zip Code 56484
Phone (218) 547-3552

Shores of Leech Lake Campground
PO Box 327
Zip Code 56484
Phone (218) 547-1819

Bayview Resort & Campground
PO Box 58
Zip Code 56484
Toll Free (800) 487-8694
Phone (218) 547-1595
Fax (218) 547-4819

Akeley
Brauhaus
Phone (218) 652-2478

Dorset
Dorset Cafe
Phone (218) 732-4072

LaPasta
Phone (218) 732-3831

Dorset House
Phone (218) 732-5556

Companeros
Phone (218) 732-7624

Woodstock North Gifts
Phone (218) 732-8457

Park Rapids
Ament's Heartland Bakery
Phone (218) 732-4275

Y-Steak House
Phone (218) 732-4565

Walker
Village Square Ice Cream
Phone (218) 547-1456

Zona Rosa
Phone (218) 547-3558

The Wharf
Phone (218) 547-3777

Information Heartland Trail

Giuliana's Upscale Pasta
Phone (218) 547-4825

Pepper's Beach Bar & Grill
Phone (218) 547-1662

Walker Bay Coffee Co
Phone (218) 547-1183

GROCERIES

Park Rapids
J & B Foods
(218) 732-3368

Walker
Bieloh's IGA
(218) 547-1624

BIKE RENTAL

Akeley
Hardware Hank
Phone (218) 652-2369

Park Rapids/Dorset
Gurney's Bike Repair & Rental
Phone (218) 732-8624

Walker
Back Street Bike and Ski Shop
Phone (218) 547-2500
Web www.backstreetbike.com

BIKE REPAIR

Akeley
Hardware Hank
Phone (218) 652-2369

Park Rapids/Dorset
Gurney's Bike Repair and Rental
Phone (218) 732-8624

Walker
Back Street Bike and Ski Shop
Phone (218) 547-2500
Web www.backstreetbike.com

FESTIVALS AND EVENTS

Akeley
June
Paul Bunyan Days
Fish fry, treasure hunt, pie social, cake walk, kiddy parade and grand parade on Sunday afternoon, arts, crafts and food booths line the street, Friday night teen dance, Saturday night adult dance, Fourth Weekend
Phone (218) 652-2600

Dorset
August
Taste of Dorset
Stroll down the Boardwalk to sample a variety of foods from local restaurants. Dorset boasts the reputation of having the most restaurants per capita in the USA. First Weekend
Toll Free (800) 247-0054
Phone (218) 732-4111

Nevis
July
Water Ski Show
Nevis beach of Lake Belle Taine
Toll Free (800) 332-3474
Phone (218) 652-3474

Park Rapids
July
Hubbard County Shell Prairie Fair
Grandstand shows, demo derby, exhibitors. food vendors, midway, 4H exhibits. Fourth Weekend
Toll Free (800) 247-0054
Phone (218) 732-9672

Summertime Arts and Crafts Festival
Exhibitors, music, food vendors, local contact: Marcy Hayes, Third Weekend
Toll Free (800) 247-0054
Phone (218) 732-9439

4th of July Celebration
Firecracker Foot Race, fireworks at city beach, First Weekend
Toll Free (800) 247-0054
Phone (218) 732-4111

Headwaters of the Mississippi Rodeo
World championship PRCA rodeo and bull ride, clowns, bullfighter, kids' events, free pony rides, parades, dances, exhibitors, local contact: the Jokelas, First Weekend
Toll Free (800) 247-0054
Phone (218) 732-5587

August
Historical Society Ice Cream Social and Auction
Varies yearly from August to September, call the Historical Society for details
Phone (218) 732-5237

North Star Arts and Crafts Festival
Exhibitors, music, food vendors, local contact: Lucy Franz, First Weekend
Toll Free (800) 247-0054
Phone (218) 829-5991

Antique Tractor Show
Threshing, tractor and horse plowing, shingle making, steam engines, square dance, parade, horse and wagon rides, local contact: Elaine Rognstad, Fourth Weekend
Toll Free (800) 247-0054
Phone (218) 732-5073

September
Fall Fishing Classic
$8,000 purse, First Saturday
Toll Free (800) 247-0054

FESTIVALS AND EVENTS cont'd

Headwaters 100 Bike Ride
Highway 71 plus part of the Heartland
Trail, loops through Itasca State Park,
local contact: Rose Higgins, Fourth
Weekend
Toll Free (800) 247-0054
Phone (218) 732-3366

Walker
July
4th of July
Parade, fireworks, food, music, children's games, volleyball, horseshoes,
sumo wrestling, First Weekend
Toll Free (800) 833-1118
Phone (218) 547-1313

Moondance Jam
Moondance Fairgrounds, jam sessions, big name and regional performances, Second Weekend
Toll Free (877) 666-6526
Phone (218) 547-1055

August
Cajun Fest
Moondance Fairgrounds, Cajun style
food, parades, dancing, music direct
from Louisiana, Second Weekend
Phone (218) 547-1055

September
Annual Ethnic Fest
Downtown Walker, celebration of ethnic diversity, food vendors, craft
demos, entertainment, storytelling,
Second Weekend
Toll Free (800) 833-1118

Walker North Country Marathon
10K run/walk, 2 person team
marathon, Third Weekend
Toll Free (800) 833-1118
Phone (218) 547-3327

ALTERNATE ACTIVITIES

Tamarac National Wildlife Refuge
43,000 acres of sanctuary and breeding ground for migrating birds and
other wildlife, Visitor Center has hiking
trails and picnic area.
Phone (218) 847-2641

Akeley
Wood Tick Musical Theatre
Phone (218) 652-4200

Cass Lake
Chippewa National Forest
Drive the Woodtick Trail, hike the
Shingobee Hills or canoe the Boy River.

Park Rapids
Itasca State Park
Visit the source of the Mississippi
River, camp, bike, hike and canoe,
view stands of old-growth pine over
200 years old
Phone (218) 266-2100
Web
www.itasca.park@dnr.state.mn.us

Walker
Moondance Ranch & Wildlife Park
Wildlife park, trail rides, pony corral,
trout pond, water slide, hot tub, hay
rides, go-karts, mini golf, arcade and
restaurant
Phone (218) 547-1055
Web www.moondanceranch.com

Shopping, shopping, and more
shopping
Downtown Walker
Toll Free (800) 833-1118
Web www.leech-lake.com

Cass County Museum and Pioneer
School House
Library, archival files, photos, newspapers, also houses Indian Art Museum,
open daily 10 - 5, closed Sundays
Phone (218) 547-7251

Paul Bunyan Trail

Vital Information:

Trail Distance: 47 miles

Trail Surface: asphalt

Access Points: Baxter, Merrifield, Nisswa, Pequot Lakes, Jenkins, Pine River, Backus, Hackensack

Fees and Passes: none

Trail Website: www.paulbunyantrail.com

ABOUT THE TRAIL

Ten feet wide and recently paved, this former Burlington Northern Rail line is ideal for biking or in-line skating. The trail more or less follows Highway 371 from Backus/Brainerd to Hackensack. Eventually it will be paved to Bemidji and Lake Bemidji State Park. Most of the small towns along the trail have parks, trailside facilities, and a lake or swimming area. Views include cattail marshes, cedar swamps, small lakes and mixed farmland/woodlot. The stretches near Highway 371 are generally wooded opposite the highway and open towards the highway.

TRAIL HIGHLIGHTS

Merrifield to Nisswa: A seven mile blend of farm fields, woodlots and wetlands, the trail has an open feel to it, yet not barren. Backus to Hackensack, eight of the most remote miles on the trail, pass through cattail marshes and cedar swamp with occasional upland woods and pasture land.
Miscellaneous: From the south, begin your ride at Lion's Park in Merrifield. It has excellent restrooms, sheltered picnic area and children's play area. Check out the shopping in Nisswa, the multi-colored water tower "bobber" in Pequot Lakes, and the swimming area behind the dam at the Pine River day use park. Relax or swim at the city park in Backus.

ABOUT THE ROADS

Roads near the northern end are mostly gravel or heavily traveled. More paved, lake roads between Baxter and Nisswa, but expect traffic on weekends and holidays.

ROAD HIGHLIGHTS

Highways 17 and 1 offer a good alternate to the trail between Pequot Lakes and Pine River. See the Heartland Trail for a great connector between Hackensack on this trail and Akeley on the Heartland Trail. Hole in the Day Park Reserve and the roads around it are very attractive.

HOW TO GET THERE

Brainerd is 130 miles northwest of the Twin Cities and 113 miles southwest of Duluth. Follow 210 west about 2 miles from Brainerd to Highway 371. See city map for trail access at Baxter. All other trail towns, except Merrifield, are along Highway 371. To start at Merrifield, take Highway 25 N, about seven miles, from Brainerd.

Hackensack
Duluth
Brainerd
Minneapolis
St. Paul
Red Wing
Winona
Rochester

See Trail Map on page M9

Paul Bunyan Trail **Information**

TOURIST INFORMATION

DNR Trails and Waterways, Brainerd
Phone (218) 828-6081

Hackensack Chamber of Commerce
Toll Free (800) 279-6932
Phone (218) 675-6135

Cass County Tourism Web Site
Web www.greattimesnorth.com

Brainerd Lakes Chamber of
Commerce
Toll Free (800) 450-2838
Phone (218) 829-2838

Pine River Chamber of Commerce
Phone (218) 587-4000

Backus City Hall
Phone (218) 947-3221
Fax (218) 947-3221
Email clerk@uslink.net
Web www.backusmn.com

Pequot Lakes Tourist Information
Toll Free (800) 950-0291
Phone (218) 568-8911
Web www.pequotlakes.com

Nisswa Chamber of Commerce
Toll Free (800) 950-9610
Phone (218) 963-2620
Web www.nisswa.com

LODGING

Motels/Resorts
Backus
Mountain View Resort
590 Wood St North
Zip Code 56435
Phone (218) 947-3233

Bayside Cabins
206 Rosalind Ave W
Zip Code 56435
Toll Free (800) 840-3344
Phone (218) 947-3344
Fax (218) 947-4144
Email bayside@uslink.net
Web www.baysidecabins.com

Baxter
Country Inn & Suites
1220 Dellwood Dr North
Zip Code 56425
Toll Free (800) 456-4000
Phone (218) 828-2161

Hackensack
John's Hyde-A-Way Bay Resort
3489 Ford Dr NW
Zip Code 56452
Toll Free (800) 309-5253
Phone (218) 675-6683
Fax (218) 675-6683

Pinewood Resort
3826 Pinewood Rd NW
Zip Code 56452
Phone (218) 675-6249

Happiness Resort on Ten Mile Lake
4609 Happiness Lane NW
Zip Code 56452
Phone (218) 675-6574
Email happiness@uslink.net

Shady Shores Resort
5445 Lower Ten Mile Lake Rd NW
Zip Code 56452
Phone (218) 675-6540

Newman Nies Cabin
4975 Woodland Dr NW
Zip Code 56452
Phone (218) 675-6913

Birch Haven Resort
P.O. Box 243
Zip Code 56452
Phone (218) 675-6151

Bradley's Resort
P.O. Box 444
Zip Code 56452
Phone (218) 675-6690
Fax (218) 675-5381
Email bearcove@uslink.net
Web www.bearcove.com

Fishtales Resort
P.O. Box 294
Zip Code 56459
Phone (218) 963-2415

Merrifield
Train Bell Resort
Zip Code 56465
Toll Free (800) 252-2102
Phone (218) 829-4941

Nisswa
Gull Bay Cabins
924 Bishop Dr
Zip Code 56468
Toll Free (800) 900-7997
Phone (218) 963-7997
Web www.gullbaycabins.com

Good Ol' Days Resort
Box 358
Zip Code 56468
Toll Free (800) 950-8520
Phone (218) 963-2478
Fax (218) 568-6116
Email pri.resorts@ibm.net
Web www.pri/resorts.com

Eagles Nest
1516 Poplar Ave
Zip Code 56468
Toll Free (800) 922-0440
Phone (218) 963-2336

Alluring Pines Resort Estate
P.O. Box 202
Zip Code 56468
Phone (218) 963-2694
Email alluring@nisswa.net

Information Paul Bunyan Trail

Nisswa Motel
P.O. Box 45
Zip Code 56468
Phone (218) 963-7611
Web www.33net.com/nisswamotel

Days Inn
24186 Smiley Rd
Zip Code 56468
Phone (218) 963-3500

Treehouse Cottage
P.O. Box 83
Zip Code 56468
Phone (218) 568-8480

Pequot Lakes
Bradmor Motel
Rt. 2 Box 440
Zip Code 56472
Phone (218) 568-4366

Meadow Ridge Guest House
Rt 2 Box 38
Zip Code 56472
Toll Free (888) 668-7669
Phone (218) 568-5680

Pequot Cottage Motel
HC83 Box 13
Zip Code 56472
Phone (218) 568-5410

Hay Lake Lodge Lakeside Townhomes
Rt 1 Box 35
Zip Code 56472
Toll Free (800) 429-5253
Phone (218) 568-8811
Web www.haylakelodge.com

AmericInn Lodge & Suites
Highway 371 & Cty 16
P.O. Box 579
Zip Code 56472
Toll Free (800) 568-8400
Phone (218) 568-8400
Web www.americinnpequotlakes.com

Pine River
Norway Brook Motel
2729 State 371 SW
Zip Code 56474
Toll Free (800) 950-7330
Phone (218) 587-2118
Fax (218) 587-5269

Pine River Travelodge
2684 State 371 SW
P.O. Box 466
Zip Code 56474
Toll Free (800) 587-7878
Phone (218) 587-4499

Bed & Breakfast
Brainerd
Whitely Creek Homestead
2166 Highway 210 NE
Zip Code 56401
Phone (218) 829-0654
Fax (218) 825-7828
Email whitelycrk@aol.com

Merrifield
Crystal Swan Inn
HC 86, Box 5
Crystal Lake Rd
Zip Code 56465
Phone (218) 828-8343
Email cryswan@uslink.net

Pequot Lakes
Upper Hay Hideaway
34088 North Oak Dr
Zip Code 56472
Phone (218) 568-4249

Camping
Backus
Lindsay Lake Campground
3781 State Highway 87 NW
Zip Code 56435
Phone (218) 947-4728
Email farrellt@uslink.net
Web www.lindseylake.com

Eagle Wing Campground
1588 36th Ave SW
Zip Code 56435
Phone (218) 587-2090
Email ddcamp@uslink.net

Brainerd
Greer Lake State Forest Campground
1601 Minnesota Dr
Zip Code 56401
Phone (218) 828-2565

Rock Lake State Forest Campground
1601 Minnesota Dr
Zip Code 56401
Phone (218) 828-2565

Crow Wing State Park Campground
3124 State Park Rd
Zip Code 56401
Phone (218) 829-8022
Web www.dnr.state.mn.us

Hackensack
Quietwoods Campground & Resort
4755 Alder Lane NW
Zip Code 56452
Phone (218) 675-6240

Nie's Cabins & Campsites
5003 Woodland Lane NW
Zip Code 56452
Phone (218) 675-6389

Nisswa
Fritz's Resort & Campground
P.O. Box 803
Zip Code 56468
Phone (218) 568-8988

Pequot Lakes
Clint Converse State Forest
Box 27
Zip Code 56472
Phone (218) 568-4566

Tall Timbers Campground
RR3 Box 7
Zip Code 56472
Phone (218) 568-4041

LODGING cont'd

Rager's Acres
1680 64th St SW
Zip Code 56472
Phone (218) 568-8752

Pine River
Doty's River View RV Park
3040 16th Ave SW
Zip Code 56474
Phone (218) 587-4112
Email tdoty564@uslink.net

RESTAURANTS

Backus
Foot Hills Saloon & Rest.
Phone (218) 947-3321

Willard's Saloon & Eatery
Phone (218) 947-3832

Salty Dog Saloon & Eatery
Phone (218) 947-4446

Hackensack
Up North Cafe
Phone (218) 675-5300

Yukon Sports Bar & Grille
Phone (218) 675-7756

Pauly's River House
Phone (218) 675-6200

Jenkins
Jenkins VFW Post 3839
Phone (218) 568-8664

A-Pine Family Restaurant
Phone (218) 568-8353

The Nest Restaurant
Phone (218) 568-5821

Nisswa
Nisswa Grille
Phone (218) 963-4717

Adirondack
Phone (218) 963-2568

Ye Olde Pickle Factory
Phone (218) 963-9910

Ganley's Family Rest.
Phone (218) 963-2993

Grand View Lodge
Phone (218) 963-3146

Nisswa Country Store
Phone (218) 963-0465

Norway Ridge
Phone (218) 543-6136

Country Cookin' Cafe
Phone (218) 963-3326

Quarterdeck Boathouse
Phone (218) 963-7537

Pequot Lakes
Plaid Duck
Phone (218) 568-7440

MarketPlace Deli
Phone (218) 568-4244

The Butcher Block
Phone (218) 568-9950

Preserve Steak House
Phone (218) 963-2234

Sibley Station
Phone (218) 568-4177

Sugar Shack
Phone (218) 568-6999

Tasty Pizza North
Phone (218) 568-4404

Timber Ridge Supper Club
Phone (218) 568-6070

Oasis Family Restaurant
Phone (218) 568-4428

Pine River
Cottage Cafe
Phone (218) 587-2588

Red Pine Supper Club
Phone (218) 587-3818

Pine Wood Cafe
Phone (218) 587-2267

JJ's Luncheon & Pizza
Phone (218) 587-3922

Norway Ridge
Phone (218) 543-6136

Pine River Legion
Phone (218) 587-9151

Al's Bakery and Coffee
Phone (218) 587-2545

Walker
The Grain Bin
Toll Free (877) 666-6526
Phone (218) 547-1055

GROCERIES

Hackensack
Mark's Market
(218) 675-6825

Nisswa
Schafer's Foods
(218) 963-2265

Pequot Lakes
Northern Food King
(218) 568-5995

BIKE RENTAL

Backus
Bayside Cabins
Toll Free (800) 840-3344
Phone (218) 947-3344

Brainerd
Trailblazer Bikes
Phone (218) 829-8542

Easy Rider Bicycle & Sport
Toll Free (800) 880-5156
Phone (218) 829-5516

Hackensack
Mike's
Phone (218) 675-6976

Information Paul Bunyan Trail

BIKE RENTAL cont'd

Merrifield
Train Bell Resort
Toll Free (800) 252-2102
Phone (218) 829-4941
Web www.trainbellresort.com

Nisswa
Bunyan Bike Shuttle and Rental
Phone (218) 568-8422
Web www.nisswa.com

Pine River
Doty's Riverview RV Park
Phone (218) 587-4112

BIKE REPAIR

Brainerd
Easy Riders Bicycle and Sport Shop
Phone (218) 829-5516

Hackensack
Mike's
Phone (218) 675-6976

Nisswa
Carlson Hardware
Phone (218) 963-7645

BIKE SHUTTLE

Nisswa
Bunyan Bike Shuttle and Rental
Phone (218) 568-8422
Web www.nisswa.com

FESTIVALS AND EVENTS

Backus
May
Annual Yard Sale
Sponsored by Lions Club,
Memorial Day Weekend
Phone (218) 947-3221

Old Timer's Weekend
Old time music, horseshoe tournament, ice cream bars and Sloppy Joe's
at Firehall, Call Bert Eveland
Phone (218) 947-3569

Annual Smelt Fry
First Weekend
Phone (218) 947-3221

July
Fly-in Breakfast
Pancake breakfast at municipal airport,
sponsored by Lions Club, Last Sunday
Phone (218) 947-3221

August
Annual Cornfest
Corn feed, parade, games, music, tal-
ent show (kids and adult divisions),
Second Saturday
Phone (218) 947-3221

Brainerd
June
Crow Wing Encampment
Fur trade era encampment with crafts
of the era, shooting demonstration,
leather and beadworking, at Crow
Wing State Park following 10 mile
canoe trip from Kiwanis Park,
Sponsored by Crow Wing County
Muzzle Loaders, First Sunday
Phone (218) 829-8022

July
Eastern Star Antique Show
Regional vendors, National Guard
Armory, Fourth Weekend
Phone (218) 829-6787

Art in the Park
Juried artists, entertainment, food,
Gregory Park, 1st weekend after
the 4th
Toll Free (800) 450-2838
Phone (218) 829-5278

4th of July Celebration
Festivities spread out over
several days
Toll Free (800) 450-2838
Phone (218) 829-5278

October
Northwoods Arts Festival
Regional and local artists, community
and senior center, First Weekend
Toll Free (800) 279-6932
Phone (218) 675-6135

Fall Service and Fun Day
At Deep Portage Conservation and
Reserve, environmental learning activi-
ties, food, entertainment, Third
Weekend
Phone (218) 682-2325

Hackensack
Lions Pancake Breakfast
Community Building, 7:30 - 11:00 am,
First Sunday of every month

Kids Fishing Contest
At city pier from 11:00 to 1:00, every
Tuesday mid-June to mid-August
Toll Free (800) 279-6932
Phone (218) 675-6135

Flea Market
Parking lot of Sacred Heart Church,
Second Wednesdays summer months
Phone (218) 675-6101

June
Sweetheart Canoe Derby
Canoe races, food vendors, craft fair,
Third Weekend
Toll Free (800) 279-6932
Phone (218) 675-6135

Sweetheart Days
Mid-week event including antique car show, parade, horseshoe tourney, carnival, and street dance, Preceded by performances of "Ballad of Lucette," a light operetta, at the Community Building, Second Weekend
Toll Free (800) 279-6932
Phone (218) 675-6135

July
Volunteer Fire Dept Fundraiser
BBQ & Dance, Third Weekend
Toll Free (800) 279-6932
Phone (218) 675-6135

August
Krazy Days
Lions Club grills pork-on-a-stick, Jaycees corn on the cob, special sales, annual weightlifting championship, street dance on Saturday night, Second Weekend
Toll Free (800) 950-9610
Phone (218) 963-2620

Nisswa
Turtle Races
Behind the Chamber of Commerce, 2:00 pm every Wednesday afternoon Mid-June through August
Toll Free (800) 950-9610
Phone (218) 963-2620

June
Nisswa Naturally Day
Learn about animal track identification, gathering mushrooms, beekeeping, wild rice harvesting, and loons, crafters, loon calling contest, native foods, Third Saturday
Toll Free (800) 950-9610
Phone (218) 963-2620

July
Freedom Day Parade
Fourth of July celebration, stagecoach rides, food court, parade, no fireworks
Toll Free (800) 950-9610
Phone (218) 963-2620

Arts and Crafts Festival
Juried show, food concessions, Fourth Weekend
Toll Free (800) 950-9610
Phone (218) 963-2620

Garden Club Show
Hosted by Nisswa Garden Club at Grand View Convention Center, Fourth Weekend
Toll Free (800) 950-9610
Phone (218) 963-2620

Pequot Lakes
July
July 4th Celebration
Kids' parade, baby race, liar's contest, bed races, pie eating contest, haystack, greased pole, foot races, food, fireworks
Toll Free (800) 950-0291
Phone (218) 568-8911

Bean Hole Days
150 gallons of Pequot Lakes baked beans cooked overnight in the ground, served between noon and 2 pm, arts and crafts, Bobberland Wayside Trail Park, Wednesday following the 4th of July
Toll Free (800) 950-0291
Phone (218) 568-8911

September
Pequot Lakes Arts and Crafts Fair And Taste of Pequot, regional arts and crafts, local food vendors, Trailside, Third Weekend
Toll Free (800) 950-0291
Phone (218) 568-8911

Pine River
Duck Races
Decoys only, Pine River Dam, 1:00 pm every Friday late June through mid-August
Toll Free (800) 728-6926
Phone (218) 587-4000

Flea Market
Every Friday at the fairgrounds, late June through mid-August
Toll Free (800) 728-6926
Phone (218) 587-4000

Free Fishing Seminars
Every Tuesday, 10 am to noon, late June through mid-August
Toll Free (800) 728-6926
Phone (218) 587-4000

June
Summerfest
Craft and sidewalk sales, band and gospel music, parade, golf, softball and horseshoe tournaments, fly-in breakfast at the airport, Legion steak fry, firemen's street dance, Fourth Weekend
Toll Free (800) 728-6926
Phone (218) 587-4000

July
Pine River Art Show
Exhibits, sales, demonstrations, snacks, Pine River Elementary, Fourth Weekend
Toll Free (800) 728-6926
Phone (218) 587-4000

Cass County Fair
Varies, usually third weekend in July
Toll Free (800) 728-6926
Phone (218) 587-4000

Information Paul Bunyan Trail

October

Heritage Days
Quilt show, various exhibits, food, music, Pine River churches, First Weekend
Toll Free (800) 728-6926
Phone (218) 587-4000

ALTERNATE ACTIVITIES

Pillsbury State Forest
Phone (218) 828-2565

Brainerd
Crow Wing County Historical Society
Local history, logging, railroad and mining history, located in the old county jail/sheriff's residence, call for hours
Phone (218) 829-3268

Northland Arboretum
Hiking trails, picnic area, learning center
Phone (218) 829-8770

Crow Wing State Park
Remains of the town of Old Crow Wing, site of the confluence of Crow Wing and Mississippi Rivers, hiking trails
Phone (218) 829-8022

Kart Kountry at Vacation Land Park
Bumper cars, batting cages, Can-Am family track
Phone (218) 963-3545

Paul Bunyan Amusement Center
Rides, attractions, arcades, miniature golf
Phone (218) 829-6342

This Old Farm Antique Museum
Thousands of antiques including cars, tractors, steam engines, also sawmill, blacksmith shop, shingle mill, log house, one-room school house, old time saloon and sweet shop
Phone (218) 764-2915

Crosby
Croft Mine Historical Park
Take a narrated ride down into the depths of a mine
Phone (218) 546-5466

Hackensack
Deep Portage Conservation Reserve
Environmental learning center, nature trails, interpretive center, between Longville and Hackensack
Phone (218) 682-2325
Web www.deep-portage.org

Merrifield
River Treat
Shuttle service, canoe trips, full or half days, bring your own or rent
Phone (218) 765-3172

Nisswa
Nisswa Family Fun Center
Water slides, hot tubs, rollerblade track (skate rental), snack stand, children's recreation area, heated wading pool
Phone (218) 682-2325

Pequot Lakes
Bump and Putt Family Fun
Bumper boats, mini golf, water wars, hoops, basketball, battery powered 4-wheeler track for kids
Phone (218) 568-8833

Pine River
Trout Lake Riding Stable
Horseback riding and hay rides
Phone (218) 543-4277

Canoe the Pine River
Shuttle service available at Doty's RV Park and Pardner's Resort
Phone (218) 587-4112

Walker
Moondance Ranch & Wildlife Park
Trail rides, pony corral, wildlife park, petting zoo, pow wows, gift shop, restaurant
Toll Free (877) 666-6526
Phone (218) 547-1055
Web www.moondanceranch.com

Vital Information:

Trail Distance: 70 miles

Trail Surface: asphalt

Access Points: Hinckley, Finlayson, Willow River, Moose Lake, Carlton, Duluth

Fees and Passes: none

Trail Website: www.mungertrail.com

See Trail Map on page M12

ABOUT THE TRAIL

A long trail with some exceptionally beautiful and historic areas. The trail from Carlton to Duluth is the best. Smooth enough for in-line skaters, the trail passes over a steep gorge of the St. Louis River, runs along a diversion canal for the hydro-electric plant, and offers a bird's eye view of Duluth Harbor. Hinckley, the southern terminus, is best known for the Hinckley Fire Storm of September 1, 1894. The trail follows the escape route that carried residents from town to Skunk Lake, an 18 inch deep water hole where passengers buried themselves in mud and water to escape the intense heat of the fire. For additional information about the firestorm, stop at the Hinckley Fire Museum in downtown.

TRAIL HIGHLIGHTS

Start in Carlton and pull over a short distance later at one of the bump out observation platforms on the bridge overlooking the St. Louis River, with its fast flowing waters and rocky outcrops. Further east, the trail passes a diversion canal for the hydro-electric plant, touches the northern edge of Jay Cooke State Park, passes through impressive rock cuts and offers a view of Duluth Harbor, then drops down to water level. The eastern edge is a short distance from the Lake Superior Zoo, a favorite stopping point for kids and adults alike. If you have time, try the Alex Laveau Memorial Trail from Carlton to Wrenshall, a pretty little trail with rock cuts, creeks and Jay Cooke State Park all in less than 3 miles.

ABOUT THE ROADS

The roads near the southern half of the trail are nearly as flat as the trail.

Traffic is moderate around Sandstone, less as you get further north. Highway 61 runs parallel to the trail from Hinckley to Carlton. A decent alternate to the trail, but quite flat. The northern roads are much more interesting. See trail maps for details.

ROAD ROUTE HIGHLIGHTS

Branch out from Wrenshall for quiet, rolling hills and a scenic loop around Chub Lake or continue on the Alex Laveau Trail to Highway 23 for a road loop back to West Duluth. Highway 210 through Jay Cooke is very pretty, very hilly, and sometimes busy with park traffic. Sandstone's attractive business district has a pleasant feel with its village park, 75 year old brick front buildings, and natural landscape plantings in front of the Evangelical Free Church. The loop around Sturgeon Lake hugs the shoreline for a couple of miles, then heads out into the country before coming back to town. A short out and back on Highway 46 will give the best lake views. A combination of roads with paved shoulders will eventually connect with a trail through Moose Lake State Park near Moose Lake.

HOW TO GET THERE

Carlton is east of Interstate 35 on Highway 210, about 15 miles from Duluth. To get to the West Duluth trailhead, take Interstate 35 to Highway 23 in West Duluth and go southwest. See city map for details. Hinckley is about 70 miles south of Duluth on Interstate 35. Take Highway 48 west from I-35 to Highway 61. See trail map for details to the trailhead. All other points can be accessed by following Highway 61 north. See trail map.

Information Willard Munger Trail

Sandstone Chamber of Commerce
Phone (320) 245-2271

Finlayson City Hall
Phone (320) 233-6472

Duluth Convention and Visitors Bureau
Toll Free (800) 438-5884
Phone (218) 722-4011
Web www.visitduluth.com

Carlton Civic Center
Phone (218) 384-4229

Willow River Mercantile
Phone (218) 372-3137

Moose Lake Chamber of Commerce
Toll Free (800) 635-3680
Phone (218) 485-4145
Email
mlchamber@mooselake.mn.com
Web www.mooselake-mn.com

Hinckley Visitors Bureau
Toll Free (800) 996-4566
Web www.hinckleymn.com

Munger Trail Towns Association
Toll Free (888) 263-0586
Web www.munger-trail.com

LODGING

Motels/Resorts

Barnum
Northwoods Motel & Cottages
3716 Main St
Zip Code 55707
Toll Free (800) 228-6951
Phone (218) 389-6951

Carlton
Americinn Motel
Highway 210 & I-35
Zip Code 55718
Toll Free (800) 634-3444
Phone (218) 384-3535
Fax (218) 384-3870

Cloquet
AmericInn Motel
111 Big Lake Rd
Zip Code 55720
Toll Free (800) 634-3444
Phone (218) 879-1231
Fax (218) 879-2237
Web www.americinn.com

Duluth
Willard Munger
7408 Grand Ave
Zip Code 55807
Toll Free (800) 982-2453
Phone (218) 624-4814
Fax (800) 982-2453
Email munger@computerpro.com
Web www.mungerinn.com

Mountain Villas
9525 West Skyline Pky
Zip Code 55810
Toll Free (800) 642-6377
Phone (218) 624-5784
Web www.visitduluth.com/mtvillas

AmericInn Motel & Suites
185 Highway 2
Zip Code 55810
Toll Free (800) 634-3444
Phone (218) 624-1026
Fax (218) 624-2818
Email amerdul@uslink.net
Web www.americinn.com

Spirit Mountain Travelodge
9315 Westgate Blvd
Zip Code 55810
Toll Free (800) 777-8530
Phone (218) 628-3691
Email travelodge@duluth.com

Finlayson
Waldheim Resort
906 Waldheim Ln
Zip Code 55735
Phone (320) 233-7405
Web www.waldheimresort.com

Banning Junction Super 8 Motel
2811 Highway 23
Zip Code 55735
Toll Free (800) 800-8000
Phone (320) 245-5284
Fax (320) 245-2233

Hinckley
Days Inn
104 Grindstone Court
Zip Code 55037
Toll Free (800) 559-8951
Phone (320) 384-7751

Holiday Inn Express
I-35, Exit #183
Zip Code 55037
Toll Free (800) 558-0612
Phone (320) 384-7171
Web www.holidayinnhinckley.com

Hinckley Gold Pine Inn
I-35 at MN 48 Hinckley Exit
Zip Code 55037
Toll Free (888) 384-6112
Phone (320) 384-6112
Web www.goldpinebw.com

Moose Lake
Moose Lake Motel
125 South Arrowhead Lane
Zip Code 55767
Phone (218) 485-8003

AmericInn Lodge & Suites
400 Park Place Dr
Zip Code 55767
Toll Free (800) 634-3444
Phone (218) 485-8885
Web www.americinn.com

Sturgeon Lake
Sturgeon Lake Motel
I-35 and Exit 209
Zip Code 55783
Phone (218) 372-3194

LODGING cont'd

Willow River
Squirrel Cage
8144 County Highway 61
Zip Code 55795
Phone (218) 372-3181

Bed and Breakfast

Duluth
Stanford Inn
1415 East Superior St
Zip Code 55805
Phone (218) 724-3044
Email stanford_inn@hotmail.com
Web www.visitduluth.com/stanford

A. Charles Weiss Inn
1615 East Superior St
Zip Code 55812
Toll Free (800) 525-5243
Phone (218) 724-7016
Web www.duluth.com/acweissinn

The Historic Cotton Mansion
2309 East 1st St
Zip Code 55812
Toll Free (800) 228-1997
Phone (218) 724-6405
Web www.cottonmansion.com

The Firelight Inn
2211 East 3rd St
Zip Code 55812
Toll Free (888) 724-0273
Phone (218) 724-0272
Web www.duluth.com/firelightinn

A.G. Thomson House
2617 East 3rd St
Zip Code 55812
Toll Free (877) 807-8077
Web www.visitduluth.com/

The Ellery House
28 South 21st Ave East
Zip Code 55812
Toll Free (800) 355-3794
Phone (218) 724-7639
Web www.visitduluth.com/elleryhouse

Finlayson
Giese's Inn
770 Aitkin County 23
Zip Code 55735
Phone (320) 233-6429

Hinckley
Dakota Lodge B&B
Rt 3, Box 178
Zip Code 55037
Phone (320) 384-6052
Web www.dakotalodge.com

Down Home B&B
RR2, Box 178
Zip Code 55037
Toll Free (800) 965-8919
Phone (320) 384-0396
Fax (320) 384-0397
Email lorraine@pinenet.com

Sturgeon Lake
Hidden Ponds Country Inn
3581 County Line Rd
Zip Code 55783
Toll Free (888) 485-0400
Phone (218) 485-0400
Email sue@hiddenponds.com
Web www.hiddenponds.com

Camping

Carlton
Jay Cook State Park Campground
500 Highway 210 East
Zip Code 55718
Phone (218) 384-4610
Web www.dnr.state.mn.us

Finlayson
Waldheim Resort
906 Waldheim Ln
Zip Code 55735
Phone (320) 233-7405
Web www.waldheimresort.com

Hinckley
Snake River State Forest Campground
312 Fire Mounument Rd
Zip Code 55037
Phone (320) 384-6146

Moose Lake
Moose Lake City Campground
PO Box Jl
Zip Code 55767
Phone (218) 485-4761

Red Fox Campground & RV Park
PO Box 10
Zip Code 55767
Toll Free (800) 569-4181
Phone (218) 485-0341

Willow River State Forest Campground
Forester
Rt2, 701 South Kenwood
Zip Code 55767

Moose Lake State Park Campground
4252 County 137
Zip Code 55767
Toll Free (888) 646-6367
Phone (218) 485-5420

Proctor
Buffalo Valley Camping
2590 Guss Rd
Zip Code 55810
Phone (218) 624-9901

Sandstone
Banning Junction State Park
PO Box 643
Zip Code 55072
Phone (320) 245-5273

Sturgeon Lake
Sun Bay Mobile Home & Campground
RR 1 Box 800
Zip Code 55783
Phone (218) 485-4869

Timberline Campground
9152 Timberline Rd
Zip Code 55783
Phone (218) 372-3272

Information Willard Munger Trail

LODGING cont'd

Edelweiss Campground and Resort
Rt 2, Box 108
Zip Code 55783
Phone (218) 372-3363

Willow River
Wilderness Campground
Long Lake Rd
Zip Code 55795
Phone (218) 372-3993

RESTAURANTS

Barnum
Wyndtree Family Restaurant
Phone (218) 485-8712

Carlton
Iverson Inn Bar & Grill
Phone (218) 879-9948

Hinckley
Tobies Restaurant & Bakery
Phone (320) 384-6174

Moose Lake
Art's Cafe
Phone (218) 485-4602

Poor Gary's Pizza
Phone (218) 485-8020

Sandstone
Jan/Gary's Ice Cream/Pizza
Phone (320) 245-5411

Maggie's Colonial Cafe
Phone (320) 245-2481

Banning Junction
Phone (320) 245-9989

GROCERIES

Carlton
Woodland Foods
(218) 384-9910

Hinckley
Daggett's Supervalu Foods
(320) 384-6185

Sandstone
Chris' Food Center
(320) 245-2229

Sandell's Super Valu
(320) 245-2331

BIKE RENTAL

Carlton
Cloquet Cyclery at Persnickety
Phone (218) 384-3367
Email cloquetcyclery@yahoo.com

Duluth
Willard Munger Inn
Toll Free (800) 982-2453
Phone (218) 624-4814

Hinckley
St. Croix State Park
Phone (320) 384-6591

Antiques America
Phone (320) 384-7272

BIKE REPAIR

Cloquet
Cloquet Cyclery
Phone (218) 879-5212
Fax (218) 878-2906
Email cloquetcyclery@yahoo.com
Web www.cloquetcyclery.co-inc.net

Duluth
Ski Hut
Phone (218) 624-5889
Fax (218) 624-5955
Email skihut@ibm.net
Web www.theskihut.com

Stewart's Bikes and Sports
Phone (218) 724-5101
Fax (218) 724-8372
Email stewarts.duluth@juno.com

Moose Lake
Coast to Coast
Phone (218) 485-4467

Sandstone
True Value
Phone (320) 245-2325

FESTIVALS AND EVENTS

Barnum
August
Carleton County Fair
Exhibits, displays, talent show, horse
races, demolition derby, games, rides,
Third Weekend
Phone (218) 384-3898

Duluth
May
Memorial Day Parade
Along Grand Ave in West Duluth
Toll Free (800) 438-5884
Phone (218) 722-4011

June
Park Point Art Fair
Fine arts and crafts exhibitions by
regional artists and artisans, recreation
area at Park Point, Fourth Weekend
Toll Free (800) 438-5884
Phone (715) 398-5970

MS 150 Bike Tour
Duluth to Anoka, three day event,
Spend Saturday night in Hinckley,
Second Weekend
Toll Free (800) 582-5296
Phone (612) 335-7900

Grandma's Marathon
26 miles, third Saturday of June
Phone (218) 727-0947

FESTIVALS AND EVENTS cont'd

July
Lake Superior Shakespeare Festival
Live performances by touring
Shakespeare troupes, arts, crafts, and
food from Elizabethan England, Leif
Erickson Park, Third Weekend
Toll Free (800) 438-5884

Fourth Fest
Food, arts and crafts, nationally known
music groups, fireworks, Bayfront
Festival Park
Toll Free (800) 438-5884
Phone (218) 722-4011

August
International Folk Festival
Celebration of multi-culturalism
through music, food, arts and crafts,
Leif Erickson Park, First Weekend
Toll Free (800) 438-5884
Phone (218) 722-7425

Bayfront Blues Festival
Blues and jazz bands play all weekend
in open air concerts, food vendors and
beer garden, Bayfront Festival Park,
Second Weekend
Toll Free (800) 438-5884
Phone (715) 394-6831

Finlayson
July
July 4th Celebration
Street dance, parade, coronation, fire-
works, music, games, boat parade,
July 3rd and 4th
Phone (320) 233-6472

September
White Pine Threshing Show
Living history display, variety of older
working machinery including working
printing press, blacksmith shop, shingle
mill, food booths, daily parade of old tractors and machinery, Labor Day Weekend
Phone (320) 592-3781

Hinckley
Art in the Park
Free entertainment, food, Monday
evenings at West Side Park, mid-June
to mid-August
Toll Free (800) 996-4566
Phone (320) 384-7837

June
MS 150
Overnights in Hinckley at West Side
Park, music, entertainment, food ven-
dors, City wide garage sale, Second
Weekend
Toll Free (800) 582-5296
Phone (612) 335-7900

July
Annual Grand Celebration Powwow
More than 1000 dancers, singers, and
drummers from throughout the
Western Hemisphere compete for cash
prizes, held at Powwow Grounds adja-
cent to Grand Casino Hinckley, Third
Weekend
Toll Free (800) 472-6321
Phone (320) 384-7777

Corn and Clover Carnival
Grand parade, kiddie parade,
pageant, talent show, pedal tractor
pull, food and entertainment, antique
appraisals, midway rides and games,
always the weekend after the 4th
Toll Free (800) 996-4566
Phone (320) 384-7837

August
S.U.N. 75
In-line skating event, Hinckley to
Duluth, two days on the trail, overnight
in Moose Lake, First weekend
Toll Free (800) 582-5296
Phone (612) 335-7900

Moose Lake
July
4th of July Carnival
Pancake breakfast, kiddy races,
parade, coronation, fireworks
Toll Free (800) 635-3680
Phone (218) 485-4145

Agate Days
Gem and mineral show, sponsored by
the Moose Lake Historical Society,
hunt for agates and quarters along
Main Street, First Weekend
Phone (218) 485-4327

August
Depot Fest
Corn feed, sidewalk sales, First
Weekend
Toll Free (800) 635-3680
Phone (218) 485-4145

Community Night on the Trail
Kids' games, music, trail run, luminar-
ies, mid-week evening in mid-August.
Sponsored by Moose Lake Historical
Society, call for exact date.
Toll Free (800) 635-3680
Phone (218) 369-6090

Sandstone
July
Lions Club Pig Roast & Garage Sale
City wide garage/sidewalk sales and
fund raising pig roast, Third Weekend
Phone (320) 245-5241

August
Quarry Days
Quarry tours, exhibits, parade, bingo,
food stands, children's games, street
dance, Second Weekend
Phone (320) 245-5127

World Championship Rodeo
Sandstone Riders Arena, weekend
after Quarry Days
Phone (320) 245-2715

Information Willard Munger Trail

October

Taste of Sandstone
Ethnic food, plane rides, fall bazaar, quilt and historic displays, quarry tours, logging, geology, and local history, Sandstone Elementary School & History and Art Center, First Weekend
Phone (320) 245-5241

Willow River
July
Willow River Days
Coronation, parade, run, softball tournament, dances, food stands, Fourth Weekend
Phone (218) 372-3733

ALTERNATE ACTIVITIES

Carlton
Superior White Water Raft Tours
Professionally guided raft tours on the St. Louis River, minimum age 12
Phone (218) 384-4637

Carlton Minnesota Wild Winery
Outside McGregor, open for tastes and tours, seven days a week
Toll Free (800) 328-6731
Phone (218) 768-4917

Finkes' Berry Farm
Pick your own strawberries in July and blueberries in August
Phone (218) 384-4432

Jay Cooke State Park
Camping, interpretive programs, bike and horse trails, hike on part of the Grand Portage of the St. Louis River
Phone (218) 384-4610
Web www.dnr.state.mn.us

Duluth
Great Lakes Aquarium
Over thirty interactive exhibits
Phone (218) 525-2265
Email info@glaquarium.org
Web www.glaquarium.org

Grand Slam Family Fun Center
30,000 square feet of baseball, golf, bumper cars, laser tag, spaceball, adventure playland and pizza parlor
Phone (218) 722-5667
Web www.funusa.net

St. Louis County Heritage and Art Center
Four museums under one roof, Lake Superior Railroad Museum, Duluth Children's Museum, St. Louis County Historical Society, and Duluth Art Institute
Toll Free (888) 733-5833
Phone (218) 727-8025
Email b.houle@excite.com
Web www.computerpro.com/-depot

Glensheen
Tour the historic Congdon Mansion
Toll Free (888) 454-4536
Phone (218) 726-8910
Web www.d.umn.edu/glen

Lake Superior Maritime Visitor Center
Film shows, model ships and exhibits, next to Aerial Lift Bridge
Phone (218) 727-2497

Lake Superior Zoological Gardens
Home to more than 25 endangered and threatened species from around the world, near West Duluth trailhead
Phone (218) 733-3777

Berry Pine Farms
Pick your own raspberries and strawberries, jams and jellies for sale
Phone (218) 721-3250

North Shore Scenic Railroad
Narrated train rides on vintage trains, excursions range from romantic to family fun
Toll Free (800) 423-1273
Phone (218) 722-1273
Email nssr@cpinternet.com
Web www.cpinternet.com/-lsrm

Hinckley
St. Croix State Park
Camping, swimming, hiking, biking, fishing
Phone (320) 384-6591

Hinckley Fire Museum
Interprets great fire of 1894 through artifacts, testimony, and video, two blocks from the trailhead
Toll Free (800) 582-5296
Phone (320) 384-7378

Moose Lake
Moose Lake City Beach
Swimming, fishing pier
Phone (218) 485-4145

Sandstone
Audubon Center of the North Woods
Environmental learning center, hiking trails, interpretive center
Phone (320) 824-5264

Banning State Park
Canoeing, hiking, kayaking, ice cave, quarry ruins, Wolf Creek Falls
Phone (320) 245-2668

Sandstone History and Art Center
Diorama of Sandstone Quarry, historical artifacts, rotating art exhibits
Phone (320) 245-2131

Scanlon
River Inn
River rafting on the St. Louis River
Phone (218) 879-2760

Vital Information:

Trail distance: 28 miles

Trail Surface: asphalt

Access Points: Sauk Centre, Melrose, Freeport, Albany, Avon

Fees and passes: none

Trail Website:
www.lakewobegontrails.com

ABOUT THE TRAIL

Named for the mythical town of Lake Wobegon from Garrison Keillor's "Prairie Home Campanion," the trail passes through five towns that could easily have been the model for Lake Wobegon. This is a land with deep roots in agriculture. The trail is mostly flat and wide open. Woodlands are limited to a few short stretches, so bring sunscreen. Sauk Centre, at the western end of the trail, is the home of Nobel Prize winning author Sinclair Lewis. Avon, on the eastern side, has the most lakes and woods near the trail. The trail comes right up next to I-94 between Albany and Freeport where the noise from the freeway is quite noticeable.

TRAIL HIGHLIGHTS

The churches along the trail are distinctive buildings with beautiful bell towers, and steeples. St. Mary's in Melrose is on the National Register of Historic Places, but be sure to see St. Paul's in Sauk Centre, Sacred Heart in Freeport, Seven Dolors in Albany and the Church of St. Benedict in Avon. Memoryville, near Melrose, is a unique theme park next to the trail. The six-mile stretch from Albany to Avon is the most scenic part of the trail, with a mix of woods, lakes and prairie.

ABOUT THE ROADS

Mostly paved, low traffic roads through rolling farmland. The terrain breaks up the endless fields of crops enough to keep the routes interesting. The best roads generally skirt a lakeshore or wind along low rises.

ROAD HIGHLIGHTS

Highway 173 south out of Melrose is a must ride, even if you only ride to Highway 30, then turn around and ride back to town. It rises and dips as it follows a ridge with scenic views, trees and nice little twists and turns. Highway 154, north of Albany, is a rolling twisting mix of woodlots and farm fields. Pelican Lake Road, .2 miles west of St. Anna, follows the eastern shoreline of Pelican Lake. Small lake cabins line the shore and farm fields butt up against the eastern edge of the road. For a heavenly tour of the area, sign up for the annual Tour of Saints bike ride. See Festivals and Events for more information.

HOW TO GET THERE

Avon is about 15 miles west of St. Cloud on I-94. All trail towns are directly accessible from the interstate.

Duluth

Sauk Centre
Avon

Minneapolis
St. Paul
Red Wing

Winona

Rochester

See Trail Map on page M16

Information Lake Wobegon Trail

Freeport Chamber of Commerce
Phone (320) 836-2112

Melrose Chamber of Commerce
Phone (320) 256-7174

Avon Chamber of Commerce
Phone (320) 356-7922

Albany Area Chamber of Commerce
Phone (320) 845-7777
Fax (320) 845-2346
Web www.albanymnchamber.org

Sauk Centre Chamber of Commerce
Phone (320) 352-5201
Web www.saukcentre.com

LODGING

Motels/Resorts
Albany
Country Inns & Suites
820 Shamrock Lane
Zip Code 56307
Toll Free (800) 456-4000
Phone (320) 845-2145

Avon
AmericInn Motel
304 Blattner Dr
Zip Code 56310
Toll Free (800) 634-3444
Phone (320) 356-2211
Fax (320) 356-2211

Melrose
Super 8 Motel
Zip Code 56352
Toll Free (800) 800-8000
Phone (320) 256-4261

Sauk Centre
Hillcrest Motel
Zip Code 56378
Phone (320) 352-2215

Super 8 Motel
Zip Code 56378
Toll Free (800) 800-8000
Phone (320) 352-6581

AmericInn Motel
1230 Timberlane Dr
Zip Code 56378
Toll Free (800) 634-3444
Phone (320) 352-2800
Fax (320) 352-2800

Palmer House
Highway 71, 1 mile north of I-94
Zip Code 56378
Toll Free (888) 222-3431
Phone (320) 352-3431

Gopher Prairie Motel
South Main and I-94
Zip Code 56378
Toll Free (800) 341-8000
Phone (320) 352-2275

Camping
Melrose
Sauk River Park
Zip Code 56352
Phone (320) 256-4278

Monticello
Lake Maria State Park Campground
11411 Clementa Ave NW
Zip Code 55362
Phone (612) 878-2325
Web www.dnr.state.mn.us

Richmond
El Rancho Manana
27302K Ranch Rd
Zip Code 56368
Phone (320) 597-2740

Sauk Centre
Sinclair Lewis Campgrounds
Along Sauk River in town
Zip Code 56378
Phone (320) 352-3831

Sauk Rapids
Birch Lake State Forest Campground
940 Industrial Dr #103
Zip Code 56379
Phone (320) 255-4276

RESTAURANTS
Albany
Jim & Gloria's Restaurant
Phone (320) 845-4631

Albany Restaurant
Phone (320) 845-2090

Dawn's Cafe
Phone (320) 845-4233

Avon
Main Street Cafe
Phone (320) 356-7733

Rascals Rest. & Lounge
Phone (320) 356-7880

Mr. G's Pizza & Subs
Phone (320) 356-7396

Burger Treat
Phone (320) 356-7946

Bill's Bar & Grill
Phone (320) 356-7753

P.J.'s Supper Club
Phone (320) 356-7349

Freeport
Charlie's Cafe
Phone (320) 836-2105

Ackie's P.I.
Phone (320) 836-2695

Melrose
The Countryside
Phone (320) 256-3000

Joyce's Cafe
Phone (320) 256-3225

RESTAURANTS cont'd

Sauk Centre

Palmer House Restaurant
Phone (320) 352-3431

Ding Dong Cafe
Phone (320) 352-6853

River's Edge Dining
Phone (320) 352-6505

Main Street Cafe
Phone (320) 352-5396

Jackie's Uptown Cafe
Phone (320) 352-6601

Red Carpet
Phone (320) 352-5397

Hennington's
Phone (320) 352-2591

Trucker's Inn
Phone (320) 352-3429

GROCERIES

Avon
Dahlin's Supermarket
(320) 356-7472

Freeport
Corner Store
(320) 836-2164

Melrose
Ernie's Jubilee Foods Deli

BIKE REPAIR

St. Cloud
Granite City Schwinn
Phone (320) 251-7540

Bike & Sport
Toll Free (888) 292-2453
Phone (320) 252-4537

Out-N-About Gear
Toll Free (800) 371-9036
Phone (320) 251-9036

FESTIVALS AND EVENTS

Albany
August
Heritage Day
Saturday only, two parades, firefighters
water fight, beer garden, food
vendors, mini-carnival, fireworks,
First Weekend
Phone (320) 845-7777

Avon
June
Spunktacular Days
Parade, water ski show, music, beer
garden, carnival, 5k run, Third or fourth
weekend
Phone (320) 356-7922

Cold Springs
Tour of Saints Bike Ride
50 and 35 mile tours through rich
green and rolling landscape
Web www.tourofsaints.com
Phone (320) 363-1311

Freeport
June
Freeport Crazy Days
Sidewalk sales, food vendors, First
Weekend
Phone (320) 836-2112

July
Parrish Festival
Parade, music, dance, food vendors,
beer garden, kids' games, Second
Weekend
Phone (320) 836-2112

Melrose
June
Independence Day Celebration
Parade, carnival rides, food vendors,
fireworks, Sauk River Park
Phone (320) 256-7174

Sauk Centre
July
Sinclair Lewis Days
Craft sales, parade, pageant, dance,
games, activities for kids, Third
Weekend
Phone (320) 352-5201

ALTERNATE ACTIVITIES

Albany
North Park
Picnic area, playground
Phone (320) 845-4244

Avon
Swimming beach
Beach and observation tower across
from bike trail
Phone (320) 356-7922

Melrose
Jaycee Park
Picnic area, playground, close to trail
Phone (320) 256-4278
Fax (320) 256-7174
Email chamber@meltel.net
Web www.melrosemn.org

Melrose Area Historical Society
Large collection of antique memorabil-
ia of the area, adjacent to trail
Phone (320) 256-4996

Birch Lake State Forest
Camping, boating, hiking trails
Phone (320) 255-4276
Web www.dnr.state.mn.us

Sauk Centre
Sinclair Lewis Park
Shelter, picnic area, Wednesday night
band concerts in the summer
Phone (320) 352-5201
Fax (320) 352-5202
Email chamber@saukcentre.com
Web www.saukcentre.com

ALTERNATE ACTIVITIES cont'd

Sinclair Lewis Museum and
Boyhood Home
1880 story and a half home furnished
with period furnishings, across the
street from Sinclair Lewis' birth place,
Open Memorial Day to Labor Day
Phone (320) 352-5202

Sauk Centre Area Historical Society
19th century artifacts housed in the
Bryant Public Library
Phone (320) 352-3016
Fax (320) 352-5202
Email chamber@saukcentre.com
Web www.saukcentre.com

Vital Information:

Trail Distance: 24 miles

Trail Surface: limestone

Access Points: 13th Ave in Plymouth, Parker's Lake, Vicksburg Lane, Stubb's Bay Park, Watertown

Fees and Passes: none

See Trail Map on page M18

ABOUT THE TRAIL

Originally a short line electric railway developed to take vacationers to resorts on Medicine Lake and Lake Minnetonka, the Luce Line eventually hauled grain and lumber before it was abandoned in 1970. Many remnants of the trail's railroad history still line the right of way.

TRAIL HIGHLIGHTS

The eastern end of the trail passes through remnants of the Big Woods and low density residential areas with large wooded lots. The woods continue as a buffer all the way to Watertown, but the land to the north and south opens into rural farmland. Numerous lakes and cattail marshes line the entire length of the trail.

ABOUT THE ROADS

Generally low traffic and smooth surfaced, the roads that parallel the trail offer a pleasant return route with medium rolling hills. Traffic is heavier near the parks on weekends and everywhere during weekday rush hour.

ROAD HIGHLIGHTS

Highway 26 is an ex-urban road with a mix of residential and farm land, low traffic, smooth surface and rolling hills. Roads in the Wayzata/Orono area pass through quiet residential streets with large houses and big lots. Wander off the beaten path for a look at some beautiful old estates. Baker Park Reserve offers a wide range of recreational facilities including swim-ming and bike trails. Highway 19 to the Park Reserve is generally low traffic and wide, but can get crowded with vehicles going to the Park. Lake Rebecca is another great park, but traffic is heavier on routes to the park. For more route information in this area, pick up a copy of the Twin Cities Bike Map by Little Transport Press.

HOW TO GET THERE

The eastern terminus begins in Plymouth, a suburb of Minneapolis. Take Interstate 494 to Highway 6. Go east on Highway 6 to Highway 61 (Xenium Lane) and south to 13th Ave Turn right on 13th. The trailhead is at the base of Interstate 494, less than half a mile on 13th. This trailhead will eventually move east to the southern tip of Medicine Lake. Parker Lake and Vicksburg Lane access points have better facilities. To get to either, go west on Highway 6. See city map for details. Watertown, the western terminus, can be reached by taking Highway 12 west to Delano, then take Highways 16/27 south. See trail map for details on access to Watertown and other points along the trail.

Information Luce Line Trail

Watertown City Offices
Phone (952) 955-2681
Fax (952) 955-2695
Email water2@ix.netcom.com

DNR Trails and Waterways Area Office
Phone (952) 826-6750
Fax (952) 826-6767
Web www.dnr.state.mn.us

Long Lake Chamber of Commerce
Phone (952) 473-1329

Northwest Suburban Chamber of
Commerce
Phone (763) 420-3242
Fax (763) 420-5964
Email info@nwschamber.com
Web www.nwschamber.com

Greater Wayzata Chamber of
Commerce
Phone (952) 473-9595
Fax (952) 473-6266
Email admin@wayzatachamber.com
Web www.wayzatachamber.com

Plymouth Park and Rec
Phone (763) 509-5200
Fax (763) 509-5207
Web www.ci.plymouth.mn.us

LODGING

Motels/Resorts
Plymouth
Comfort Inn Plymouth
3000 Harbor Lane
Zip Code 55447
Toll Free (877) 668-9330
Web www.bestlodging.com/sites/

Country Inn & Suites
210 Carlson Parkway North
Zip Code 55447
Toll Free (877) 668-9330

Radisson Hotel & Conference Center
3131 Campus Dr
Zip Code 55441
Toll Free (877) 668-9330

Camping
Plymouth
Baker Park Reserve
3800 Cty 24
Zip Code 55359
Phone (763) 559-6700
Web www.hennepinparks.org

RESTAURANTS

Orono
Culver's Family Restaurant
Phone (952) 471-7500

Plymouth
Panera Bread
Phone (763) 551-0954

Italianni's
Phone (952) 449-6433

Montagu's Sand. & Coffee
Phone (763) 550-1766

Wayzata
D'Amico & Sons
Phone (952) 476-8866

Wayzata Legion Post 118
Phone (952) 473-7678

Wayzata Bar & Grill
Phone (952) 473-5286

Jade Fountain
Phone (952) 473-4646

Gianni's Steakhouse
Phone (952) 404-1100

Blue Point Rest. & Oyster Bar
Phone (952) 475-3636

Black's Ford
Phone (952) 473-2940

GROCERIES
Plymouth
Rainbow Foods
(952) 476-6994

Erickson's New Market
(952) 473-1387

Cub Foods
(763) 559-2110

Wayzata
Lund's Food Stores
(952) 476-2223

BIKE REPAIR
Long Lake
Gear West Ski Bike Run
Phone (952) 473-0093

Plymouth
Plymouth Schwinn Cycling
Phone (763) 553-0331

Wayzata
Sports Hut
Phone (952) 473-8843

FESTIVALS AND EVENTS
Long Lake
June
Buckhorn Days
Friday and Saturday historic tribute to
the Buckhorn Place, fishing tourna-
ment, volleyball tournament, carnival,
kids' games, music, water ski show,
family fun, Fourth Weekend
Phone (952) 473-0890

August
Corn Days
Corn feed, beer tent, wine tasting,
food stands, children's events, music,
fun run, parade, bingo, St. George
Catholic Church, Second Weekend
Phone (952) 475-3739

FESTIVALS AND EVENTS cont'd

Maple Plain
Summer Celebration
Antique flea market, sidewalk sale, street vendors, turkey barbeque, used book sale, Third Weekend
Phone (763) 479-4222

August
Polo Classic
Polo and cricket matches, pony rides, picnic, dancing, gourmet food, fund raiser for Children's Home Society, West End Farm, First Weekend
Phone (651) 646-7771

October
Fall Festival
Scarecrow contest, farmers market, antique and flea market, concessions, kids' games, Second Weekend
Phone (763) 479-4222

Watertown
July
Rails to Trails Festival
Fire muster parade, kids' games, pet parade, Taste of Watertown, food fair, fun run, Christian music festival, Fourth Weekend
Phone (952) 955-2681

Wayzata
September
James J. Hill Days
Weekend after Labor Day, kids' games, arts and crafts fair, food booths, parade, historical displays, antique show, dachshund races
Phone (952) 473-9595

ALTERNATE ACTIVITIES

Long Lake
Wolsfeld Woods
DNR Scientific and Natural Area, 185 acres with hiking trails, Woodlands, blooming wildflowers in spring, Highway 6 at Brown Rd
Phone (651) 296-6157

Maple Plain
Baker Park Reserve
Fishing, swimming, hiking, picnicking, play area, concessions, bike trail
Phone (763) 479-2964
Web www.hennepinparks.org

Homestead Orchard
Spring strawberries, fall raspberries and appple picking, picnic table, hayrides, petting zoo, pumpkin patch and observation beehive, year round pre-arranged group hayrides
Phone (763) 479-3186
Web www.homesteadorchard.com

Orono
Wood-Rill
400 year old growth forest, DNR Scientific & Natural Area located on Old Long Lake Rd
Phone (651) 296-6157

Plymouth
Clifton E. French Park
Fishing, swimming, hiking, picnicking, play area, concessions, bike trail
Phone (763) 559-8891
Fax (763) 550-9460
Web www.hennepinparks.org

Severs Farm Market and Corn Maze
Seasonal summer produce, pick your own pumpkins, corn maze mid-August to Halloween
Phone (763) 974-5000
Web www.severscornmaze.com

Rockford
Lake Rebecca Park Reserve
Picnicking, play area, mountain bike trails, boat rentals
Phone (763) 479-2964
Web www.hennepinparks.org

Wayzata
Trolley Rides
Free trolley departs from the historic Wayzata Depot and circulates throughout the commercial district from mid-May to mid-October, Wednesday evening concerts at the depot, June into August
Phone (952) 473-9595

SW Regional LRT Trails

Vital Information:

Trail Distance: North Trail 16 miles, South Trail 12 miles

Trail Surface: limestone

Access Points: North-Hopkins, Excelsior, Victoria; South-Hopkins, Edenvale Park, Miller Park, Lake Riley Park, Chaska

Fees and Passes: none

ABOUT THE TRAILS

These two former rail beds may someday become light rail corridors for the western suburbs. Until then, they supply bicycle escape routes to the western edges of the sprawling Twin Cities. The northern route is the older trail. It passes through the old wealth of Lake Minnetonka on its way to Carver Park Reserve. Marinas, mansions and money give way to a mix of rural land and suburban sprawl until the trail ends at the little town of Victoria. Carver Park Reserve is readily accessible from Victoria and worth the visit. The southern trail is being extended east toward Minneapolis. To the west it passes through a blend of new wealth and middle class subdivisions with a mix of lakes, parks and restored prairie.

TRAIL HIGHLIGHTS

Both trails begin in Hopkins, a suburb that has maintained a very comfortable, human-scale downtown. Stop in historic Excelsior for a stroll down Main Street, then take a shaded break at Excelsior Commons on the shore of Lake Minnetonka. Minnetonka has its own system of bike trails. The most interesting begins behind the Minnetonka High School and runs down to Purgatory Park, a 6 mile round trip including the trail through Purgatory Park. See trail map for details. The southern LRT trail skirts Shady Oak Lake and Lake Riley, then opens to a grand view of the Minnesota River and the Minnesota Valley Wildlife Refuge. From here to the southern trailhead at Bluff Creek Drive, the trail drops quickly. The 1 mile extension southwest of the trail-head runs through hillside fields, then ends abruptly at Highway 212. From this point, road routes will take you to downtown Chaska with its tree lined town square and older brick buildings. Go south on Chestnut Street, (Highway 41) to the town square. See city map.

ABOUT THE ROADS

Expect traffic on the roads in this area. The three main routes shown here connect the two trails together to create several loop options. For more information about road and trail routes in this area, pick up a copy of the Twin Cities Bike Map by Little Transport Press.

ROAD ROUTE HIGHLIGHTS

Smithtown Road offers a quiet alternate to the trail. Low rolling hills and large estates dot this short stretch of road. Highways 43 and 10 still hold their rural charm and connect the two trails as they pass through rolling hills and open farm land.

HOW TO GET THERE

Hopkins is just off Highway 169 west of Minneapolis. Take Excelsior Blvd (Highway 3) west about half a mile to 8th Ave South. The southern trail begins at the back of the park-and-ride lot on the south side of Excelsior Blvd. You can park here for the north trail as well and take 8th Ave to half a block north of Main Street. The trail begins behind a row of bushes. See city map for details. See the trail map for highway routes to other access points along the north and south trails.

Duluth

Hopkins Minneapolis
Victoria St. Paul
Chanhassen Red Wing

Winona

Rochester

See Trail Map on page M20

TOURIST INFORMATION

Chaska Chamber of Commerce
Phone (952) 448-5000
Fax (952) 448-4261
Email chaska@chaska_chamber.org
Web www.chaska_chamber.org

Eden Prairie Chamber of Commerce
Phone (952) 944-2830
Fax (952) 944-0229
Email adminj@epchamber.org
Web www.epchamber.org

Eden Prairie City Hall
Phone (952) 949-8300
Fax (952) 949-8390
Web www.edenprairie.org

Excelsior Area Chamber of Commerce
Phone (952) 474-6461
Fax (952) 474-3139
Web www.excelsioronline.com

Twin West Chamber of Commerce
Phone (612) 540-0234
Web www.twinwest.com

LODGING

Motels/Resorts

Chanhassen
Country Suites by Carlson
591 West 78th St
Zip Code 55317
Phone (952) 937-2424

Hopkins
The Hopkins House
1501 Highway 7
Zip Code 55305
Toll Free (800) 328-6024
Phone (952) 935-7711
Fax (952) 933-3621

Minnetonka
Minneapolis Marriott Southwest
5801 Opus Pky
Zip Code 55343

Phone (952) 935-5500
Fax (952) 935-2718

Bed and Breakfast

Chaska
Bluff Creek B&B
1161 Bluff Creek Dr
Zip Code 55318
Phone (952) 445-2735
Email jmeggen@aol.com

The Peacock Inn
314 Walnut St
Zip Code 55318
Phone (952) 368-4343
Email innkeeper@peacockn.com

Excelsior
James H Clark House
371 Water St
Zip Code 55331
Phone (952) 474-0196
Web www.bbonline.com

Camping

Victoria
Carver Park Reserve
7200 Victoria Drive
Zip Code 55386
Phone: (763) 559-6700
Web www.hennepinparks.org

RESTAURANTS

Excelsior
The Bean & Wine Cafe
Phone (952) 474-7428

Hopkins
Hoagies Restaurant
Phone (952) 938-0078

Mainstreet Bar & Grill
Phone (952) 938-2400

The Big 10 Restaurant
Phone (952) 930-0369

Hopkins Best Steak House
Phone (952) 938-0078

Michelangelo Cafe
Phone (952) 938-2211

Minnetonka
Snuffy's Malt Shop
Phone (952) 475-1850

Zaroff's Delicatessen
Phone (952) 545-9090

Schlotzsky's
Phone (952) 933-9775

Market Bar-B-Que
Phone (952) 475-1770

Sherlock's Home
Phone (952) 931-0203

Sidney's Pizza Cafe
Phone (952) 933-1000

GROCERIES

Hopkins
Tait's SuperValu
(952) 938-6301

BIKE RENTAL

Chanhassen
Bokoo Bikes
Phone (952) 934-6468

Chaska
The Bicycle Shop
Phone (952) 448-9911

Excelsior
Area Wide Cycle
Phone (952) 474-3229

BIKE REPAIR

Chanhassen
Bokoo Bikes
Phone (952) 934-6468

BIKE REPAIR cont'd

Chaska
The Bicycle Shop
Phone (952) 448-9911

Eden Prairie
Prairie Cycle and Ski
Phone (952) 942-8685

Excelsior
Area Wide Cycle
Phone (952) 474-3229

Hopkins
Now Bikes and Fitness
Phone (952) 935-8207

FESTIVALS AND EVENTS

Chaska
June
Taste of Chaska
Wednesday evening sometime in
June, call chamber for date
Phone (952) 448-5000

July
River City Days
Music, arts and crafts show, kids'
games, food booths, City Square Park,
Fourth Weekend
Phone (952) 448-5000

Eden Prairie
June
MN Festival of Jazz on the Prairie
Staring Lake Amphitheater, usually
Second Sunday
Phone (952) 949-8453

Lions Club Schooner Days Festival
Round Lake Park, family activities, carnival rides, softball tourney, 1st weekend in June or last weekend in May
Phone (952) 937-8972

July
4th of July celebration
Round Lake and Staring Lake Parks,
triathlon, softball tourney, mixed dou-
bles tennis, fireworks
Phone (952) 949-8453

August
Eden Prairie Lions Club Corn feed
Round Lake Park, First Saturday
Phone (952) 937-8972

Diverse City/Taste on the Prairie
Staring Lake Amphitheater, food
booths and entertainment, usually the
second Sunday
Phone (952) 949-8453

SunBonnet Day
Cummins Grill Homestead, old fash-
ioned ice-cream social, usually third
Sunday
Phone (952) 949-8453

October
Oktoberfest
Staring Lake Amphitheater Celebrates
German background of the community,
entertainment, food, children's activi-
ties, hay rides, noon to 6, First Sunday
Phone (952) 949-8453

Excelsior
May
Memorial Day Parade
Patriotic program and parade
Phone (952) 474-6461

Excelsior Boat Show
Boat displays in Lyman Park, food ven-
dors, ride the Excelsior Streetcar, Third
Weekend
Phone (952) 474-6461

June
Art on the Lake
200 juried artists from all over the U.S,
food, music, kids' activities, at
Commons Park on Lake Minnetonka,
Second Weekend
Phone (763) 474-6461

July
Fireman's Dance
Annual Friday night street dance spon-
sored by Excelsior Volunteer Fire Dept,
Third Weekend
Phone (952) 474-6461

Old Fashioned Fourth of July
Kids' parade, kids' fishing contest,
sand castle contest, 10k fun run, food
and entertainment, evening perfor-
mance by Minnesota Orchestra, fireworks off Excelsior Bay
Phone (952) 474-6461

September
Apple Day
Apples, antiques, art, accessories,
autumn harvest, entertainment, family
fun, Third Saturday
Phone (952) 474-6461

Hopkins
July
Raspberry Festival
10 day celebration including golf tourney, Grand Day Parade, kids' fishing
contest, music in the park, softball, volleyball, bike race, tent dances, 5-mile
run, Second Weekend
Phone (952) 931-0878

ALTERNATE ACTIVITIES

Chanhassen
Minnesota Landscape Arboretum
Over a thousand acres of rolling hills, grand vistas, display gardens, and plant collections, three mile drive/bike, hiking trails, picnic facilities, restaurant
Phone (952) 443-1400
Fax (952) 443-2521
Email bonnie@arboretum.umn.edu
Web www.arboretum@umn.edu

Eden Prairie
Summer Concert Series
Staring Lake Amphitheater, 7:00pm
Sun, Wed, and Fri evenings mid-June through mid-August
Phone (952) 949-8453

Excelsior
Water Street shops
Antique and specialty shops, restaurants, Minnesota Transportation Museum, old train depot
Phone (952) 474-6461

Minnetrista
Lake Minnetonka Regional Park
Swimming, play area, boat launch
Phone (952) 474-4822

Victoria
Boorsma Farm
Farmer's market, pick your own strawberries and raspberries
Phone (952) 443-2068

Grimm Farm
Located in Carver Park, historic farm house under construction as an interpretive center
Phone (763) 559-9000
Web www.hennepinparks.org

Carver Park Reserve
3300 acres of marsh, tamarack swamp, rolling hills, wooded areas, lots of lakes, camping, hiking, biking, in-line skating, fishing, bird watching, picnic areas, fishing pier, boat launch, access to LRT Trail
Phone (763) 559-9000
Web www.hennepinparks.org

Lowry Nature Center
Located within Carver Park Reserve, hiking trails, free Sunday afternoon family programming, "Habitat" educational play area
Phone (952) 472-4911
Fax (952) 472-5420
Web www.hennepinparks.org

Gateway Trail

See Trail Map on page M22

Vital Information:

Trail distance: 17 miles

Trail Surface: asphalt

Access Points: Cayuga St (St. Paul, no parking), Arlington Ave, Phalen-Kellor Park, Flicek Park (Maplewood), Hadley Ave, numerous streets, Pine Point Park

Fees and passes: none

ABOUT THE TRAIL

Part of the Willard Munger Trail, which will eventually run from St. Paul to Duluth, the Gateway provides an urban escape route from near downtown St. Paul to the countryside at Pine Point Park. The trail is very popular, for good reasons, and heavily used by bicyclists, in-line skaters and walkers, especially on weekends and holidays.

TRAIL HIGHLIGHTS

The western end, in St. Paul, passes golf courses, parks, cemeteries and other green spaces. Spur trails circle through Phalen Park near Keller and Phalen Lakes. The central portion runs along Highway 36 and is not attractive, but it does offer ice cream and fast food stops near the trail. North of Highway 36, the trail moves into a semi-rural area with lakes, fields and trees. Quite attractive, especially so close to an urban center. The trailhead at Pine Point has bathrooms, running water and some shade.

ABOUT THE ROADS

Flat to low rolling, the roads toward the northeastern end of the trail pass mostly through farm fields and wide open spaces. Traffic is generally low, but can spike occasionally or change because of new developments in the ex-urban lands around the city. For more road information, refer to the Twin Cities Bike Map by Little Transport Press.

ROAD HIGHLIGHTS

Take an out-and-back loop to Square Lake Park, about four and a half miles northeast of the Pine Point Trailhead. The lake is pretty and clear. The park has a public beach and bathhouse. Withrow is a quiet little town just beyond the relentless urban sprawl. Traffic on Highways 9 and 66 will vary with the time of day and day of the week. The Demontreville Loop circles and passes between lakes, trees and housing developments. The little spur between Lakes Demontreville and Olson is at water's edge and passes through an older development with mature trees and narrow roads.

HOW TO GET THERE

See city and trail maps for details.

TOURIST INFORMATION

Greater Stillwater Chamber of
Commerce
Phone (651) 439-4001
Fax (651) 439-4035
Email chamber@stillwtr.com
Web www.ilovestillwater.com

St. Paul Convention and Visitors
Bureau
Toll Free (800) 627-6101
Phone (651) 265-4900
Fax (651) 265-4999
Email spcvb@stpaulcvb.org
Web www.stpaulcvb.org

DNR
Toll Free (888) 646-6367
Phone (651) 296-6699
Fax (651) 297-3618
Email info@dnr.state.mn.us
Web www.dnr.state.mn.us

LODGING

Motels/Resorts
Maplewood
Best Western Inn
1780 East County D
Zip Code 55109
Toll Free (800) 528-1234
Phone (651) 770-2811

Bed and Breakfast
Marine on St. Croix
ASA Parker House
17500 St. Croix Trail North
Zip Code 55047
Toll Free (888) 857-9969
Phone (651) 433-5248
Email asaparkr@pressenter.com
Web www.asaparker.com

Camping
Hastings
Afton State Park
6959 Keller Ave South
Zip Code 55047
Phone (651) 436-5391
Web www.dnr.state.mn.us

Marine on St. Croix
William O'Brien State Park
16821 O'Brien Trail North
Zip Code 55047
Phone (651) 433-0500
Web www.dnr.state.mn.us

RESTAURANTS

Stillwater
Dock Cafe
Phone (651) 430-3770

Gasthaus Bavarian Hunter
Phone (651) 439-7128

GROCERIES

Stillwater
Rainbow Foods
(651) 439-9299

BIKE RENTAL

North St. Paul
Lowry's Bikes
Phone (651) 770-6340

St. Paul
Como Bike Shop
Phone (651) 488-9078

BIKE REPAIR

Maplewood
Strauss Skates and Bicycles
Toll Free (888) 770-1344
Phone (651) 770-1344
Fax (651) 770-2486

St. Paul
Como Bike Shop
Phone (651) 488-9078
Email contact through website
Web www.hunterbc.net

Stillwater
St. Croix Bike and Skate
Phone (651) 439-2337
Fax (651) 351-5434

FESTIVALS AND EVENTS

St. Paul
May
Festival of Nations
Multicultural celebration at
RiverCentre, First Weekend
Toll Free (800) 627-6101
Phone (651) 265-4900

Cinco de Mayo Mexican Fiesta
Parade, food and entertainment, West
side of St. Paul, First Weekend
Toll Free (800) 627-6101
Phone (651) 222-6347

June
Grand Old Day
Parade, entertainment, crafts, food
and activities along Grand Ave
First Weekend
Toll Free (800) 627-6101
Phone (651) 699-0029

July
A Taste of Minnesota
4th of July celebration at the State
Capitol grounds with music, food,
and fireworks
Toll Free (800) 627-6101
Phone (651) 291-5600

Information Gateway Trail

August
Irish Festival
Irish music, dancing, food, and crafts, at University of St. Thomas, Second Weekend
Toll Free (800) 627-6101
Phone (651) 474-7411

Minnesota State Fair
One of the largest state fairs in the U.S., Fourth Weekend
Toll Free (800) 627-6101
Phone (651) 642-2200

Stillwater
May
Rivertown Art Fair
Arts, crafts, food, entertainment, in Lowell Park, Third Weekend
Phone (651) 439-4001

June
Music on the Waterfront
Free outdoor concerts at Lowell Park Wednesday evenings
Phone (651) 439-4001

Taste of Stillwater
Sampling of Stillwater's finest restaurants all under one tent, live music, Third Weekend
Phone (651) 439-4001

July
Fourth of July
Parade and fireworks on the St. Croix
Phone (651) 439-4001

Lumberjack Days
Exhibitions, competitions, parade, 10K and half marathon runs, craft fair, food vendors, music, kids' games and rides, fireworks, Fourth Weekend
Phone (651) 439-4001

September
Oktoberfest
Polka bands and food, at Gasthaus Bavarian Hunter, Last two full weekends in September
Phone (651) 439-7128

October
Fall Colors Fine Art and Jazz
Juried fine art, jazz bands and food vendors, at Lowell Park, First Weekend
Phone (651) 439-4001

ALTERNATE ACTIVITIES

Marine on St. Croix
William O'Brien State Park
Camping, hiking, interpretive programs, canoeing (rentals available), swimming, picnicking
Phone (651) 433-0500
Fax (651) 433-0504
Web www.dnr.state.mn.us

Roseville
Harriet Alexander Nature Center
Trails through marsh, prairie and forest
Phone (651) 415-2161

St. Paul
Minnesota Children's Museum
Interactive children's museum geared to kids under 10 years old and their families
Phone (651) 225-6000
Fax (651) 225-6006
Email cm@mcm.org
Web www.mcm.org

Paddleford Packet Boat Company
Sternwheeler riverboat cruises on the Mississippi, from Harriet Island
Toll Free (800) 543-3908
Phone (651) 227-1100
Fax (651) 227-0543
Email www.riverrides.com
Web www.riverrides.com

Down In History Tours
Several tours, including the popular St. Paul Gangster Tour, haunts and hideouts of America's most notorious gangsters. Others include the Rivers and Roots Tour, The Caves Tour, and The Victorian Tour
Phone (651) 292-1220
Fax (651) 224-0059
Web www.downinhistory.com

Farmers Market
290 East 5th St Saturday mornings, May to October
Phone (651) 227-8101

Como Park Zoo and Conservatory
Zoological exhibits, botanical gardens, with summer concerts at Lakeside Pavilion
Phone (651) 487-8200
Fax (651) 487-8203
Web ci.stpaul.mn.us/depts/parks

Minnesota Brewing Company
One hour free brewery tour by appointment only
Phone (651) 290-8209l
Web www.grainbelt.com

Minnesota Museum of American Art
Diverse collection of American Art, including paintings, crafts and sculptures
Phone (651) 292-4355
Fax (651) 292-4340
Web www.mtn.org/mmaa

Fitzgerald Theater
Home of Garrison Keillor's "A Prairie Home Companion"
Phone (651) 290-1221
Fax (651) 290-1195
Web www.prairiehome.org

ALTERNATE ACTIVITIES cont'd

Capitol City Trolley
Historical tours of downtown St. Paul,
Thursdays, by reservation only
Phone (651) 223-5600
Fax (651) 793-8731

Minnesota State Capitol Tours
Tour the House, Senate, Supreme
Court, and governor's reception room
Toll Free (800) 657-3773
Phone (651) 296-2881
Fax (651) 297-1502
Email statecapitol@mnhs.org
Web www.mnhs.org

Phalen Keller Park
Picnic areas, walking and bike trails,
swimming, Wheelock Pky at Arcade St
Phone (651) 266-6400

Science Museum of Minnesota
Hands on science exhibits, world class
collection of fossils and artifacts,
Omnitheater
Toll Free (800) 221-9444
Phone (651) 221-9444
Fax (651) 221-4777
Web www.smm.org

Stillwater

Aamodt's Apple Farm and St. Croix
Vineyard
Pick your own or buy, hayrides, hot air
balloon rides
Phone (651) 439-3127
Web www.aamodtsapplefarm.com

Antique shopping
Minnesota's antique mecca,
downtown area
Phone (651) 439-7700

Nature's Nectar
Local honey, comb honey, beeswax
products, call ahead
Phone (651) 439-8793
Email natnec@quest.net

Wolf Brewery Caves
10,000 square feet of caves, open for
afternoon tours, Spring through Fall
Phone (651) 439-3588
Fax (651) 439-0019

Rockin' R Ranch
Carriage and hay rides, lessons,
trail rides
Phone (651) 439-6878

Minnesota Zephyr
Elegant, restored dining train along the
St. Croix River Valley with hits of the
40s and 50s by the Zephyr Cabaret
Toll Free (800) 992-6100
Phone (651) 430-3000
Web www.minnesotazephyr.com

Historic tours
Guided tours of downtown Stillwater
Phone (651) 439-4001
Fax (651) 439-4035
Email chamber@stllwtr.com
Web www.ilovestillwater.com

Northern Vineyards
Downtown Stillwater, wine tasting,
tours by appointment
Phone (651) 430-1032
Email northernvineyards@att.net
Web www.northernvineyards.com

White Bear Lake

Pine Tree Apple Orchards of White
Bear Lake
Pick your own strawberries and
apples. pumpkin patch, wagon rides,
hiking in the orchards
Phone (651) 429-7202
Fax (651) 429-4593

Cannon Valley Trail

Vital Information:

Trail Distance: 20 miles

Trail Surface: asphalt

Access Points: Cannon Falls, Welch Village, Red Wing

Fees and Passes: Wheel Pass $2.00/day, $10.00 season. No charge for children under 18.

Trail Website:
www.cannonvalleytrail.com

See Trail Map on page M24

ABOUT THE TRAIL

This former Chicago Great Western Rail Line runs along the south side of the Cannon River from Cannon Falls to Red Wing. Views from the trail include panoramic overlooks near Cannon Falls and intimate river bottom near Red Wing. The trail drops at a steady rate from Cannon Falls on the west to Red Wing on the east. Watch for old railway mileposts and a wide variety of wildflowers.

TRAIL HIGHLIGHTS

The bluffs come right up to the trail on the south and the river drops away to the north between Cannon Falls and Anderson Memorial Rest Area, creating spectacular panoramic views of the river and a damp micro environment supporting ferns, mosses and lichens. An eagle's nest has been spotted about 4 miles east of Welch Village Station near the Cannon River Turtle Preserve.

ABOUT THE ROADS

This is bluff country. The marked routes are hilly, smooth, low traffic and rural in character. Ride all the way from end to end or cut back to the trail at the halfway point, near Welch Village. Roads to the north of the Cannon River tend to be gravel. Expect to climb from the trail to all road routes.

ROAD ROUTE HIGHLIGHTS

County Road 1 climbs from the Mississippi River Valley in Red Wing to the rural highlands of Goodhue County. Once out of the river valley, expect rolling ridge top to the town of White Rock, then more pronounced up and down to Highway 25. Traffic is heavy near Red Wing, so consider the alternate route laid out in the Red Wing City Map. Highway 25 climbs long and steady out of Cannon Falls, then settles into rolling ridge top to Highway 1. Highway 7 connects the trail to the tiny town of Vasa via a long climb, then rolls up and down to Highway 1. Check out the Vasa Museum and the nearby Lutheran Church on the hill. The cemetery next to the church has tombstones dating back to the middle 1800s. Cannon Bottoms and Colischan roads offer an interesting diversion. These minimum maintenance, gravel roads delve into the heart of the Mississippi River floodplain. Colischan Rd is at water level and sometimes underwater. Ride as far as you feel comfortable. Wide tires work best.

HOW TO GET THERE

Cannon Falls is off Hwy 52, about midway between the Twin Cities and Rochester. Red Wing is 45 miles southeast of St. Paul on Highway 61. To get to Welch Village, at the midpoint of the trail, take Hwy 7 south from Hwy 61, about 8 miles west of Red Wing. Watch for the Welch Village signs. See city maps for directions to trailheads in Cannon Falls and Red Wing.

Cannon Valley Trail, Cannon Falls
Phone (507) 263-0508
Fax (507) 263-5843
Email info@cannonvalleytrail.com
Web www.cannonvalleytrail.com

Cannon Valley Trail, Welch
Phone (651) 258-4141

Cannon Falls Chamber of Commerce
Phone (507) 263-2289
Fax (507) 263-2785
Email tourism@cannonfalls.org
Web www.cannonfalls.org

Red Wing Visitor and Convention
Bureau
Toll Free (800) 498-3444
Phone (651) 385-5934
Fax (651) 388-0991
Email visitorinfo@redwing.org
Web www.redwing.org

LODGING

Motels/Resorts
Cannon Falls
Caravan Motel
Highway 52
Zip Code 55009
Phone (507) 263-4777

Edgewood Motel
Highway 52
Zip Code 55009
Phone (507) 263-5700

Best Western Saratoga Inn
Highway 52 & County 24
Zip Code 55009
Phone (507) 263-7272

Red Wing
Super 8 Motel
232 Withers Harbor Dr
Zip Code 55066
Toll Free (800) 800-8000
Phone (651) 388-0491

St. James Hotel
406 Main St
Zip Code 55066
Toll Free (800) 252-1875
Phone (651) 388-2846
Web www.st-james-hotel.com

Rodeway Inn
Highway 61 & Withers Harbor Dr
Zip Code 55066
Toll Free (800) 228-2000
Phone (651) 388-1502

Parkway Motel
3425 Highway 61 West
Zip Code 55066
Toll Free (800) 762-0934
Phone (651) 388-8231

Days Inn
Highways 61 & 63
Zip Code 55066
Toll Free (800) 325-2525
Phone (651) 388-3568

Best Western Quiet House & Suites
Highway 61 & Withers Harbor Dr
Zip Code 55066
Toll Free (800) 528-1234
Phone (651) 388-1577

AmericInn
1819 Old West Main
Zip Code 55066
Toll Free (800) 634-3444
Phone (651) 385-9060
Fax (651) 385-8139

Bed and Breakfast
Cannon Falls
Quill and Quilt
615 Hoffman St
Zip Code 55009
Toll Free (800) 488-3848
Phone (507) 263-5507
Web www.quillandquilt.com

Country Quiet Inn
37295 112th Ave Way
Zip Code 55009
Toll Free (800) 258-1843
Phone (651) 258-4406
Email country@rconnect.com

Red Wing
The Golden Lantern Inn
721 East Ave
Zip Code 55066
Toll Free (888) 288-3315
Phone (651) 388-3315
Email goldenla@win.bright.net
Web www.goldenlantern.com

Lawther Octagon House B&B
927 West 3rd St
Zip Code 55066
Phone (651) 388-8483

Moondance Inn
1105 West 4th St
Zip Code 55066
Phone (651) 388-8145
Fax (651) 388-9655

Red Wing Blackbird
722 West 5th St
Zip Code 55066
Phone (651) 388-2292
Web www.pressenter.com/-blakbird/

The Candlelight Inn
818 West 3rd St
Zip Code 55066
Toll Free (800) 254-9194
Phone (651) 388-8034
Email candlerw@rconnect.com
Web www.candlelightinn-redwing.com

Welch
Hungry Point Inn
One Olde Deerfield Rd
Zip Code 55089
Phone (651) 437-3660

Information Cannon Valley Trail

LODGING cont'd

Camping
Cannon Falls
Cannon Falls Campground
30365 Oak Lane
Zip Code 55009
Phone (507) 263-3145
Fax (507) 263-5138

Lake Byllesby Regional Park
Campground
7650 Echo Point Rd
Zip Code 55009
Phone (507) 263-4447

Lake City
Dorer Memorial Hardwood State Forest
1801 South Oak
Zip Code 55041
Phone (651) 345-3216

Red Wing
Hay Creek Valley Campground
31673 Highway 58 Blvd
Zip Code 55066
Toll Free (888) 388-3998
Phone (651) 388-3998

Welch
Hidden Valley Campground
27173 144th Ave
Zip Code 55089
Phone (651) 258-4550

RESTAURANTS

Cannon Falls
Lorentz Meats & Deli
Toll Free (800) 535-6382
Phone (507) 263-3617

Hi-Quality Bakery
Phone (507) 263-2221

Dairy Inn
Phone (507) 263-4141

Pizza Man
Phone (507) 263-5553

Piccadilly's Circus
Phone (507) 263-2014

Ellie's
Phone (507) 263-2296

Dudley's Pizza & Sandwich
Phone (507) 263-4000

Cuppa Caffe
Phone (507) 263-2580

Brewster's Bar & Grill
Phone (507) 263-5020

Red Wing
Staghead
Phone (651) 388-6581

Lily's Coffee House & Flowers
Phone (651) 388-8797

Braschler's Bakery & Coffee Shop
Phone (651) 388-1589

Eagles Nest Coffee House
Phone (651) 388-1280

Randy's Restaurant
Phone (651) 388-1551

Tea Room & Gift Shoppe
Phone (651) 388-2250

Marie's Casual Dining & Lounge
Phone (651) 388-1896

Liberty's Rest & Lounge
Phone (651) 388-8877

GROCERIES

Cannon Falls
Cannon SuperValu
(507) 263-3643

Red Wing
County Market
(651) 388-8258

BIKE RENTAL

Cannon Falls
Trail Station & Bicycle Works
Phone (507) 263-5055

Red Wing
Outdoor Store
Phone (651) 388-5358
Email outdoor@pressenter.com
Web www.outdoorstore.forabike.com

Four Seasons Bike
Phone (651) 385-8614

BIKE REPAIR

Cannon Falls
Cannon Falls Trail Station
Phone (507) 263-5055

Lindahl Tire and Battery
Phone (507) 263-2111
Fax (507) 263-5896

Red Wing
Four Seasons Bike
Phone (651) 385-8614

Outdoor Store
Phone (651) 388-5358
Fax (651) 388-7802
Email outdoor@pressenter.com
Web www.outdoorstore.forabike.com

BIKE SHUTTLE

Cannon Falls
Trail Station and Bicycle Works
Phone (507) 263-5055

FESTIVALS AND EVENTS

Cannon Falls
Farmer's Market
Saturdays at downtown city parking lot
during growing season.
Phone (507) 263-2289

FESTIVALS AND EVENTScont'd

Voices of the Valley
Natural and cultural resource people along the trail to answer questions on a variety of topics, May through Sept, 1st Saturday
Phone (507) 263-0508

May

Memorial Day Parade
Parade and service at Colvill Memorial
Phone (507) 263-2289

June

National Trails Day
Music, refreshments, and other programs in addition to Voices of the Valley programs, First Saturday
Phone (507) 263-0508

Cannon Falls Classic
60 mile bike race on county roads and up to 30 mile tour on trail, Second Saturday
Phone (507) 263-2289

July

Cannon Valley Fair
Parade, carnival, harness racing, exhibits and fireworks, First Weekend
Phone (507) 263-2289

Little Log House Antique Power Show
Antique and classic tractor show, flea market, craft sale, home of the replica of the famed Hastings Spiral Bridge, Third Weekend
Phone (507) 263-2289

August

Cruisin' Days
Friday night '50s car cruise and dance, Saturday merchant Crazy Days, Sunday Classic car show, First Sunday
Phone (507) 263-2289

September

Community Wide Garage Sale
Third Saturday after Labor Day
Phone (507) 263-2289

October

Sogn Valley Craft Fair
Arts, crafts, and local farm produce at the Edgewood Restaurant, First Weekend
Phone (507) 263-5700

Red Wing

May

85 Mile Garage Sale
Residents and stores in the thirteen river towns around Lake Pepin participate in a huge garage sale spectacular. First Weekend
Toll Free (888) 999-2619

July

Red Wing Collectors' Society
Auctions, sales, and swaps of Red Wing Pottery, Second Weekend
Toll Free (800) 977-7927
Phone (651) 385-5934

August

River City Days
Parade, family events, arts and crafts, carnival, fireworks, at Bay Point Park, First Weekend
Toll Free (800) 762-9516
Phone (651) 388-4719

October

Fall Festival of Arts
Juried art festival featuring 75 artists, Minnesota book fair, film festival and music, childrens' activities, food and entertainment, downtown, Second Weekend
Toll Free (800) 762-9516
Phone (651) 388-7569

Sheep Dog Trials
Farmers and ranchers from throughout the US and Canada compete. Cty 1 and 200th Ave, Second Weekend
Toll Free (800) 852-4422
Phone (651) 385-5934

ALTERNATE ACTIVITIES

Cannon Falls

Countryside Antique Mall
Over 40 antique dealers under one roof
Phone (507) 263-0352

Downtown Cannon Falls
29 downtown properties listed on the National Registry of Historic Places
Phone (507) 263-2289
Fax (507) 263-2785
Email tourism@cannonfalls.org
Web www.cannonfalls.org

Cannon Falls Historical Museum
Local history, call library for hours
Phone (507) 263-2804

Frontenac

Frontenac State Park
Wooded bluffs with scenic views, camping, boating, fishing, picnic areas, Explore Old Frontenac—historic river town
Phone (651) 345-3401

Red Wing

Antique shopping and architecture walking tour, downtown
Toll Free (800) 498-3444
Phone (651) 385-5934

Levee Park

Downtown on the Mississippi River, docking site of Mississippi steamboats
Toll Free (800) 498-3444
Phone (651) 385-5934

Information Cannon Valley Trail

ALTERNATE ACTIVITIES cont'd

Barn Bluff and Sorin's Bluff
Miles of bluff hiking above Red Wing
Phone (800) 498-3444

Historic Pottery District
Antique Alley, Redwing Pottery
salesroom, Pottery Place, factory out-
lets, specialty shops, eateries and
antique dealers, Old West Main St
Toll Free (800) 498-3444
Phone (651) 385-5934

Sheldon Theatre
Oldest municipally owned theater in
the US, call for schedule
Toll Free (800) 899-5759
Phone (651) 385-3667
Web www.sheldontheatre.com

Goodhue County Historical Society
Kid-friendly historical museum
Phone (651) 388-6024
Web www.goodhistory.org

Vital Information:

Trail distance: 12 miles

Trail Surface: asphalt

Access Points: Willmar, Spicer, New London

Fees and passes: none

ABOUT THE TRAIL

A little gem in the otherwise flat lands of western Minnesota. The trail is in the heart of a glacial moraine, the end point of a vast glacier that pushed south out of Canada. Because of the moraine, lakes, cattail marshes, rolling hills and numerous wooded pockets of land surround the trail. Spicer is the logical trailhead. It's in town within blocks of Green Lake at Spicer City Park. Willmar has better facilities inside the Civic Center building including bathrooms, showers and drinking water, but the trailhead itself is located near the end of the gigantic paved parking lot of the Civic Center, an uninviting spot without a single tree or rest bench to aid the trail user.

TRAIL HIGHLIGHTS

The most interesting section is from Spicer north. This is a short trail overall, so you should be able to ride to the abrupt end of the trail at the intersection of 187th Ave NE and Riverview Lane. The southern portion of the trail moves into flatter land with larger farm fields and fewer lakes. The trail is still quite attractive, but the northern section sets a pretty high standard by comparison.

ABOUT THE ROADS

Much of the road route follows the Glacial Ridge Trail, a locally designated scenic route that follows the rising and falling terrain of the terminal moraine. Quite a few hills, some tall, but the climbs and descents are moderately steep at the worst. Traffic is low, scenery is high and the roads are in good condition. Although the number of roads is limited, the quality is outstanding.

ROAD HIGHLIGHTS

Highway 40 winds its way over a large climb in the first mile and a half east of the trail, then drops down to County 4 and Indian Beach Road along the eastern shore of Green Lake. Indian Beach Road is a cabin road. It passes small to mid sized cabins and year round homes as it follows the eastern shore back to Spicer. The reward at the end of the loop is a city park with beach and nearby restaurants and drinking establishments.

HOW TO GET THERE

Willmar is 100 miles west of the Twin Cities on Highway 12. Turn right on County 9 just before Highway 71. County 9 becomes 3rd St NE. Go 1.8 miles north, until you cross the trail, turn left and go 0.1miles to the Willmar Trailhead. To get to Spicer, continue on Highway 12 to Highway 71, go north to the Highway 23 exit. Highway 23 runs into Spicer. The trailhead is half a block off the Highway.

See Trail Map on page M26

Information Glacial Lakes State Trail

Willmar Chamber of Commerce
Phone (320) 235-0300
Fax (320) 231-1948
Email kwarner@willmar.com
Web www.willmarareachamber.com

Willmar Convention and Visitors
Bureau
Toll Free (800) 845-8747
Phone (320) 235-3552
Fax (320) 231-1948
Email michelle@seeyouinwillmar.com
Web www.seeyouinwillmar.com

New London Chamber of Commerce
Phone (320) 354-7111
Fax (320) 354-4001
Email nlcity@tds.net
Web www.ci.new-london.mn.us

City of Spicer
Phone (320) 796-5562
Fax (320) 796-2044
Email spicer06.tds.net
Web www.spicermn.com

LODGING

Motels/Resorts
Spicer
Ye Old Mill Inn Resort
7911 North Shore Dr
Zip Code 56288
Phone (320) 796-2212

Willow Bay Resort
5280 132nd Ave NE
Zip Code 56288
Phone (320) 796-5517
Email vkratt@mail.tds.com
Web www.willowbayresort.com

Park Lane Resort
355 Lake Ave South
Zip Code 56288
Phone (320) 796-5540

Little Morgandale Resort
6231 150th Ave NE
Zip Code 56288
Phone (320) 796-5150

Northern Inn Hotel & Suites
154 Lake Ave South
Zip Code 56288
Toll Free (800) 941-0423
Phone (320) 796-2091
Web www.northerninn.com

Lakeview Motel
15150 Highway 23 NE
Zip Code 56288
Phone (320) 796-2224

Island View Resort on Nest Lake
5910 132nd Ave NE
Zip Code 56288
Toll Free (800) 421-9708
Phone (320) 796-2775

Indian Beach Resort
13412 Indian Beach Rd
Zip Code 56288
Phone (320) 796-5616

Cedar Point Resort
4808 132nd Ave NE
Zip Code 56288
Phone (320) 796-5146
Email cfilley@willmar.com
Web www.cedarpointresort.com

Willmar
Hi-Way 12 Motel
609 Highway 12 East
Zip Code 56201
Phone (320) 235-4500

Holiday Inn & Willmar Conference
2100 Highway 12 East
Zip Code 56201
Toll Free (800) 465-4329
Phone (320) 235-6060
Web www.holidayinnwillmar.com

Lakeview Inn
1212 Business Highway 71 North
Zip Code 56201
Toll Free (800) 718-3424
Phone (320) 235-3424

Cozy Inn
1809 1st St South
Zip Code 56201
Phone (320) 231-3714

Comfort Inn
2200 Highway 12 East
Zip Code 56201
Toll Free (800) 228-5150
Phone (320) 231-2601
Web www.comfortinnwillmar.com

AmericInn of Willmar
2404 Highway 12 East
Zip Code 56201
Toll Free (800) 632-3444
Phone (320) 231-1962
Fax (320) 231-1962
Web www.americinn.com

Viking Motel
616 Business Highway 71 North
Zip Code 56201
Toll Free (800) 835-0176
Phone (320) 235-5211

Days Inn Willmar
225 28th St SE
Zip Code 56201
Toll Free (800) 329-7466
Phone (320) 231-1275
Web www.daysinnwillmar.com

Super 8 Motel
2655 1st St South
Zip Code 56201
Toll Free (800) 800-8000
Phone (320) 235-7260

Colonial Inn
1102 1st St South
Zip Code 56201
Toll Free (800) 396-4445
Phone (320) 235-4444

LODGING cont'd

Bed and Breakfast

Spicer

Green Lake Inn
152 Lake Ave North
Zip Code 56288
Toll Free (888) 660-3068
Phone (320) 796-6523

Spicer Castle
11600 Indian Beach Rd
Zip Code 56288
Toll Free (800) 821-6675
Phone (320) 796-5870
Email spicercastle@spicercastle.com
Web www.spicercastle.com

Willmar

The Buchanan House B&B
725 SW 5th St
Zip Code 56201
Toll Free (800) 874-5534
Phone (320) 235-7308
Web
www.thebuchananhousebandb.com

Country Guest House
719 Monongalia Ave SW
Zip Code 56201
Phone (320) 235-4742
Email vonnie@willmar.ruralink.com

Camping

New London

Sibley State Park
800 Sibley Park Rd NE
Zip Code 56273
Phone (320) 354-2055
Web www.dnr.state.mn.us

Spicer

Kandiyohi County Park #5
12381 North Shore Dr
Zip Code 56288
Phone (320) 796-5564
Web www.co.kandiyohi.mn.us/depts/
cntypark.htm

Block's Whistle Stop
334 Lake Ave North
Zip Code 56288
Phone (320) 796-5786

Cedar Point Resort
4808 132nd Ave NE
Zip Code 56288
Phone (320) 796-5146
Email cfilley@willmar.com
Web www.cedarpointresort.com

Indian Beach Resort
13412 Indian Beach Rd
Zip Code 56288
Phone (320) 796-5616

Island View Resort on Nest Lake
5910 132nd Ave NE
Zip Code 56288
Toll Free (800) 421-9708
Phone (320) 796-2775

Little Morgandale Resort
6231 150th Ave NE
Zip Code 56288
Phone (320) 796-5150

Starbuck

Glacial Lakes State Park
25022 Cty 41
Zip Code 56381
Phone (320) 239-2860

RESTAURANTS

New London

Jimmy's Pizza
Phone (320) 354-5683

Riverside Cafe
Phone (320) 354-2124

McKale's
Phone (320) 354-2007

Agape Coffe House
Phone (320) 354-7017

American Legion
Phone (320) 354-2284

Hillcrest Rest & Truck Stop
Phone (320) 354-4545

Spicer

American Legion
Phone (320) 796-5542

Melvin's Restaurant
Phone (320) 796-2195

Annie's Downtown Diner
Phone (320) 796-5355

O'Neils Food & Spirits
Phone (320) 796-6524

Papa's Pizza Place
Phone (320) 796-2040

Spicer Castle
Phone (320) 796-5556

Little Crow Country Club
Phone (320) 354-2214

Green Lake Inn
Phone (320) 796-6523

Willmar

Willmar Blue Heron
Phone (320) 235-4448

Bixby's Cafe
Phone (320) 235-2929

Jake's Pizza
Phone (320) 235-1714

Applebee's Grill & Bar
Phone (320) 214-8816

American Legion
Phone (320) 235-8136

GROCERIES

New London

Big Store
(320) 354-2206

Spicer

Jahnke Foods
(320) 796-2163

Information Glacial Lakes State Trail

GROCERIES cont'd

Willmar

Cash Wise Foods
(320) 235-2485

Cub Foods
(320) 231-0060

Super Fair Foods
(320) 235-4466

BIKE RENTAL

Spicer

Spicer Bike and Sports
Phone (320) 796-6334
Email spicerbike_sports@excite.com

BIKE REPAIR

Spicer

Spicer Bike and Sports
Phone (320) 796-6334
Fax (320) 796-6386
Email spicerbike_sports@excite.com

Willmar

Rick's Schwinn and Sports Center
Phone (320) 235-0202
Fax (320) 235-0202

FESTIVALS AND EVENTS

New London

May

Historical Society Spring Festival
Lefse and rosette making demos, hot dishes, home cooked food, bluegrass music, Memorial Day
Phone (320) 354-2990

July

New London Water Days
Coronation, petting zoo, pony rides, home cooked food booths, games, dunking tank, talent show, fireworks, Third Weekend
Phone (320) 354-7111

August

New London/New Brighton Antique Car Run
Vintage auto parade, pancake breakfast, steak dinner at the Legion, Saturday drive from New London to New Brighton, Second Weekend
Phone (320) 354-7111

New London Music Fest
Professional musicians perform and teach hands-on workshops. Call for exact weekend.
Phone (320) 354-7111

Spicer

July

July 4th Celebration
Parade, flea market, free entertainment, food vendors, boat parade on Green Lake, street dance, fireworks, First Weekend
Phone (320) 796-5562

Willmar

June

Willmar Fest
Parade, water show, firefighters water fight, block party, coronation, food vendors, carnival, fireworks, Fourth Weekend
Phone (320) 231-2048

August

Kandiyohi County Fair
Exhibits, food, entertainment, Second Weekend
Phone (320) 235-0886

September

Celebrate Arts/Celebrate Coffee
Original arts and crafts, sales, demos, music, children's arts activities, free gourmet coffee, Fourth Weekend
Phone (320) 231-0430

ALTERNATE ACTIVITIES

New London

Monongalia Historical Society
Area archival information, variety of displays, open Thursday through Sunday
Phone (320) 354-2990

Kandiyohi County Park
Camping, large swimming area, store and restaurant, boat rentals
Phone (320) 354-4453

Shopping
Antique, arts, and crafts shopping

Little Crow Players
Performances at the historic theater, call for schedule
Phone (320) 354-2559

Sibley State Park
Camping, interpretive center, daily programs, swimming, biking and hiking trails, boat and canoe rentals, volleyball area, horseshoe pits, "Mt. Tom" monument and observation deck
Phone (320) 354-2055
Fax (320) 354-2372
Web www.dnr.state.mn.us

Prairie Woods Environmental Learning Center
Weekend family programs, interpretive hiking trails
Phone (320) 354-5894
Fax (320) 354-4890
Email pwelc@wecnet.com

Spicer

Downtown park
Sheltered picnic area, playground, fishing pier
Phone (320) 796-5562
Fax (320) 796-2044
Email spicer06.tds.net
Web www.spicermn.com

ALTERNATE ACTIVITIES cont'd

Saulsbury swimming beach
Volleyball and basketball courts, picnic
area, boat access
Phone (320) 796-5562
Fax (320) 796-2044
Email spicer06.tds.com
Web www.spicermn.com

Wally's Water Slide
300 ft. water slide, mini-golf course,
arcade, food concessions
Phone (320) 796-6666
Email rolf@tds.net

Willmar
Robbin's Island
Park, swimming beach, biking and
walking trails
Phone (320) 235-4913

Kandiyohi Historical Society
1893 house, antique locomotive, variety of exhibits
Phone (320) 235-1881
Email kandhist@wecnet.com

Sakatah Singing Hills Trail

Vital Information:

Trail Distance: 38 miles

Trail Surface: asphalt

Access Points: Faribault, Warsaw, Morristown, Sakatah Lake State Park, Waterville, Elysian, Madison Lake, Mankato

Fees and Passes: none

See Trail Map on page M28

ABOUT THE TRAIL

Running from a narrow, wooded valley called "Wardlaws Ravine" in Mankato through Sakatah Lake State Park and to the edge of Faribault, this trail passes through a number of attractive small towns and skirts large and small lakes. The trail has relatively new pavement smooth enough for in-line skating. Trail towns offer parks, museums, and historic buildings. A marked bike route from the trailhead south along Highway 22 will take you to the Depot in downtown Mankato. The 10 mile Red Jacket Trail begins at the Depot and follows the river front south to the town of Rapidan. The highlight of the Red Jacket Trail is the Red Jacket Trestle, 80 feet high and 550 feet long. The Red Jacket Trail is not shown in this guide.

TRAIL HIGHLIGHTS

The western section, from Mankato to Madison Lake has the most diversity. It climbs through the heavily wooded, narrow valley of "Wardlaws Ravine", then opens up to wildflowers and farmland on the way to Madison Lake. The Elysian trail access is set in a pleasant little park with drinking water, modern bathrooms and a sheltered picnic area. The trail stops at each edge of Waterville, but the road route connector is well marked and follows quiet residential streets. Pull off the trail at Sakatah State Park and head up to the lake for a pleasant break. Do the same a few miles further east at Morristown, where a short side trip will take you to the historic dam site and a quiet park along the Cannon River. The trail east of Morristown follows Highway 60 and loses some of its charm as a result.

ABOUT THE ROADS

The roads near the middle and eastern portions of the trail offer the best riding. They undulate over low to medium rollers past farm fields and woodlots, and skirt a number of mid-sized lakes. The routes on the trail map offer only a hint of the road riding options in this area. The roads near Mankato tend to have more, and faster moving, traffic.

ROAD ROUTE HIGHLIGHTS

Piles of sawdust inside and outside the steam powered Geldner Saw Mill on the west edge of German Lake, northwest of Elysian, indicate that it is a working museum. The wide range of cutting and milling tools are visible even when the museum is closed because of wide mesh steel grated doors. Highway 131 on the north edge of Sakatah Lake is a quiet, winding road with great views of Sakatah Lake State Park across the water. The roads north of the trail between Morristown and Faribault pass through gently rolling farmland and offer a great alternate to the trail.

HOW TO GET THERE

Take the Highway 60 exit off Interstate 35 at Faribault. The nearest trail access is at the Dairy Queen just west of the Interstate. See city map. All trail towns can be accessed from Highway 60 as you head west. The Mankato Trailhead is near the eastern edge of Mankato. Take the Highway 22 exit off Highway 14. Go north to Lime Valley Road. The trailhead is on the left, 0.2 miles north on Lime Valley Road.

TOURIST INFORMATION

Sakatah Singing Hills State Trail Office
Toll Free (800) 507-7787
Phone (507) 267-4772
Web www.dnr.state.mn.us

Waterville Chamber of Commerce
Phone (507) 362-4609
Email lmesk@prairie.lakes.com
Web www.watervillemn.com

Faribault Chamber of Commerce
Toll Free (800) 658-2354
Phone (507) 334-4381
Fax (507) 334-1003
Email amys@faribaultmn.org
Web www.faribaultmn.org

Mankato Area Convention and
Visitors Bureau
Toll Free (800) 657-4733
Phone (507) 345-4519
Fax (507) 345-4451
Email maccb@mnic.net
Web www.makato.com

Elysian Tourism Center
Toll Free (800) 507-7787
Phone (507) 267-4040
Fax (507) 267-4750
Email elysian@frontiernet.net
Web www.mnlakesregion.com

Morristown City Hall
Phone (507) 685-2302
Fax (507) 685-2632
Email motown@means.net

Southern Minnesota Lakes
Region Association
Toll Free (800) 507-7787
Phone (507) 267-4040
Web www.mnlakesregion.com

LODGING

Motels/Resorts
Elysian
Lotus Lodge Motel
Across the Road from Trail
Rt 1 Box 128A
Zip Code 56028
Phone (507) 267-4212

Faribault
AmericInn Motel & Suites
1801 Lavender Dr
Zip Code 55021
Toll Free (800) 634-3444
Phone (507) 334-9464
Fax (507) 334-0616

Super 8 Motel
2509 Lyndale Ave North
Zip Code 55021
Toll Free (800) 800-8000
Phone (507) 334-1634

Select Inn
4040 Highway 60 West
Zip Code 55021
Toll Free (800) 641-1000
Phone (507) 334-2051

The Lyndale Motel
904 Lyndale Ave North
Zip Code 55021
Toll Free (800) 559-4386
Phone (507) 334-4386

Knights Inn
841 Faribault Rd
Zip Code 55021
Toll Free (800) 843-5644
Phone (507) 334-1841

Galaxie Inn & Suites
1401 Highway 60 West
Zip Code 55021
Toll Free (800) 341-8000
Phone (507) 334-5508

Madison Lake
Sakatah Trail Resort
Rt 1 Box 174
Zip Code 56063
Phone (507) 267-4000

Point Pleasant Resort
400 Sheppard Circle
Zip Code 56063
Phone (507) 243-3611

Mankato
Comfort Inn
131 Apache Place
Zip Code 56002
Phone (507) 388-5107

Riverfront Inn
1727 North Riverfront Dr
Zip Code 56002
Phone (507) 388-1638

Holiday Inn Downtown
101 East Main St
Zip Code 56002
Toll Free (800) 465-4329
Phone (507) 345-1234

Waterville
Lakeview Resort
North Shore Lake Sakatah
PO Box 164
Zip Code 56096
Phone (507) 362-4616

Bed and Breakfast
Faribault
Cherub Hill Bed & Breakfast
105 1st Ave NW
Zip Code 55021
Toll Free (800) 332-7254
Phone (507) 334-5508

Information Sakatah Singing Hills Trail

LODGING cont'd

Mankato
Butler House
704 South Broad St
Zip Code 56002
Phone (507) 387-5055

Camping
Elysian
Silver's Resort
North Shore Lake Elysian
PO Box 205
Zip Code 56028
Phone (507) 267-4694

Faribault
Camp Faribo Campground/RV Park
21851 Bagley Ave
Zip Code 55021
Toll Free (800) 689-8453
Phone (507) 332-8453

Le Mieux Resort & Campground
7710 Cedar Lake Blvd
Zip Code 55021
Phone (507) 334-5334

Roberds Lake Resort & Campground
18192 Roberds Lake Blvd
Zip Code 55021
Toll Free (800) 879-5091

Maiden Rock Campground
22661 Dodge Ct
Zip Code 55021
Toll Free (800) 657-4776
Phone (507) 685-4430
Email cmrfern@clear.lakes.com

Morristown
Maiden Rock Campground
PO Box 326
Zip Code 55052
Toll Free (800) 657-4776
Phone (507) 685-4430
Email cmrfern@clear.lakes.com

Waterville
Sakatah Lake State Park Campground
Rt 2, Box 19
Zip Code 56096
Phone (507) 362-4438
Web www.dnr.state.mn.us

O'Leary's Cabins & Campground
420 1st St North
Zip Code 56096
Phone (507) 362-8379

Lakeview Resort
North Shore Lake Sakatah
PO Box 164
Zip Code 56096
Phone (507) 362-4616

Kamp Dels
North Shore Lake Sakatah
Zip Code 56096
Phone (507) 362-8616
Web www.kampdels.com

RESTAURANTS
Faribault
El Tequila Mexican Rest
Phone (507) 332-7490

The Depot Bar and Grill
Phone (507) 332-2825

Bernie's Grill
Phone (507) 334-7476

Long Cheng Chinese Rest
Phone (507) 334-3002

Mankato
Applebee's
Phone (507) 386-1010

Coffee Hag
Phone (507) 387-5533

Stoney's Fine Dining
Phone (507) 387-4813

McGoff's Irish Pub & Eatery
Phone (507) 387-4000

Jazz Club
Phone (507) 387-5100

Charley's Rest & Lounge
Phone (507) 388-6845

BW-3
Phone (507) 625-9464

Bagel Brothers
Phone (507) 625-2245

Warsaw
Channel Inn
Phone (507) 685-4622

Waterville
The Waterville Cafe
Phone (507) 362-8977

Pirates' Galley Drive In
Phone (507) 362-4497

Livingood Bakery
Phone (507) 632-8337

Gilligan's Bar & Grill
Phone (507) 632-4111

GROCERIES
Elysian
D & B Foods
(507) 267-4447

Faribault
Faribault Foods
(507) 334-5521

Hy Vee Food Store
(507) 334-2085

Rainbow Foods
(507) 334-1661

Waterville
Veen's Super Valu
(507) 362-8188

BIKE RENTAL

Mankato
A-1 Bike Shop
Phone (507) 625-2453

Waterville
Ron's Hardware Hank
Phone (507) 362-4308

BIKE REPAIR

Faribault
The Village Pedaler
Phone (507) 332-2636

Mankato
A-1 Bike Shop
Phone (507) 625-2453

Waterville
Ron's Hardware Hank
Phone (507) 362-4308
Fax (507) 362-4308

FESTIVALS AND EVENTS

Elysian
July
Fourth of July Festival
Parade, kids' fishing contest, kids'
tractor pull, milk jug regatta, pageant,
dance, car show, flea market, 3 day
event
Phone (507) 267-4708

Rookies' Triathlon
Seven age categories with a .4 mile
swim, 8 mile bike, 4 mile run, Saturday
after the 4th, Call Jeannie Zwart
Phone (507) 267-4231

Faribault
Farmers Market
Every Saturday morning during grow-
ing season, at Central Park
Phone (507) 334-8474

June
Heritage Days
Celebrating the diverse heritage and
cultures that comprise Faribault,
parade, carnival, street dance, arts
and crafts show, volleyball and softball
tourneys, kids' fishing contest, bike
tour, truck pull, tours of historical buildings, Third Weekend
Toll Free (800) 658-2354
Phone (507) 334-4381

Rock Island Art Festival
Fifty artists showing their wares, class-
es for adults and children throughout
the event, entertainment, food,
Heritage Park, same weekend as
Heritage Days
Phone (507) 332-7372

July
Rice County Free Fair
Food, derby races, coronation, rodeo,
five day event at the fairgrounds, Third
Weekend
Toll Free (800) 658-2354
Phone (507) 334-4381

September
Tree Frog Music Festival
Music, art, food, twenty diverse music
acts, original art, food booths, beer
garden, children's activities, at Teepee
Tonka Park, Third Weekend
Toll Free (800) 658-2354
Phone (507) 334-4381

Balloon Air-a-Rama
Hot air balloon exhibition, antique air-
craft display, glider demonstrations,
airplane rides, food vendors, at
Municipal Airport, Second Weekend
Toll Free (800) 658-2354
Phone (507) 334-4381

October
Taste of Faribault
Sample food from local vendors at the
American Legion, Third Thursday
Toll Free (800) 658-2354
Phone (507) 334-4381

Madison Lake
July
Paddlefish Days
Parade, street dance, tractor pull, food
fair, fun run, fire department open
house, Fourth Weekend
Phone (507) 243-3011

Mankato
July
North Mankato
Vikings Training Camp
At Blakeslee Field, Minnesota State
University Mankato, mid July through
mid August
Toll Free (800) 657-4733
Phone (507) 345-4519

Fourth of July
Music, food, and fireworks
Toll Free (800) 657-4733
Phone (507) 345-4519

September
Mankato Mdewakanton Pow Wow
Native food, crafts, ceremonial danc-
ing, and singing, Land of Memories
Park, Second or third weekend
Toll Free (800) 657-4733
Phone (507) 345-4519

Morristown
June
Dam Days
Twilight parade Friday, carnival, family
events, kids' parade, lawn mower pull,
car show, American Legion steak fry,
First weekend after Memorial Day
Phone (507) 685-4155

Information Sakatah Singing Hills Trail

August

City Wide Garage Sales
Maps available at the community hall,
First Saturday
Phone (507) 685-2302

Bois Plume Rendezvous
Celebration of the frontier, with fur
trade fun, teepees, black powder competitions, and food vendors, across
from Camp Maiden Rock, one mile
west of Morristown, Fourth Weekend
Phone (507) 685-2240

Waterville
May

City Garage Sales and
Classic Car Show
Car show downtown, garage sale
maps available at printing office,
Third Saturday
Phone (507) 362-4609

June

Bullhead Days
Pageant, carnival, grand parade, kids'
parade, food stands (including deep
fried bullhead), demolition derby, 10k
run and bike race, tractor pull, mud
drag races, kids' fishing contest,
Second Weekend
Phone (507) 362-4609

ALTERNATE ACTIVITIES

Elysian
Okaman Cervidae Elk Farm
View a majestic herd of elk at restored
historic farm
Phone (507) 267-4338

Klondike Hill
Highest point in three counties offering
a beautiful panoramic view, one of the
first Jesse James gang campsites
Phone (507) 267-4708

LeSueur County Historical
Society Museum
Displays and tours, open weekends
Phone (507) 267-4620

Elysian City Park and Beach
Public swimming beach, sand volley-
ball courts, picnic shelters
Phone (507) 267-4708

Faribault
Faribault Woolen Mills
Tour the mill and shop the outlet store
Toll Free (800) 448-9665
Phone (507) 334-1644
Fax (507) 334-9431
Web www.faribowool.com

Faribault Art Center
Local artists on display, pottery and
basket making, downtown Faribault
Phone (507) 332-7372

Rice County Historical
Society Museum
Varied exhibits, tours of Alexander
Faribault House and historical one
room log cabin school, call for hours
Phone (507) 332-2121

Countryside Berries
Pick your own strawberries
Phone (507) 332-8761

River Bend Nature Center
Forest, prairie, wetland, and riverbank,
nine miles of marked trails, call for
programs
Phone (507) 332-7151
Email riverbnd@deskmedia.com

Mankato
Minneopa State Park
Native prairie area, hiking and bird-
watching, interpretive drive, explore
the only major waterfall in southwestern Minnesota, old stone mill and van-
ished village, camping, picnicking,
paved bike trail

Phone (507) 389-5464
Fax (507) 389-5174
Web www.dnr.state.mn.us

Blue Earth County Heritage Center
Varied exhibits, Victorian home tour
Phone (507) 345-5566
Email bechs@juno.com
Web
www.ic.mankato.mn.us/reg9/bechs

Highland Summer Theater
Four musicals and plays presented
during the summer season at
Minnesota State University, call for
brochure
Phone (507) 389-2118
Web www.msutheatre.com

Waterville
Minnesota Fish Hatchery
Two miles west of Waterville on Cty 14,
call for tours
Phone (507) 362-4223

Sakatah Lake State Park
Camping, picnicking, hiking, canoe
and boat rentals, playground, swimming, fishing, interpretive center, five
miles of trails
Phone (507) 362-4438

Douglas Trail

Vital Information:

Trail Distance: 12 miles

Trail Surface: asphalt

Access Points: Pine Island, Douglas, Rochester

Fees and Passes: none

See Trail Map on page M30

ABOUT THE TRAIL

This short, very popular trail has two great access points, at Pine Island and Douglas, and a surprising number of amenities. The trail passes primarily through flat, rich agricultural land and ends on the north side of Rochester. The Mayo Clinic and most of the city's services are 10 miles from the trailhead.

TRAIL HIGHLIGHTS

Watch for irregular knobs of land protruding above the landscape about 3.5 miles south of Pine Island, followed by a slight rise into a wooded hillside. The trailhead in Douglas provides a pleasant, shaded rest stop.

ABOUT THE ROADS

Flat near the north and south ends of the trail, hilly and scenic just north of Douglas, these rural, lightly traveled roads cross the trail and pass near it, but offer an entirely different look at the land.

ROAD ROUTE HIGHLIGHTS

Going north from Douglas, County 3 climbs for about a mile to a ridgetop with great overviews of the valley below. Then it's up and down for another half dozen miles until payback time with a long, swift, scenic descent into the flatlands. Finish by entering the south end of Pine Island. See city map for route through town to the trailhead. Roads south of Douglas are generally scenic, low traffic and rural, nothing dramatic, but quite pleasant.

HOW TO GET THERE

Pine Island is just off Highway 52, about 70 miles south of the Twin Cities. Take the Highway 11 exit. Trailhead is half a mile west of the highway. See city map. Rochester is 83 miles south of the Twin Cities on Highway 52. Take the 14th St NW/15th St NW exit. Go west on 14th St NW to Valleyhigh Drive. Turn right. Valleyhigh becomes Olmsted County 4. Continue to trailhead. Distance from intersection of 14th and Valleyhigh Drive to trailhead is 2.1 miles. See city map.

55

Information Douglas Trail

Rochester Convention and
Visitors Bureau
Toll Free (800) 634-8277
Phone (507) 288-4331
Fax (507) 288-9144
Email info@rochestercvb.org
Web www.rochestercvb.org

LODGING

Motels/Resorts
Rochester
Country Inn & Suites
4323 Highway 52 North
Zip Code 55901
Toll Free (800) 456-4000
Phone (507) 285-3335

Hawthorne Inn & Suites
2829 NW 43rd St
Zip Code 55901
Toll Free (800) 527-1133
Phone (507) 281-1200

Microtel Inn & Suites
4210 Highway 52 North
Zip Code 55901
Toll Free (800) 245-9535
Phone (507) 286-8780
Fax (507) 286-8885

AmericInn Hotel & Suites
5708 Highway 52 North Frontage Rd
Zip Code 55901
Toll Free (800) 634-3444

Bed and Breakfast
Rochester
Hilltop B&B
1735 3rd Ave NW
Zip Code 55901
Phone (507) 282-6650

Inn at Rocky Creek B&B
2115 Rocky Creek Dr N
Zip Code 55906
Toll Free (888) 388-1019
Phone (507) 288-1019
Web
www.bbhost.com/innatrockycreek

Camping
Pine Island
Wazionja Campground
6450 120th St NW
Zip Code 55963
Phone (507) 356-8594

Rochester
Silver Lake RV Park
1409 North Broadway
Zip Code 55904
Phone (507) 289-6412

Brookside RV Park
516 17th Ave NW
Zip Code 55901
Phone (507) 288-1413

RESTAURANTS

Rochester
Brass Lantern
Phone (507) 289-2468

Michaels Steaks & Seafood
Phone (507) 288-2020

Culvers of Rochester
Phone (507) 281-8538

Wong's Cafe
Phone (507) 282-7514

Legends of Rochester
Phone (507) 287-9333

GROCERIES

Rochester
Good Food Store Co-op
(507) 289-9061

Numerous Supermarkets

BIKE REPAIR

Rochester
Bicycle Sports, Inc.
Phone (507) 281-5007
Fax (507) 280-5878
Email gritman@bicyclesportsinc.com
Web www.bicyclesportsinc.com

FESTIVALS AND EVENTS

Rochester
May
Med City Marathon
Marathon and 2 & 4 person relay,
Sunday before Memorial Day, Website:
www.medcitymarathon.com, Fourth
Weekend
Phone (507) 282-1411

June
Mayowood Garden Tour and
Flower Show
Tour the Mayowood Mansion and
several private gardens, Last
Saturday in June
Toll Free (800) 634-8277
Phone (507) 282-9447

Rochesterfest
Street dance, parade, live music, food
vendors and family entertainment,
Week long celebration, mid-June
Toll Free (800) 634-8277
Phone (507) 285-8769

Down By The Riverside Concerts
Free evening concerts by various
musical groups, Mayo Park, mid-July
through mid-August, call for schedule
Toll Free (800) 634-8277
Phone (507) 288-4331

July

Olmsted County Fair
Exhibits, food and entertainment, at
the fairgrounds, Fourth Weekend
Toll Free (800) 634-8277
Phone (507) 282-0519

4th of July Celebration
Water Ski Club performs at Silver
Lake, food vendors and fireworks,
First Weekend
Toll Free (800) 634-8277
Phone (507) 288-4331

August

Greek Festival
Music, food, and dance, call Father
Nick for info and location
Phone (507) 282-1529

Threshing Show
Food, demos of early crafts and 19th
century era threshing show, Olmsted
County History Center. Website:
www.olmstedhistory.com, Second
Weekend
Toll Free (800) 634-8277
Phone (507) 282-9447

September

Fall Harvest Fest
Nature related activities and crafts,
canoeing, rock climbing wall, minnow
races, live music and food wagon,
Quarry Hill Nature Center
Website:
www.rochester.k12.mn.us/quarryhill/
Third Weekend
Phone (507) 281-6114

Three Rivers Rendezvous
Participants dressed as early frontiers-
men live in replica teepees and frontier
tents, cook over open fires and
demonstrate their mastery of early
skills. Olmsted County History Center
grounds. Website: www.olmstedhisto-
ry.com. Fourth Weekend
Toll Free (800) 634-8277
Phone (507) 282-9447

Olmsted County Gold Rush Days
Antique show, flea market and food
vendors at the fairgrounds, Website:
www.iridescenthouse.com, three weekends during the season
Phone (507) 288-0320

ALTERNATE ACTIVITIES

Rochester

Rochester Art Center
Fine arts and crafts, ongoing exhibits,
free admission
Phone (507) 282-8629
Fax (507) 282-7737
Web www.rochesterusa.com/artcenter

Olmsted County History Center &
Museum
Pictures, maps, diaries, exhibits,
restored pioneer log cabin and one-
room schoolhouse
Phone (507) 282-9447
Web www.olmstedhistory.com

Quarry Hill Nature Center
Hiking trails, bike trail that connects to
town, interactive displays and exhibits,
1700 gallon aquarium, live bee display,
life-size model T-Rex head
Phone (507) 281-6114
Fax (507) 287-1345
Email grmunson@rochester.k12.mn.us
Web
www.rochester.k12.mn.us/quarryhill/

Silver Lake Park

Biking, rollerblading, jogging, paddle-
boat and canoe rentals, picnicking,
children's adventure playground, outdoor pool
Phone (507) 281-6160
Fax (507) 281-6165
Web www.ci.rochester.mn.us/park

Sekapp Orchard
Pick your own strawberries and
raspberries
Phone (507) 282-4544

Mayo Clinic Tours
Behind the scenes tour, learn about
Mayo's historical origins, art, and
architecture
Phone (507) 284-9258

Root River Trail

Vital Information:

Trail Distance: 43 miles

Trail Surface: asphalt

Access Points: Fountain, Lanesboro, Whalan, Peterson, Rushford, Houston

Fees and Passes: none

See Trail Map on page M31

ABOUT THE TRAIL

A former Milwaukee Road railbed running through the blufflands and Amish country of southeast Minnesota, the trail follows and crosses the Root River as it passes beneath towering bluffs. The scenery is exceptional and the wildlife abundant. Expect to see hawks and vultures riding wind currents near the bluffs, wild turkeys in the woods, and deer in the open fields. Lanesboro, with its entire Main Street designated a historic district, is the best known town on the trail, but Rushford offers a unique museum in its two story depot and Whalan is known for its pies.

TRAIL HIGHLIGHTS

Check out the Karst landscape near Fountain. Karst is a type of topography characterized by sinkholes, caves and underground channels. The Harmony-Preston Valley Trail begins just east of the Isinours Unit. See Harmony–Preston Valley Trail for details. The dam and road cut on the western edge of Lanesboro create a dramatic first impression of the trail if you start from Lanesboro and ride west. East of Lanesboro, the trail hugs the Root River for some miles as it squeezes between the bluffs and the river. The trail has recently been extended to Houston on the eastern edge, but experienced extensive flood damage. Check for current trail conditions before riding east of Rushford.

ABOUT THE ROADS

From the Valley of the Root River to the top of the bluffs, the roads will lead you through all the terrain that you only see from the trail. The options are endless, sometimes the hills will feel the same. Low traffic, generally good asphalt, watch for Amish vehicles, buffalo farms and 40 mile per hour descents off the bluffs. Expect to climb in any direction as you go away from the Root River.

ROAD ROUTE HIGHLIGHTS

Highway 13 from Houston climbs steeply through a couple of 10 mph switchbacks to the ridgetop. Highway 30 is quite flat from Arendahl to several miles east of Highway 25, then begins a rapid descent towards Rushford. The first few miles of the descent pass through a narrow, intimate valley. Highways 21 and 10, south of the trail, have been re-paved recently. The climb from Lanesboro to Highway 12 is long and fairly steep. Watch for the buffalo farm at the intersection of Highways 10 and 12.

HOW TO GET THERE

Fountain, the western terminus, is about 30 miles south of Rochester on Highway 52. Continue on Highway 52 to Preston to start on the Preston-Harmony Trail. Take Highway 52 past Preston to Highway 16 for access to Lanesboro and other towns along the trail. From the east, take Interstate 90 west from LeCrescent about 25 miles to Highway 16. Rushford, near the eastern terminus, is about 10 miles south of Interstate 90 on Highway 16. See trail and city maps for details.

TOURIST INFORMATION

Root River Trail Center, Lanesboro
Phone (507) 467-2552

Lanesboro Office of Tourism
Toll Free (800) 944-2670
Phone (507) 467-2696

Historic Bluff Country Visitors Bureau
Toll Free (800) 428-2030
Phone (507) 886-2230
Email hbc@means.net
Web www.bluffcountry.com

Rushford Historic Depot
Phone (507) 864-7560

Rushford City Hall
Phone (507) 864-2444
Fax (507) 864-7003
Email rushford@means.net
Web www.rushford.net

LODGING

Motels/Resorts

Lanesboro
Green Gables Inn
303 West Sheridan
Zip Code 55949
Toll Free (800) 818-4225
Phone (507) 467-2936
Email green@rconnections.com

Brewster's Red Hotel
Zip Code 55949
Phone (507) 467-2999

Peterson
Geneva's Hideaway
87 Centennial St
Zip Code 55962
Phone (507) 875-7733

Wenneson Hotel
425 Prospect St
PO Box 11
Zip Code 55962
Phone (507) 875-2587

Bed and Breakfast

Fountain
Main Street Inn
RR1 Box2B
Zip Code 55935
Phone (507) 268-4375

Houston
The Bunkhouse Lodge
501 South Jefferson
Zip Code 55943
Phone (507) 896-2080
Web
www.bluffcountry.com/bunkhouse.htm

Addie's Attic B&B
117 South Jackson St
Zip Code 55943
Phone (507) 896-3010
Web
www.bluffcountry.com/addies.htm

Lanesboro
Sleepy Nisse B&B
701 Kenilworth Ave South
Zip Code 55949
Phone (507) 467-2268

Mrs. B's Inn & Restaurant
Downtown Lanesboro
Zip Code 55949
Toll Free (800) 657-4710
Phone (507) 467-2154

Berwood Hill Inn
Zip Code 55949
Toll Free (800) 803-6748
Phone (507) 765-2391
Web www.berwood.com

Cozy Quilt Cottage
Zip Code 55949
Phone (507) 467-3314

Cady Hays House
500 Calhoun Ave
Zip Code 55949
Phone (507) 467-2621

Rushford
River Trail Inn
PO Box 357
Zip Code 55971
Toll Free (800) 584-6764
Phone (507) 864-7886

Sweet Dreams B&B
RR1, Box 19
Zip Code 55971
Phone (507) 864-2462

Meadows Inn B&B
900 Pine Meadow Lane
Zip Code 55971
Phone (507) 864-2378

Camping

Lanesboro
Eagle Cliff Campground & Lodging
RR1, PO Box 344
Zip Code 55949
Phone (507) 467-2598

Sylvan Park/Riverview Campground
City Park in Lanesboro
Zip Code 55949
Phone (507) 467-3722

Peterson
Peterson RV Campground
Zip Code 55962
Phone (507) 875-2587

Preston
The Old Barn Resort
Rt 3, Box 57
Zip Code 55965
Toll Free (800) 552-2512
Phone (507) 467-2512
Web www.exploreminnesota.com

Rushford
North End Park
City Park in Rushford
Zip Code 55971
Phone (507) 864-7720

Information Root River Trail

RESTAURANTS

Fountain
White Corner Cafe
Phone (507) 268-4334

Lanesboro
Mrs. B's Restaurant
Toll Free (800) 657-4710
Phone (507) 467-2154

River Trail Coffee
Phone (507) 467-2368

Lanesboro Cheese & Deli
Phone (507) 467-7000

Nicks Ribs
Phone (507) 467-0101

Old Village Hall
Phone (507) 467-2962

Peterson
Judy's Country Cafe
Phone (507) 875-2424

Preston
Old Barn Resort
Toll Free (800) 552-2512
Phone (507) 467-2512

Rushford
McGeorge's Steak & Burger
Phone (507) 864-7654

Mill Street Inn
Phone (507) 864-2929

The Creamery
Phone (507) 864-7214

Whalan
The Overland Inn
Phone (507) 467-2623

GROCERIES

Fountain
Willie's Grocery & Locker

Rushford
Rushford IGA
(507) 864-2878

BIKE RENTAL

Houston
Class Cycle Bikes of Houston
Phone (507) 896-9433

Lanesboro
Capron Hardware
Toll Free (800) 726-5030
Phone (507) 467-3714

Historic Scanlan House
Toll Free (800) 944-2158
Phone (507) 467-2158
Email scanlanbb@aol.com
Web www.scanlanhouse.com

Little River General Store
Toll Free (800) 994-2943
Phone (507) 467-2943
Email lrgenstore@aol.com
Web www.lrgeneralstore.com

Eagle Cliff Campground
Phone (507) 467-2598

Root River Outfitters
Phone (507) 467-3400
Email rro@means.net

Rushford
Root River Bait and Tackle
Phone (507) 864-7004

BIKE REPAIR

Houston
Class Cycle Bikes of Houston
Phone (507) 896-9433
Fax (507) 896-9433

Lanesboro
Little River General Store
Toll Free (800) 994-2943
Phone (507) 467-2943
Fax (507) 467-3574
Email lrgenstore@aol.com
Web www.lrgeneralstore.com

FESTIVALS AND EVENTS

Lanesboro
Farmers Market
Fresh produce, baked goods, and crafts by Amish farmers, Saturday mornings, June through October in Sylvan Park
Toll Free (800) 944-2670
Phone (507) 467-2696

June
Art in the Park
Artisans and crafters, entertainment, demos, food, children's activities, photography contest, Father's Day
Toll Free (800) 944-2670
Phone (507) 467-2696

August
Buffalo Bill Days
Parade, flea market, brat and beer garden, live theater, volleyball and softball tourneys, dance, pony rides, First Weekend
Toll Free (800) 944-2670
Phone (507) 467-2696

October
Oktoberfest
German Polkafest featuring food, beer, and dance music, First Saturday
Toll Free (800) 944-2670
Phone (507) 467-2696

Peterson
June
Gammel Dag Fest
City-wide celebration, parade, food vendors, Third Weekend
Phone (507) 875-2587

Rushford

July

Frontier Days

Parade, crafts, antiques, food, dance, kids' games, horseback and pony rides, volleyball and softball tourneys, Creekside Park, Third Weekend

Phone (507) 864-7720

Whalan

May

Root River Sykkle Tur

Lefse and soapmaking demos, church food, "stand still" parade, Third Weekend

Toll Free (800) 944-2670

Phone (507) 467-2696

ALTERNATE ACTIVITIES

Fountain

Fillmore County History Center

Collection of artifacts describing heritage of Fillmore County, huge tractor collection, airplane memorabilia, genealogy services (weekdays only)

Phone (507) 268-4449

Lanesboro

Cornucopia Art Center

Local and regional artists, year round exhibits

Phone (507) 467-2446

Fax (507) 467-4446

Email cac2446@means.net

Little River General Store

Canoe rentals

Toll Free (800) 994-2943

Phone (507) 467-2943

Fax (507) 467-3574

Email lrgenstore@aol.com

Web www.lrgeneralstore.com

Commonweal Theatre Company

Live professional theater from Shakespeare to musicals, call for schedule

Toll Free (800) 657-7025

Phone (507) 467-2525

Fax (507) 467-2468

Email info@commonwealtheatre.org

Web www.commonwealtheatre.org

Eagle Bluff Environmental Learning Center

4.5 miles of hiking trails, bat condominium, raptor viewing from the bluffs, treetop-high ropes course, by reservation

Toll Free (888) 800-9558

Phone (507) 467-2437

Fax (507) 467-3583

Email hello@eagle-bluff.org

Web www.eagle-bluff.org

State Fish Hatchery

Tour the largest trout hatchery in Minnesota

Phone (507) 467-3771

Fax (507) 467-2556

Email edstork@dnr.state.mn.us

Eagle Cliff Campground

Canoe, kayak, innertube rentals

Phone (507) 467-2598

Web www.lanesboro.com

Lanesboro Canoe Rental

Canoe rentals

Phone (507) 467-2948

Root River Outfitters

Canoe rentals

Phone (507) 467-3400

Email rro@means.net

Scenic Valley Winery

Tasting, wine and gift shop

Toll Free (888) 965-0250

Phone (507) 467-2958

Fax (507) 467-2640

Peterson

State Fish Hatchery

Tours by appointment

Phone (507) 875-2625

Fax (507) 875-2625

Web www.dnr.state.mn.us

1877 Peterson Station Museum

Close to trail

Phone (507) 875-2551

Rushford

Root River Bait & Tackle

Canoe and innertube rentals

Phone (507) 864-7004

Rushford Historic Depot

Depot, schoolhouse, church and jail, close to trail

Phone (507) 864-7004

Harmony-Preston Valley Trail

Vital Information:

Trail distance: 18 miles

Trail Surface: asphalt

Access Points: Preston, Harmony

Fees and passes: none

ABOUT THE TRAIL

A spur off the Root River Trail, it has enough character to merit independent status. The trail begins near the Isinours Unit near the west end of the Root River Trail and follows the south branch of the Root to Preston. From Preston it follows Camp Creek south for several miles then climbs quickly to the top of the ridge near Harmony. This trail crosses the creek many times and runs neither flat nor straight, making it a welcome addition to the trails of Minnesota.

TRAIL HIGHLIGHTS

Camp Creek is a quiet trout stream running through small woodlots and along the edge of farms and horse pastures. It's almost always shaded and quiet. Watch for small, seldom used concrete access bridges across the creek. If you don't feel up to climbing to Harmony, consider a bike shuttle to the town and an effortless ride down from the hilltop to the edge of Camp Creek. North of Preston, the trail has all the charm and more variety of terrain than any section of the Root River Trail. For a short side trip follow the 1 mile Trout Run Trail along the Root River in Preston.

ABOUT THE ROADS

From hilltop to river bottom, expect a large change in elevation including either steep climbs or quick descents. Traffic on Highway 22 near Harmony is moderate. Highway 15 and the two mile section of Highway 22 that is gravel are low traffic and very scenic.

ROAD HIGHLIGHTS

Highway 17 will be under construction through 2001, then should become a very smooth road with a shoulder. If you don't mind gravel, ride Highway 15 and 22 south from Preston. Highway 22 is gravel, but the scenery is more intimate and interesting than Highway 17.

HOW TO GET THERE

Preston is about 40 miles south of Rochester on Highway 52. Continue south on Highway 52 to Harmony for a hilltop start.

Duluth

Minneapolis
St. Paul
Red Wing
Rochester
Winona
Preston
Harmony

See Trail Map on page M33

TOURIST INFORMATION

Preston Area Tourism Association
Toll Free (888) 845-2100
Phone (507) 765-2100

Harmony Visitor Information
Toll Free (800) 288-7153
Phone (507) 886-2469
Email visit@means.net
Web www.harmony.mn.us

LODGING

Motels/Resorts
Harmony
Country Lodge Motel
PO Box 656
Zip Code 55939
Toll Free (800) 870-1710
Phone (507) 886-2515

Bed and Breakfast
Harmony
Harmony Guest House
115 2nd Ave SW
Zip Code 55939
Phone (507) 886-4331

The Bunk House/Slim's Woodshed
160 1st St NW
Zip Code 55939
Phone (507) 886-3114
Email slims_ws@means.net

Selvig House
140 Center St East
Zip Code 55939
Toll Free (888) 887-2922
Phone (507) 886-2200

Michel Farm Vacation
Zip Code 55939
Toll Free (800) 752-6474
Phone (507) 886-5392

Park Place Guest House
33 Main Ave South
Zip Code 55939
Phone (507) 886-2266

Preston
Country Hearth Inn
Zip Code 55965
Toll Free (888) 443-2784
Phone (507) 765-2533

Sunnyside Cottage of Forestville
RR2, Box 119B
Zip Code 55965
Phone (507) 765-3357

Jailhouse Historic Inn
PO Box 422, 109 Houston NW
Zip Code 55965
Phone (507) 765-2181

Camping
Harmony
Harmony Campground
Zip Code 55939
Phone (507) 886-2469

Preston
Hidden Valley Campground
Zip Code 55965
Phone (507) 765-2467

Fillmore County Fairgrounds Camping
Zip Code 55965
Phone (507) 765-2425

Maple Springs Campground
RR2, Box 129B
Zip Code 55965
Phone (507) 352-2056
Web www.exploreminnesota.com

The Old Barn Resort
Rt 3, Box 57
Zip Code 55965
Toll Free (800) 552-2512
Phone (507) 467-2512
Web www.exploreminnesota.com

RESTAURANTS

Harmony
Harmony House
Phone (507) 886-4612

Intrepid Traveler
Phone (507) 886-2891

Wheelers Bar and Grill
Phone (507) 886-4444

Preston
Branding Iron
Phone (507) 765-3388

Bowlwinkles Cantina
Phone (507) 765-2522

Community Market & Deli
Phone (507) 765-5245

Brick House on Main
Toll Free (888) 999-1576
Phone (507) 765-9820

Victory Cafe
Phone (507) 765-2492

GROCERIES

Harmony
IGA
(507) 886-2225

Preston
IGA
(507) 765-2465

BIKE RENTAL

Harmony
Country Lodge Motel
Toll Free (800) 870-1710
Phone (507) 886-2515
Email ctrylodg.@means.net
Web www.exploreminnesota.com/

Preston
Old Barn Resort
Toll Free (800) 552-2512
Phone (507) 467-2512

Brick House Coffee House
Toll Free (888) 999-1576
Phone (507) 765-9820
Email sendme@sendmeminnesota.com
Web www.bluffcountry.com/

Information Harmony-Preston Valley Trail

BIKE REPAIR

Preston
P M Bike and Repair
Phone (507) 765-2314

FESTIVALS AND EVENTS

Forestville
July
4th of July at Forestville
Based on 4th of July in 1899, music, speeches, children's games, Historic Forestville, located in Forestville State Park, First Weekend
Toll Free (888) 727-8386
Phone (507) 765-2785

September
Evening of Leisure
Saturday evening only, recreation of 1899 summer leisure time through music, toys, games, and food, Historic Forestville, First Weekend
Toll Free (888) 727-8386
Phone (507) 765-2785

1899 Harvest Day
Saturday only, corn harvest, apple cider pressing, quilting bee, heirloom seed saving, Fourth Weekend
Toll Free (888) 727-8386
Phone (507) 765-2785

Harmony
July
4th of July
Parade, kids' games, fireworks
Toll Free (800) 288-7153
Phone (507) 886-2469

September
Fall Foliage Fest
Amish tours, horse and wagon rides, food vendors, shopping, scarecrow contest, toad races, sheep shearing and spinning, fish fry at the Legion, Fourth Weekend
Toll Free (800) 288-7153
Phone (507) 886-2469

Preston
May
Trout Day and Sykkle Tur
Parade, bike ride, craft show, food vendors, street dance, car show, Third Weekend
Toll Free (888) 845-2100
Phone (705) 765-2100

July
Fillmore County Fair
Exhibits, food, entertainment, Third Weekend
Toll Free (888) 845-2100
Phone (507) 765-2100

September
Fall Fest
Saturday only, hay wagon rides, chicken BBQ, city wide garage sales, Fourth Weekend
Toll Free (888) 845-2100
Phone (507) 765-2100

ALTERNATE ACTIVITIES

Forestville
Forestville/Mystery Cave State Park
Trout fishing, camping, 17 mile shared hiking and horseback trail system, tours of Mystery Cave, the longest cave in Minnesota
Phone (507) 352-5111
Fax (507) 352-5113
Web www.dnr.state.mn.us

Historic Forestville
Daily living history program with costumed interpreters, located in Forestville State Park
Toll Free (888) 727-8386
Phone (507) 765-2785
Fax (507) 765-2785
Email forestville@mnhs.org
Web www.mnhs.org

Harmony
Harmony Roller Rink
Indoor roller skating
Phone (507) 886-4444

Michel's Amish Tours
Personal guide through Amish country
Toll Free (800) 752-6474
Phone (507) 886-5392
Web www.bluffcountry.com/michel.htm

Slim's Wood Shed
Woodcarving museum/workshop, hand carved circus caricatures display, woodcarving supplies and gift shop
Phone (507) 886-3114
Fax (507) 886-3115
Email slims_ws@means.net
Web www.web-site.com/slimswood-shed/

Austin's Goat Farm
200 baby angora goats produce mohair for knitters to create a variety of hand-crafted pieces, gift shop, tours
Phone (507) 886-6731
Email mohair@means.net
Web www.bluffcountry.com/austins.htm

Amish Country Tours
Minibus and car tours of Amish farms
Phone (507) 886-2303
Email amish@means.net
Web www.shawcorp.com/amish

ALTERNATE ACTIVITIES cont'd

Harmony Toy Museum
Over 4,000 toys on display
Phone (507) 867-3380

Niagara Cave
Daily guided tours, 60 foot
underground waterfall, gift shop
Toll Free (800) 837-6606
Phone (507) 886-6606
Fax (507) 886-6432
Email niagara@means.net
Web www.niagaracave.com

Preston
Amish Tours
Personal or group tours to Amish
homes, including furniture and basket
making demonstrations, quilts and produce for sale
Phone (507) 765-2477

Preston Apple and Berry Farm
Apples, cider, baked goods, bedding
plants through June, pick your own
strawberries June and July
Phone (507) 765-4486

Gandy Dancer Trail

Vital Information:

Trail Distance: 45 miles

Trail Surface: limestone

Access Points: St. Croix Falls, Centuria, Milltown, Luck, Frederic, Lewis, Siren, Webster, Danbury

Fees and Passes: Wisconsin State Trail Pass; $3.00 daily fee or $10 for an annual pass. State Trail passes are good on all Wisconsin State Trails.

See Trail Map on page M35

ABOUT THE TRAIL

This former SOO Line railroad bed follows Highway 35 from St. Croix Falls to Danbury. Small towns dot the trail at 4 to 7 mile intervals providing plenty of access points and opportunities to start or stop. I saw more variety of wildlife on this trail than any other, in part because I rode sections in a light rain when no one else was on the trail. The southern end of the trail has a bit too much underbrush too close to the riding surface creating a tunnel effect. Selective clearing to create occasional scenic vistas would do wonders for this part of the trail.

TRAIL HIGHLIGHTS

Frederic has endorsed the trail. The town has rebuilt the historic depot and developed other facilities for bicyclists. Coon Lake Park, about half a mile east of the trail in Frederic, offers a shady, restful lakeside stop. See city map. The trail skirts several lakes and passes through bogs and cattail marshes for several miles north and south of Siren. At the far north end, the trail makes a high dramatic crossing of the Yellow River just south of Danbury. Although the improved surface ends at Highway 77 in Danbury, it is worth walking or riding a fat tired bike 0.4 miles north to the bridge over the St. Croix River. The bridge, about 300 feet long and 100 feet above the river, overlooks a pristine portion of the St. Croix. ATVs and other motorized vehicles are allowed on this stretch, so proceed with caution.

ABOUT THE ROADS

Polk and Burnett counties offer a wide selection of beautiful, low traffic roads.

Northern roads wind around lakes and weave through forests. Southern roads undulate through a mix of farmland and woodlots. Hills can be long, but the grade is usually mild to intermediate. Ride one way on the trail and return by the roads for an interesting mix of scenery and topography.

ROAD ROUTE HIGHLIGHTS

The eastern route between Luck and Centuria or St. Croix Falls looks more complicated than it really is. Most of the turns on the town roads are "T" intersections, which makes watching for the correct road easier. The route provides a very diverse, alternative to the flat and straight trail. The east and west loops between Danbury and Oakland skirt lakes, meander through a full canopy of tree crowns and generally take in a wide range of lakes and northwoods beauty. Expect rolling hills, but not a lot of dramatic climbs and descents.

HOW TO GET THERE

St. Croix Falls is about an hour from the Twin Cities. Take Interstate 35 north to Highway 8. Go east into Wisconsin. Turn south on Highway 35, toward Interstate Park, and stop at the Polk County Information Center just off the ramp. Trail begins at the information center. For mid-trail towns, stay on Highway 8 to Highway 35 North and pick up the trail at any one of the towns along the highway. Danbury, on the north end of the trail, can also be reached by taking Interstate 35 to Hinckley and heading east on Highway 48. Highway 48 becomes Highway 77 in Wisconsin.

TOURIST INFORMATION

Polk County Information, St. Croix Falls
Toll Free (800) 222-7655
Phone (715) 483-1410
Email polkinfo@lakeland.ws
Web www.polkcountytourism.com

Village of Centuria
Phone (715) 646-2300
Web www.polkcountytourism.com

Frederic Village Hall
Phone (715) 327-4294
Web www.polkcountytourism.com

Luck Village Hall
Phone (715) 472-2221
Web www.polkcountytourism.com

Webster Area Chamber of Commerce
Toll Free (800) 788-3194
Phone (715) 866-4211
Web www.mwd.com/burnett

Siren Area Chamber of Commerce
Phone (715) 349-2273

Burnett County Tourism Dept
Toll Free (800) 788-3164
Phone (715) 349-5999
Web www.mwd.com/burnett

LODGING

Motels/Resorts
Danbury
Hole in the Wall Hotel & RV Park
PO Box 129
Zip Code 54830
Phone (715) 656-4333

Ike Walton Lodge
7861 Birch St
Zip Code 54830
Phone (715) 866-7101

Frederic
Frederic Motel
807 Wisconsin Ave S

Zip Code 54837
Phone (715) 327-4496

Luck
Luck Country Inn
Highway 35 & 48
Zip Code 54853
Toll Free (800) 544-7396
Phone (715) 472-2000

Siren
The Lodge at Crooked Lake
24271 Highway 35 North
Zip Code 54872
Toll Free (877) 843-5634

Best Western Northwoods Lodge
Jct Highways 35 & 70
Zip Code 54872
Toll Free (877) 349-7800

Pine Wood Motel
2382 Highway 35 South
Zip Code 54872
Phone (715) 349-5225

St. Croix Falls
Wild River Motel
517 North Hamilton St
Zip Code 54024
Phone (715) 483-9343

Dalles House Motel
Highways 8 & 35
Zip Code 54024
Toll Free (800) 341-8000
Phone (715) 483-3206

Holiday Inn Express Hotel & Suites
Highway 8
Zip Code 54024
Toll Free (800) 465-4329
Phone (715) 483-5775

Bed and Breakfast
Danbury
Danbury Hospitality Bed & Breakfast
30750 Highways 35 & 77

Zip Code 54830
Phone (715) 656-7686

Lewis
Seven Pines Lodge
1098 340th Ave
Zip Code 54851
Phone (715) 653-2323

Siren
Forgotten Tymes Country Inn B&B
7420 Tower Rd
Zip Code 54872
Phone (715) 349-5837

St. Croix Falls
Wissahickon Farms Country Inn
2263 Maple Dr
Zip Code 54024
Phone (715) 483-3986

Amberwood Bed & Breakfast
320 McKenny St
Zip Code 54024
Phone (715) 483-9355

Taylors Falls
The Cottage B&B
950 Fox Glen Dr, Box 71
Zip Code 55084
Phone (651) 465-3595
Web www.the-cottage.com

High Woods B&B
35930 Wild Mountain Rd
Zip Code 55084
Phone (651) 257-4371
Email highwood@scc.net
Web www.highwoods.net

The Old Jail B&B
349 Government St
PO Box 203
Zip Code 55084
Phone (651) 257-4371
Email oldjail@scc.net
Web www.oldjail.com

Information Gandy Dancer Trail

Camping

Danbury
Yellow River Campground &
Canoe Rental
PO Box 67
Zip Code 54830
Phone (715) 656-4402

Frederic
Clam Falls Campground
642 335th Ave
Zip Code 54837
Phone (715) 653-2617

St Croix Falls
Interstate State Park Campground
Highway 35
Zip Code 54024
Phone (715) 483-3747
Web www.dnr.state.wi.us

Taylors Falls
Camp Waub-o-Jeeg
2185 Chisago St
Zip Code 55084
Phone (651) 465-5721

Wildwood Campground
PO Box 235
Zip Code 55084
Toll Free (800) 447-4958
Phone (651) 465-6315
Email fun@wildmountain.com
Web www.wildmountain.com

Webster
Log Cabin Hollow Resort &
Campground
27925 Lone Pine Rd
Zip Code 54893
Phone (715) 866-8255

DuFour's Pine Tree Campground
PO Box 335
Zip Code 54893
Phone (715) 656-4084

RESTAURANTS

Centuria
Al's Diner
Phone (715) 646-2931

Danbury
Ike Walton Lodge
Phone (715) 866-7101

Frederic
The Coffee Station
Phone (715) 327-8089

Bean's Country Griddle
Phone (715) 327-5513

Frederic Bakery
Phone (715) 827-5509

Luck
The Wild Goose
Phone (715) 472-4400

Main Dish
Phone (715) 472-2378

Oakwood Inn
Phone (715) 472-8987

The Luck-E
Phone (715) 472-2578

Blarney & Beans
Phone (715) 472-4700

Milltown
Milltown Drive in
Phone (715) 825-3389

Auctioneers
Phone (715) 825-3345

Siren
Main Street Cafe
Phone (715) 349-2536

Kris' Pheasant Inn
Phone (715) 349-5755

Fancy Freeze Drive In
Phone (715) 349-5209

Galen's Little Mexico
Phone (715) 349-5874

Webster
The World Famous Tap
Phone (715) 866-9950

Carson's Cafe
Phone (715) 866-7332

Yellow River Inn
Phone (715) 866-7375

GROCERIES

Danbury
Wayne's IGA
(715) 656-3456

Luck
Wayne's IGA
(715) 472-2210

Natural Alternative Food Co-op
(715) 472-8084

Milltown
Holiday Foods
(715) 825-2200

Siren
Holiday Foods
(715) 349-5563

R&M Foods
(715) 349-5656

St. Croix Falls
Marketplace
(715) 483-5178

Webster
Wayne's IGA
(715) 866-8366

Voyageur Super Value
(715) 866-4421

BIKE RENTAL

St. Croix Falls
Wissahickon Country Inn
Phone (715) 483-3986

Gandy Dancer Trail **Information**

BIKE REPAIR

St. Croix Falls
Wissahickon Country Inn
Phone (715) 483-3986

FESTIVALS AND EVENTS

Centuria
July
Centuria Memory Days
Parade, softball tournaments, craft fair,
street dance, tractor pull, classic car
show, First Weekend
Toll Free (800) 222-7655
Phone (715) 646-2300

Frederic
June
Frederic Lions Bike Race and Tour
38 mile race/tour on the scenic back-
roads around Frederic, Call Jim
Snyder for details. Second Weekend
Phone (715) 327-8750

July
Indianhead Gem & Mineral Show
Local artists showing jewelry, raw
rocks and polished rocks at the high
school, Third Weekend
Toll Free (800) 222-7655

October
Mixed Sampler Guild Quilt Show
Over 50 quilters from multiple states,
at the High School, Second Weekend
Phone (800) 222-7655

Luck
July
Lucky Days Celebration
"In and Out of Luck" Run/Race/Walk,
parade, midway, food, street dance
Third Weekend
Toll Free (800) 222-7655

Milltown
June
Fisherman's Party
Parade, food and horseshoe pitching
contests, Third Weekend
Phone (800) 222-7655

Siren
July
Fourth of July Celebration
5K run/walk, bed race, parade, boat
parade, fireworks, First Weekend
Phone (714) 349-2273

August
Crazy Day Sales
Sidewalk sale, arts and crafts, softball
tournament, volleyball tournaments,
kiddie parade, street dance and chick-
en BBQ, First Weekend
Phone (715) 349-2273

St. Croix Falls
July
Polk County Fair
Horse shows, live entertainment, trac-
tor and truck pulls, carnival rides, farm
animals, Fourth Weekend
Toll Free (800) 222-7655

Wannigan Days
Parade, fireworks, queen coronation,
craft show, Centered on lumberjack
era, Second Weekend
Toll Free (800) 222-7655

Webster
August
Gandy Dancer Days
Street dance, queen pageant, side-
walk sales, Second Weekend
Phone (800) 788-3194

ALTERNATE ACTIVITIES

Balsam Lake
Polk County Museum
Native American artifacts, lumbering
era artifacts, armed forces
Phone (715) 485-9269

Grantsburg
Crex Meadows Wildlife Area
2,399 acre refuge of prairie and
wetlands, see sandhill cranes, bald
and golden eagles, thousands of
ducks and geese, Extensive road
system and well marked informational
and directional signs
Phone (715) 463 2899

Osceola
Osceola & St. Croix Valley Railway
Experience rail travel as it was during
the first half of the century. 1916 red-
brick depot, train rides every weekend
May through October
Toll Free (800) 711-2591

St. Croix Falls
Interstate Park
Wisconsin's oldest state park, camp-
ing, hiking, interpretive center and a
truly stunning view of the scenic St.
Croix River
Phone (715) 483-3747

St.Croix National Scenic Riverway
Visitor's Center
Traces the wild St. Croix and
Namekagon Rivers for more than 250
miles, staff will help plan canoe trips
Phone (715) 483-3284
Web www.nps.gov/sach

St. Croix Festival Theater
Non-profit professional theater
productions of classical,
contemporary and forgotten works,
May through December
Phone (715) 294-2991

Information Gandy Dancer Trail

Taylors Falls

Taylors Falls Scenic Boat Tours
Four trips daily down the St. Croix
River, June through August
Toll Free (800) 447-4958
Phone (651) 465-6315
Email fun@wildmountain.com
Web www.wildmountain.com

Wild Mountain

Waterslides, Alpine Slides Go-Karts
and Canoe Rental
Toll Free (800) 447-4958
Phone (651) 465-6315
Email fun@wildmountain.com
Web www.wildmountain.com

Webster

Forts Folle Avoine Historical Park
Reconstructed 1802 Fur Trade Post, 80
acres of hiking along the Yellow River
Phone (715) 866-8890

Old Abe Trail

Vital Information:

Trail distance: 20 miles

Trail Surface: asphalt

Access Points: Lake Wissota, Jim Falls, Cornell, Brunet Island State Park

Fees and passes: Wisconsin State Trail Pass; $3 daily fee or $10 for an annual pass. State Trail passes are good on all Wisconsin State Trails.

See Trail Map on page M38

ABOUT THE TRAIL

This is one of the newest trails in western Wisconsin. With a state park at either end, the undeveloped shores of the Chippewa River near the middle and a mix of hardwood forests and agriculture for its entire length, this trail offers a scenic look at an attractive part of western Wisconsin. The trail name comes from Old Abe, a bald eagle that became the mascot of Company C of the 8th Wisconsin Infantry during the Civil War.

TRAIL HIGHLIGHTS

The middle section, just north of Jim Falls, skirts the edge of Old Abe Lake, then passes through a forest of oak, birch, maple and cherry. Look upriver at the small bridge over the pond for a picturesque view of the Coban Bridge, a 1906 overhead truss bridge. The bridge was moved to this spot during the winters of 1916 and 1917 by horse and sled when the Wissota Dam was built. The 175 foot steel structure in Cornell is the only known pulpwood stacker in the world. The visitor center at the base describes the history and operation of the stacker. The trail extends to Brunet Island State Park near Cornell. Follow the trail to the Park, then ride the 3 mile park road as it circles the island.

ABOUT THE ROADS

This is flat to rolling land. Expect a low to moderate roller coaster ride as you move toward or away from the river and flatter routes in the river floodplain and beyond the valley. Agricultural fields are small to mid-sized and intermingled with woodlots. Traffic is generally very low as long as you stay away from main connecter routes like County S and the State Highways. Highway 178 on the west side of the Chippewa River is very scenic, but traffic is high and fast and the road is narrow, not recommended.

ROAD HIGHLIGHTS

The park road in Brunet Island State Park circles the island under a canopy of evergreens. Allow time for frequent stops at beaches and picnic grounds. This is a very peaceful road where bikes generally travel as fast as automobiles. County K, north of the Coban Bridge, is closer to the river and offers a better view than the trail. For a unique experience, cross the one way Coban Bridge. The deck is wood and planks have been laid in two rows at the width of auto tires. A marker just south of the bridge highlights its history. Use caution when crossing Highway 178 to get to the marker.

HOW TO GET THERE

From the Twin Cities, take I-94 east to the Highway 29/40 exit, east of Menomonie. Follow Highway 29 east to Highway 53, on the western edge of Chippewa Falls. Go north approximately 3 miles to County S and turn right. Go east 5.5 miles on S to the intersection of County Roads S and O. The trailhead is on the north side of County S. Stay on County S to Jim Falls for a mid-trail start, or go through Jim Falls to Highway 27 then north on Highway 27 to Cornell to start at Brunet Island State Park.

Information Old Abe Trail

TOURIST INFORMATION

Cornell Development Assoc, Inc
Toll Free (800) 866-6264
Phone (715) 239-3713
Fax (715) 239-3714
Web www.cityofcornell.com

Chippewa Area Visitors Center
Toll Free (888) 723-0024
Phone (715) 723-0331
Email info@chippewachamber.org
Web www.chippewachamber.org

Wisconsin Department of Tourism
Toll Free (800) 432-8747

LODGING

Motels/Resorts
Chippewa Falls
Mallard Resort
Highway 178
Zip Code 54729
Phone (715) 288-6511

Glenn Loch
1225 Jefferson Ave
Zip Code 54729
Toll Free (800) 470-2755
Phone (715) 723-9121

HideAway Resort
5967 167th St
Zip Code 54729
Toll Free
Phone (715) 720-7367

Cornell
Pike Lake Resort
Zip Code 54732
Phone (715) 667-5224

Edgewater Motel
24250 State Highway 178
Zip Code 54732
Phone (715) 239-6295

Jim Falls
Windmill Resort
Zip Code 54748
Phone (715) 382-4349

Bed and Breakfast
Chippewa Falls
Pleasant View B&B
16649 96th Ave
Zip Code 54729
Phone (715) 382-4401

McGilvray's Victorian B&B
312 West Columbia St
Zip Code 54729
Toll Free (800) 720-1600
Phone (715) 720-1600

Cornell
The Happy Horse B & B
Highway 27 north of Cornell
Zip Code 54732
Phone (715) 239-0707

Camping
Chippewa Falls
Pine Harbor Campground
7181 185th St
Zip Code 54729
Phone (715) 723-9865

O'Neil Campground
14956 105th Ave
Zip Code 54729
Phone (715) 723-6581

Duncan Creek
12374 102nd Ave
Zip Code 54729
Phone (715) 720-4686

Lake Wissota State Park
18127 County O
Zip Code 54729
Phone (715) 382-4574
Web www.dnr.state.wi.us

Colfax
Elk Point Resort and Campground
N8535 618th St
Zip Code 54730
Phone (715) 962-3055

Cornell
Brunet Island State Park
23125 25th St
Zip Code 54732
Phone (715) 239-6888
Web www.dnr.state.wi.us

RESTAURANTS
Chippewa Falls
The Fill Inn Station
Phone (715) 723-8282

Lindsay's On Grand
Phone (715) 723-4025

Olson's Ice Cream Parlor
Phone (715) 723-4331

Sheeley House Restaurant
Phone (715) 723-6180

Water's Edge Supper Club
Phone (715) 723-0161

Bake & Brew Cafe
Phone (715) 720-2360

Cornell
Sandi's Drive In

Jim Falls
Delushi's Bar

Lake Wissota
High Shores Supper Club
Phone (715) 723-9854

GROCERIES
Chippewa Falls
Gordy's IGA
(715) 726-2500

Sokup's Market
(715) 723-4953

GROCERIES cont'd

Cornell
IGA
(715) 239-6833

Jim Falls
Cenex Convenience Mart

Lake Wissota
IGA
(715) 726-2505

BIKE RENTAL

Chippewa Falls
Spring Street Sports
Phone (715) 723-6616

BIKE REPAIR

Chippewa Falls
Spring Street Sports
Phone (715) 723-6616

FESTIVALS AND EVENTS

Chippewa Falls
May
Kiwanis Century Ride & Run
Begins Irvine Park, Memorial Day
Weekend, Fourth Weekend
Toll Free (888) 723-0024
Phone (715) 723-1198

July
Northern Wisconsin State Fair
Midway, free grandstand show, live
stock, crafts
Phone (715) 723-2861

August
Chip Dip
Tube float down the Chippewa River,
Third Weekend
Phone (715) 723-5667

Pure Water Days
Parade, Tour de Chippewa Bike Ride,
softball, craft show, fireworks,
Second Weekend
Phone (715) 723-6661

Cornell
May
Community Wide Thrift Sale
Maps of participating homes available,
Memorial Day Weekend
Phone (715) 293-3713

June
Cornell Community Fair
Tractor pull, parade, live music, Lion's
club Chicken BBQ, Mill Yard Park,
First Weekend
Phone (715) 239-3713

July
July 3rd Fireworks
The night before the fourth, Lion's Club
BBQ chicken, Mill Yard Park
Phone (715) 239-3713

August
Jubilee Days
Sidewalk merchant's sales, farmer's
market, crafter tables, food, bake
stands, First Weekend
Phone (715) 239-3713

October
Pork in the Park Polka
Roasted pork dinner, homemade pies,
activities for children, Polka Band and
dance contest, Mill Yard Park, First
Weekend
Phone (715) 239-3713

ALTERNATE ACTIVITIES

Chippewa Falls
Historic Walking Tour of Downtown
Chippewa Falls
Listed on the National Register of
Historic Places, 36 historic buildings
and points of interest, brochures avail-
able at various retail stores and Tourism
Center, 10 S Bridge St, downtown
Toll Free (888) 723-0024
Web www.chippewachamber.org

Lake Wissota State Park
Hiking, biking, camping, swimming
Phone (715) 382-4574
Web www.dnr.state.wi.us

Irvine Park and Zoo
225 acres of natural wooded areas,
the Zoo, hiking, picnicking, play-
grounds, Sunny Valley School House
Museum and Norwegian Log Home
Phone (715) 723-0051

Rose Garden/Lily Garden
Gardener's paradise, 500 roses, teas,
floribunda, grandifloras, miniatures
and climbers

Leinenkugel's Brewery Tours
1/2 hour tours until 3:00 PM every day
through summer, closed Sundays after
Labor Day
Toll Free (888) 534-6437
Phone (715) 723-5557
Web www.leinie.com

Cook Rutledge Mansion
Fine example of High Victorian
Italianate architecture
Phone (715) 723-7181

Information Old Abe Trail

Chippewa Falls Museum of Industry
& Technology
History of local manufacturing and pro-
cessing from 1840's to present including Cray Super Computer collection,
$2 for adults, $1 children under 18
Phone (715) 720-9206

Heyde Center for the Arts
Renovated High School, live theater,
musical performances, art shows,
dance and festivals
Phone (715) 726-9000

Cornell
Millyard Park
175 foot high wood stacker used from
1913 to 1972, only known pulp wood
stacker in the world, visitors center
Web www.cityofcornell.com

Brunet Island State Park
Island Park in the Chippewa River,
scenic drive, camping, swimming
and hiking
Phone (715) 239-6888

Red Cedar Trail

Vital Information:

Trail Distance: 14 miles

Trail Surface: limestone

Access Points: Menomonie, Irvington, Downsville

Fees and Passes: Wisconsin State Trail Pass, $3.00 daily fee or $10 for an annual pass. State Trail passes are good on all Wisconsin State Trails.

ABOUT THE TRAIL

This attractive trail has the feel of a Victorian era carriage road next to a canal. Downsville, at the midpoint, is an excellent starting or turn-around point for those who don't want to ride the entire trail. The Creamery, in Downsville, is a fine dining restaurant with screened in patio and wildflower gardens. The trail enters the Dunnville Wildlife Area near its southern tip, a wetland prairie in the Chippewa River floodplain. The southern end of the trail connects with the western end of the Chippewa State Trail after crossing the Chippewa River on an 860 foot railroad trestle.

TRAIL HIGHLIGHTS

Its hard to go wrong on this trail. From Menomonie to Downsville the trail and river run right next to each other. Watch for the historic site of the Downsville Cut Stone Company about two and a half miles south of Downsville. Go another mile south and enter a very remote and beautiful stretch of river. The prairie portion of the Dunnville Wildlife Area radiates a wonderful purple hue in late August. Closer to the river, the vegetation changes to erratic clumps of brush in an ever-shifting sandy shoreline. The trestle bridge offers great views of the river.

ABOUT THE ROADS

Expect a mix of woods and farmland and low to medium rollers. Traffic is low to medium on the county roads and slightly higher on the short stretches of State Highways, such as Highway 72 near Downsville. The steepest terrain is near the river.

ROAD HIGHLIGHTS

Hardscrabble Road, south of Downsville, is also hard climbing if traveling south to north. Hardscrabble is shady and lightly traveled, has excellent pavement and offers a couple of great views of the river valley to the west. If you are looking for a short diversion from the trail, this is the road to take. County Roads C and D offer a couple of steep climbs near the river, then rolling, rural panoramic views. Paradise Valley Rd parallels the trail north of Irvington from a vantage point slightly inland and higher, a quiet road with low underbrush on both sides and occasional views of the river.

HOW TO GET THERE

Menomonie is about 30 miles west of Eau Claire on Interstate 94. Take the Highway 25 exit south off Interstate 94. Go south about 2.5 miles to Highway 29 west. Go west on Highway 29 about one half mile. The trailhead is on the left side of the road just after crossing the Red Cedar River. Continue south on Highway 25 about 6 miles to Downsville.

Superior

Menomonie
Eau Claire
Wausau
Green Bay
Tomah
LaCrosse
Madison
Milwaukee

See Trail Map on page M39

Information Red Cedar Trail

Greater Menomonie Chamber of
Commerce
Toll Free (800) 283-1862
Phone (715) 235-9087
Email info@chippewavalley.net
Web www.chippewavalley.net

Menomonie.com
Phone (715) 962-4660
Email tourism@menomonie.org
Web www.menomonie.org

Red Cedar State Trail, DNR,
Menomonie
Phone (715) 232-1242
Web
www.dnr.state.wi.us/org/land/parks

Menomonie Park and Rec
Phone (715) 232-1664

LODGING

Motels/Resorts
Downsville
The Creamery Restaurant & Inn
Zip Code 54735
Phone (715) 664-8354
Fax (715) 664-8353
Email visit@www.creameryrestaurant-
inn.com
Web www.creameryrestaurant-inn.com

Menomonie
Super 8 Motel
1622 North Broadway
Zip Code 54751
Phone (715) 235-8889
Toll Free (800) 800-8000
Web www.super8.com

Motel 6
2100 Stout St
Zip Code 54751
Phone (715) 235-6901

Best Western/Holiday Manor
1815 North Broadway
Zip Code 54751
Toll Free (800) 528-1234
Phone (715) 235-9651

AmericInn
1915 North Broadway
Zip Code 54751
Toll Free (800) 634-3444
Phone (715) 235-4800
Fax (715) 235-5090
Web www.americinn.com

Bed and Breakfast
Menomonie
Cedar Trail Guest House
E4761 County C
Zip Code 54751
Phone (715) 664-8828

Hansen Heritage House
919-13th St
Zip Code 54751
Phone (715) 235-0119

Oaklawn Bed & Breakfast
423 Technology Park Dr East
Zip Code 54751
Phone (715) 235-6155

Camping
Menomonie
Twin Springs Campground
3010 Cedar Falls Rd
N6572 530th St
Zip Code 547519052
Phone (715) 235-9321

Edgewater Acres Campground
E5468 670th Ave
Zip Code 54751
Phone (715) 235-3291

RESTAURANTS

Downsville
The Creamery
Phone (715) 664-8354

Menomonie
Old 400 Depot Cafe
Phone (715) 235-1993

Kernel Restaurant
Phone (715) 235-5154

Grazi's
Phone (715) 232-8878

Bolo Country Inn
Toll Free(800) 553-2656
Phone (715) 235-5596

The Pepper Mill
Phone (715) 235-2188

Papa Murphy's
Phone (715) 233-1380

Acoustic Cafe
Phone (715) 235-1115

Ted's Pizza
Phone (715) 235-0600

GROCERIES

Menomonie
Leevers Fresh Foods
(715) 235-2108

BIKE RENTAL

Menomonie
Red Cedar Outfitters
Phone (715) 235-5431
Email redcedaroutfitters@yahoo.co
Web www.redcedartrail.com

BIKE RENTAL cont'd

Riverside Bike & Rental
Phone (715) 235-9697

BIKE REPAIR

Menomonie
Red Cedar Outfitters
Phone (715) 235-5431
Email redcedaroutfitters@yahoo.co
Web www.redcedartrail.com

Riverside Bike & Skate
Phone (715) 235-9697

BIKE SHUTTLE

Menomonie
Red Cedar Outfitters
Phone (715) 235-5431
Email redcedaroutfitters@yahoo.com
Web www.redcedartrail.com

FESTIVALS AND EVENTS

Downsville
August
Made in Dunn County, Grown in
Dunn County
A celebration of abundance featuring
arts and crafts, local food processors
and growers display their wares, pup-
pet show and other activities for kids,
at the Creamery Restaurant, Fourth
Weekend
Phone (715) 664-8355

Menomonie
Outdoor Concerts
Outdoor concerts by the Ludington
Guard Band at the Wilson Park Band
Shell at 8 pm on Tuesday evenings,
All Summer
Toll Free (800) 283-1862
Phone (715) 235-9087

July
Fourth of July Celebration
Fireworks, Wakanda Park
Toll Free (800) 283-1862
Phone (715) 235-9087

Dunn County Fair
Includes animal exhibits, rides, games
and special events, Third Weekend
Toll Free (800) 283-1862
Phone (715) 235-0032

ALTERNATE ACTIVITIES

Downsville
Empire in Pine Lumber Museum
Relive the logging camp era of Dunn
County's early days. Displays depict
operations of Knapp, Stout &
Company, once the largest white pin-
ery in the world, as well as a black-
smith shop.
Phone (715) 664-8690

Menomonie
Farmers Market
Fresh produce, crafters and artists
every Saturday from July through
October
Phone (800) 283-1862

Russell J. Rassbach Heritage Museum
Chronicles the development of Dunn
County through its extensive collection
of artifacts and photographs. Exhibits
feature a timeline from prehistoric
times to white   settlement.
Phone (715) 232-8685
Web http://discover-net.net/~dchs

Wakanda Waterpark
Outdoor swimming facility featuring a
zero depth pool that increases to 4
feet, a 230 foot long water slide, interactive water play equipment and two
lap lanes, the park also has sand volleyball courts, playground equipment,
picnic shelters, a concession stand,
and a deck with lounge chairs
Phone (715) 232-1664

Wilson Place Mansion Museum
Museum of local history, including
furnishings of lumber baron William
Wilson
Toll Free (800) 368-7384
Phone (715) 235-2283

Red Cedar Outfitters
Canoe and tube rentals
Phone (715) 235-5431
Email redcedaroutfitters@yahoo.com
Web www.redcedartrail.com

Hoffman Hills State Recreation Area

Hilly, wooded recreation area, 60 foot
observation tower at top of hill, self-
guided nature trail and hiking trails
Toll Free (888) 523-3866

Mabel Tainter Theater and
Memorial Gallery
Lavishly furnished and restored 1889
theater with exhibit gallery, features
hand-carved woodwork, bronze cast
opera seats and a rare working Steere
and Turner tracker pipe organ
Toll Free (800) 236-7675
Phone (715) 235-0111
Email mtainter@mabeltainter.com
Web www.mabeltainter.com

Bullfrog Fish Farm
Pole and bait available, hatchery tours,
catch cleaned and iced
Phone (715) 664-8775
Fax (715) 664-8870
Email bullfrog@eatmyfish.com
Web www.eatmyfish.com

Chippewa River Trail

Vital Information:

Trail Distance: 23 miles

Trail Surface: asphalt emulsion

Access Points: Eau Claire, Highway 85 Rest Stop, Caryville, Meridean

Fees and Passes: Wisconsin State Trail Pass; $3.00 daily fee or $10 for an annual pass. State Trail passes are good on all Wisconsin State Trails.

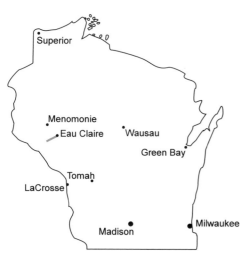

See Trail Map on page M41

ABOUT THE TRAIL

The unique aspahlt emulsion surface of this trail makes it one of the smoothest in Wisconsin, although not suitable for in-line skates. The trail runs from the park-like setting of Eau Claire's city trail through the open farmland of Caryville and into Dunnville Wildlife Area west of Meridean. The western terminus connects to the Red Cedar Trail at an 860 foot railroad trestle across the Chippewa River.

TRAIL HIGHLIGHTS

Blend two trails for a unique look at the Dunnville Wildlife Area and the Chippewa River. Start in Meridean, ride west to the trail end, cross the trestle and continue north along the Red Cedar Trail to Downsville. For an unforgettable sunset, end your day on the railroad trestle over the Chippewa River. The middle area of the trail passes through wide open farm fields, and can get a bit tedious. Consider the road alternate. The eastern edge of the trail is interesting in a different way. Beginning at the Highway 85 rest area, the trail winds along the Chippewa River, then crosses near Highway 12 on a beautiful old railroad bridge and follows the north shore past the University of Wisconsin, Eau Claire into Owen Park. The ride through town is quite pleasant with historical markers and great views of the river.

ABOUT THE ROADS

Hilly, twisting and low traffic, the best road routes start from the Highway 85 rest area. If you like hills, these are ideal roads for loops of 12 to 35 miles.

ROAD HIGHLIGHTS

Highway 85 has traffic, but the shoulder is paved. Mitchell Road is relatively flat with a beautiful full canopy tree cover. County F has long, medium rollers, surrounded by a blend of forest and fields. County W is a narrow, snakelike road. It twists and turns, climbs and descends creating scenic views and narrow, intimate trails through the woods. The southern end of County Z repeats the snakelike motions of County W, but passes through a more open landscape. Schuh and Town Hall Roads provide an interesting rolling alternate to the flatlands surrounding the trail between the Highway 85 rest area and Caryville.

HOW TO GET THERE

Eau Claire is 87 miles east of the Twin Cities on Interstate 94, and 87 miles north of LaCrosse on Highway 53. You can avoid going into Eau Claire by taking the Highway 37/85 exit off Interstate 94. Stay on Highway 85 to the rest area. Caryville is on Highway 85 further west and Meridean can be reached off Highway 85 via County O. If you start in Eau Claire, you can get on the state trail by following the Eau Claire city trail along the Chippewa River through town. See city and trail maps for details.

Chippewa Valley Convention &
Visitors Bureau
Toll Free (888) 523-3866
Phone (715) 831-2345
Fax (715) 831-2340
Email info@chippewavalley.net
Web www.chippewavalley.net

LODGING

Motels/Resorts
Eau Claire
Holiday Inn Convention Center
205 South Barstow
Zip Code 54701
Phone (715) 835-6121
Web www.basshotels.com/holiday-in

Super 8 Motel
6260 Texaco Dr
Zip Code 54703
Toll Free (800) 800-8000
Phone (715) 874-6868
Fax (715) 874-6898
Web www.super8.com

Park Inn & Suites
3340 Mondovi Rd
Zip Code 54701
Phone (715) 838-9989
Web www.parkinneauclaire.com

Quality Inn Conference Center
809 West Clairemont
Zip Code 54701
Phone (715) 834-6611
Web www.qualityinn-eauclaire.com

Ramada Conference Center
1202 West Clairemont
Zip Code 54701
Phone (715) 834-3181
Web www.ramada-eauclaire.com

Westgate Motel
1436 North Clairemont
Zip Code 54701
Phone (715) 834-3580

Holiday Inn Campus Area
2703 Craig Rd
Zip Code 54701
Phone (715) 835-2211
Web www.holiday-inn.com

Bed and Breakfast
Eau Claire
The Atrium
5572 Prill Rd
Zip Code 54701
Toll Free (888) 773-0094
Web www.atriumbb.com

Fanny Hill Inn & Dinner Theatre
3919 Crescent Ave
Zip Code 54701
Phone (715) 836-8184
Web www.fannyhill.com

Apple Tree Inn B&B
6700 Highway 53 South
Zip Code 54701
Toll Free (800) 347-9598
Web www.appletreeinnbb.com

Camping
Augusta
Woodland Campground
2002 Highway 27
Zip Code 54722
Phone (715) 286-2112

RESTAURANTS
Eau Claire
Camaraderie
Phone (715) 834-5411

Latte The Coffee Place
Phone (715) 833-0100

Racy D'Lene's Coffee
Phone (715) 834-0000

Mona Lisa's
Phone (715) 839-8969

Varone's Restaurant
Phone (715) 831-2345

Houligans
Phone (715) 836-9828

Mogie's Pub
Phone (715) 836-9666

Grand Avenue Cafe
Phone (715) 831-1100

Acoustic Cafe
Phone (715) 832-9090
Web

Stella Blues
Phone (715) 855-7777

O'Leary's Pub & Grill
Phone (715) 834-6611

GROCERIES
Eau Claire
Copps Food Center
(715) 834-3993

Randall Foods
(715) 834-2081

BIKE RENTAL
Eau Claire
Riverside Bike & Skate
Phone (715) 835-0088

BIKE REPAIR
Eau Claire
Eau Claire Cycle
Phone (715) 832-6149

Bike Doctor
Phone (715) 835-4812

Information Chippewa River Trail

BIKE REPAIR cont'd

Anybody's Bikeshop
Phone (715) 833-7100

Riverside Bike & Skate
Phone (715) 835-0088

FESTIVALS AND EVENTS

Eau Claire
July
Country Jam, USA
Outdoor country music festival with
more than thirty top national acts.
Side stage entertainment, country ven-
dors, food and camping, Summer
Festival Grounds, Web
www.countryjam.com, Third Weekend
Toll Free (800) 780-0526

August
Festival in the Pines
Arts and crafts, food vendors, games,
rides, and family entertainment,
Carson Park,
www.festivalinthepines.com, Fourth
Weekend
Toll Free (888) 611-7463
Phone (715) 552-5504

World Series Tournament
Continental Amateur Baseball
Association, held at Carson Park
Toll Free (800) 344-3866

Rendezvous Days
Crafters, games and great food,
Third Weekend
Phone (715) 831-2839

Pioneer Days
Flea Market, horse pull, steamer
games, food stand, tractor pull, cross-
cut saw competition, parade, Second
Weekend
Phone (715) 839-7678

ALTERNATE ACTIVITIES

Dunnville
Dunnville Wildlife Area
Right on the trail

Eau Claire
Chippewa Valley Museum
Ojibwe Indian culture & frontier her-
itage, includes Anderson Log House
and the one-room Sunnyview School
Phone (715) 834-7871
Fax (715) 834-6624
Web www.cvmuseum.com

Rude Trude Flyfishing Services
Learn to flyfish for brook, brown and
rainbow trout, lessons or guide service
Phone (715) 832-2377

Hank Aaron Statue
Bronze sculpture in Carson Park,
Aaron began his playing days for the
Eau Claire Bears in 1952
Toll Free (888) 523-3866

Riverside Bike & Skate
Canoes, kayaks, paddle and peddle
trips on the Eau Claire and Chippewa
Rivers
Phone (715) 835-0088

Ski Sprites Waterski Show
Water ski performances, including
bare footing, jumping, pyramids and
more, Half Moon Lake, Wednesday
and Sunday evenings at 6:30, June
through August
Phone (715) 836-9048
Web www.ecol.net/skisprites/

Fanny Hill Victoria Inn & Dinner
Theater
Professional dinner theater
performances
Toll Free (800) 292-8026
Phone (715) 836-8184
Fax (715) 836-8180
Web
www.eauclaireinfo.com/theatre.htm

Paul Bunyan Logging Camp
1900 logging era buildings, including
bunkhouse, cook shanty, heavy equipment building, blacksmith shop, and
barn, in Carson Park
Phone (715) 835-6200
Fax (715) 835-6293
Email info@paulbunyancamp.org
Web www.paulbunyancamp.org

Vital Information:

Trail Distance: 22 miles

Trail Surface: limestone

Access Points: Marshland, Perrot State Park, Trempealeau, Lytles Landing, Midway, Onalaska

Fees and Passes: Wisconsin State Trail Pass; $3 daily fee or $10 for an annual pass. State Trail Passes are good on all Wisconsin State Trails.

See Trail Map on page M43

ABOUT THE TRAIL

18 bridges, Mississippi River bottoms and open prairie mark the scenery along this trail. The Mississippi River itself is only visible if you get off the trail at Trempealeau or Perrot State Park, but you will see plenty of water as the trail crosses the many branches of the Black River. This is a very quiet, remote trail with a lot of diversity. The town of Trempealeau is worth leaving the trail to see. Ask about the outdoor music schedule at the Trempealeau Hotel and stop for a meal, the food is very good.

TRAIL HIGHLIGHTS

The bridge at Lytles Landing passes over the main branch of the Black River and well into the lowlands surrounding the Mississippi River. It's long, low and inviting. For a unique experience spend some time in the Trempealeau National Wildlife Refuge. Explore the dike road to Trempealeau Mountain plus the nature drive and various secondary roads into the vast marshland. The surface isn't as solid for bike tires as the trail, but traffic is low and the combination of prairie, wetland and natural history signs makes it worth an extended visit. Pick up a brochure at the parking lot.

ABOUT THE ROADS

Choose your route according to your riding needs. The roads are flat south of Highways 35/54 and hilly north. The flat roads pass through corn fields and open farmland. The hilly roads offer a mix of woodlots, pasture and farmland, some of it from high, scenic van-tage points. Most of the roads in this area are paved and low traffic as long as you stay off the major highways.

ROAD ROUTE HIGHLIGHTS

The county roads north of Highways 35/54 pass through deep dry valleys called coulees. This kind of riding is addictive. The road slowly rises or falls as long as you are following a creek or small river. Passing from one watershed to another, however, guarantees lots of large hills. For a flatter loop with occasional views of Lake Onalaska, a backwater of the Mississippi, try the roads around Brice Prairie. You can start near Midway and end at Lytles Landing by taking County Roads Z and ZB. Avoid County ZN, especially near Midway, because of traffic. The road route through Onalaska follows low traffic, back roads, but isn't especially interesting. It does lead to Onalaska Park, a large, well appointed city park, and to the trailhead at the Chamber of Commerce building. A connecter from the trailhead leads to the LaCrosse River Trail.

HOW TO GET THERE

Onalaska is just north of LaCrosse in southwestern Wisconsin. Take Highway 35 north from Interstate 90 to get to the trailhead. See city map. Continue north on Highway 35 to Midway or Trempealeau. From the northwest, cross the Mississippi River on Highway 54 in Winona. Highways 54 and 35 meet in Wisconsin. Watch for Marshland and the Wildlife Refuge sign for parking. Continue along Highway 35 to Trempealeau or Perrot State Park for a better starting point.

Information Great River Trail

Trempealeau Chamber of Commerce
Phone (608) 534-6780
Web www.trempealeau.net

Onalaska Center for Commerce and
Tourism
Toll Free (800) 873-1901
Phone (608) 781-9570
Web www.tourism.onalaska.wi.us

Perrot State Park and Great River Trail
Phone (608) 534-6409

LODGING

Motels/Resorts
Onalaska
Comfort Inn
1223 Crossing Meadows Dr
Zip Code 54650
Phone (608) 781-7500

Onalaska Inn
Highway 35
Zip Code 54650
Toll Free (888) 359-2619
Phone (608) 783-2270

Shadow Run Lodge
Highway 35
Zip Code 54650
Toll Free (800) 657-4749
Phone (608) 783-0020

Trempealeau
Riverview Motel
First & Main
Zip Code 54661
Phone (608) 534-7784
Email rivervw@win.bright.net

Pleasant Knoll Motel
Zip Code 54661
Phone (608) 534-6615
Email pkmotel@win.bright.net
Web www.greatriver.com/pleasantknoll

Trempealeau Hotel
150 Main St
Zip Code 54661
Phone (608) 534-6898
Web www.greatriver.com/hotel.htm

Bed and Breakfast
Onalaska
The Lumber Baron Inn B&B
421 2nd Ave North
Zip Code 54650
Phone (608) 781-8938

Rainbow Ridge Farms and B & B
W5732 Hauser Rd.
Zip Code 54650
Phone (608) 783-8181
Web www.fflax.net/~rainbow

Camping
La Crosse
Bluebird Campgrounds
Highway B, 2843 Smith Valley Rd
Zip Code 54601
Phone (608) 781-2267

Onalaska
Sias Isles/R&L Riversports
107 1st Ave South
Zip Code 54650
Toll Free (888) 269-8007
Phone (608) 783-5623
Fax (608) 269-8007

Stoddard
Goose Island Campground
Highway 35
Zip Code 54658
Phone (608) 788-7018

Trempealeau
Perrot State Park
Rt 1, Box 407
Zip Code 54661
Phone (608) 534-6409
Web www.dnr.state.wi.us

RESTAURANTS
Onalaska
Ciatti's Italian Rest.
Phone (608) 781-8686

Traditions Restaurant
Phone (608) 783-0200

Seven Bridges Rest.
Phone (608) 783-6103

Manny's Mexican Cocina
Phone (608) 781-5601

Onalaska American Legion
Phone (608) 783-3300

Onalaska Inn
Toll Free (888) 359-2619
Phone (608) 783-2270

Lakeview Rest. & Lounge
Phone (608) 781-0150

Trempealeau
Larry's Landing
Phone (608) 534-7771

Ed Sullivan's
Phone (608) 534-7775

Rock Garden Inn
Phone (608) 534-5222

Wildflower Cafe
Phone (608) 534-6866

Trempealeau Hotel
Phone (608) 534-6898

GROCERIES
Onalaska
Kwik Trip Stores
(608) 779-9364

Trempealeau
Budget Mart
(608) 534-6554

PJ's Market & Deli
(608) 534-7460

BIKE RENTAL

Onalaska

Onalaska Pro Sports
Phone (608) 783-5898
Web www.prosportsonline.net

Smith's Cycling & Fitness
Phone (608) 779-0510
Web www.smithsbikes.com

Trempealeau

Trempealeau Hotel
Phone (608) 534-6898
Web www.greatriver.com/

BIKE REPAIR

Onalaska

Smith's Cycling & Fitness
Phone (608) 779-0510
Web www.smithsbike.com

Onalaska Pro Sports
Phone (608) 783-5898
Web www.prosportsonline.net

BIKE SHUTTLE

Onalaska

Onalaska Pro Sports
Phone (608) 783-5898
Web www.prosportsonline.net

FESTIVALS AND EVENTS

Onalaska

May

Sunfish Days
Kids' fishing derby, craft fair, volleyball
and softball tourneys, carnival rides,
petting zoo, parade, live music, beer
garden, food stands. Omni Center at
Van Riper Park, Memorial Day weekend
Phone (608) 781-9570

July

Salute to the Fourth
Kids' games, craft and food booths,
beer tent, evening fireworks in conjunction with LaCrosse Symphony
Orchestra, always July 1st, regardless
of day of the week
Phone (608) 781-9566

September

Oktoberfest
Oktoberfest 100 Bicycle Tour and
Race, Rowe Park, all-service event,
trophies and prizes plus refreshments
and dinner, end of September into
October
Phone (608) 782-4630

Fall 15 Great River Walk
Four, nine, or 15 mile fitness walk
along the Great River Trail from
Onalaska to Trempealeau, shuttles and
snacks on the trail, dinner, prizes and
entertainment in Trempealeau,
advance registration required,
Saturday after Labor Day
Phone (608) 781-9570

Trempealeau

Stars under the Stars
Outdoor summer concert series featur-
ing national acts at the Trempealeau
Hotel concert grounds, Web
www.greatriver.com/hotel, All Summer
Phone (608) 534-6898

May

Reggae Sunsplash
Jamaican style music, food and crafts
from early afternoon through the
evening. Trempealeau Hotel concert
grounds, Web
www.greatriver.com/hotel
Phone (608) 534-6898

Blues Bash
Nationally and internationally famous
blues bands play from early afternoon
through the evening at the
Trempealeau Hotel concert grounds,
Web www.greatriver.com/hotel
Phone (608) 534-6898

Spring Bike Tour
10, 25 and 50 mile tours from the
Sportsman's Club, Second Weekend
Phone (608) 534-6780

July

Catfish Days
Art and craft fair, flea market, fishing
tournament, kids' games, live music,
dancing, kiddy parade, carnival, beer
tent, parade on Sunday and fireworks
in the evening, First weekend following
the 4th
Phone (608) 543-6780

ALTERNATE ACTIVITIES

Bird Watching
Bird watching along the Mississippi
River during spring and fall migration
at Highway 35 North overlooking Lake
Onalaska, two observation points with
interpretive signs
Phone (608) 783-8405

Onalaska

Upper Mississippi River National
Wildlife Refuge
Contains 200,000 acres of fish and
wildlife habitat extending 260 miles
along the Mississippi River. Popular
viewing spots include Lake Onalaska,
Trempealeau National Wildlife Refuge
and Lake Pepin near Stockholm.
Phone (507) 452-4232

Trempealeau

Lock and Dam #6
Watch boats and barges go through
the locks on the Mississippi River.
Phone (608) 534-6424

Canoe Rentals
Trempealeau Hotel
Phone (608) 534-6898
Web www.greatriver.com/hotel.htm

Canoe Shuttle
Al's Canoe Rental and Shuttle Service
Phone (608) 534-5046

Perrot State Park
1,400 acres nestle among bluffs where
the Trempealeau and Mississippi rivers
meet. Scenic hikes to the top of the
bluffs, including Brady's Bluff Prairie, a
goat prairie on the bluff rising 460 feet
above the Mississippi River
Phone (608) 534-6409

Long Lake Canoe Trail
Canoe through the Upper Mississippi
River National Wildlife and Fish
Refuge. Travel 4.5 miles in about 2
hours through slow moving water,
sloughs and islands that are a haven
for wildlife.
Phone (608) 785-9000

Trempealeau National Wildlife Refuge
View a variety of animal and plant life
in wetland, sand prairie and bottom-
land hardwood forest habitats. Roads
are gravel, but bikeable. Some go
deep into the marshlands of the
Mississippi River.
Phone (608) 539-2311

Vital Information:

Trail Distance: 21 miles

Trail Surface: limestone

Access Points: Onalaska, Medary, West Salem, Bangor, Rockland, Sparta

Fees and Passes: Wisconsin State Trail Pass; $3 daily fee or $10 for an annual pass. State Trail passes are good on all Wisconsin State Trails.

Trail Website:
www.lacrosseriverstatetrail.org

See Trail Map on page M45

ABOUT THE TRAIL

This trail has a rap for not being very scenic, and there is some justification for it, but taken selectively, and in small doses, it has some real charms. The connecting road routes are very nice, so it is possible to tie together the better parts of the trail with the scenic roads to create some very enjoyable rides. For long distance riders, the trail links the Great River Trail on the west with the Elroy-Sparta Trail to the east. It is possible to travel over 100 miles with only two minor breaks in the trail system.

TRAIL HIGHLIGHTS

Between Medary and West Salem the trail passes through the vast floodplain of the LaCrosse River. Lots of marshland, wet prairie and backwaters offer good bird watching in the spring. Veteran's Memorial Park in West Salem is a unique memorial to local veterans who died in US wars. The Dutch Creek Swimming hole, right off the trail in Bangor City Park, offers a refreshing dip in a shaded creek. Great for cooling off on a hot summer day. The native prairie east of Rockland has some nice wildflowers, but is a little disappointing as a prairie.

ABOUT THE ROADS

Take your pick. You get a little of everything from the nearly flat roads between Bangor and Sparta to the extremely long climb over Mindoro Pass. This is primarily dairy country where contour plowed fields of corn and alfalfa form a patchwork of zig zag fields mixed with pastures and woodlots. Monroe County has a cold weather theme between the county line and Sparta. Check out the road names as you ride them or cross them.

ROAD ROUTE HIGHLIGHTS

The Mindoro loop climbs to high scenic vistas and rural panoramic views. The climbs are long and challenging. The descents are exciting. Mindoro is charming. The sidewalk rises six feet above the street to create a porch-like setting with roof, railings and rest benches. Stop at Mr. Whiffles Grocery Store for a wide selection of unique sodas. If the bank is open, stop in for a look at the collection of photos showing how Mindoro Pass was cut by hand near the turn of the century. While the Mindoro Loop spends its time on the ridge, the southern loop, between Medary and Bangor, follows the creeks and valleys. From west to east, the valley walls slowly close in until the road turns and begins a long steep climb, followed by a fast descent. East of Bangor, the road routes offer a diverse, nearly flat alternate to the trail. Take the trail one way and the roads on the way back. From Hammer Road to Sparta, take the trail because Iberia carries some traffic, including trucks.

HOW TO GET THERE

Interstate 90 parallels the trail from LaCrosse to Sparta. All trail towns are easily accessible from the Interstate. To get to Medary, take the Highway 16 exit off Interstate 90, go south to County B and east on B to the trailhead.

Information LaCrosse River Trail

LaCrosse Area Convention and
Visitors Bureau
Toll Free (800) 658-9424
Phone (608) 782-2366
Web www.explorelacrosse.com

Greater LaCrosse Area Chamber of
Commerce
Toll Free (800) 889-0539
Phone (608) 784-4880
Fax (608) 784-4919
Email lse_chamber@centuryinter.net
Web www.wi.centurytel.net/lacrosse

Sparta Chamber of Commerce
Phone (608) 269-4123

LaCrosse River State Trail
Toll Free (888) 540-8434
Phone (608) 269-3350
Fax (608) 269-3350
Email
information@LaCrosseRiverStateTrail.org
Web www.laCrosseriverstatetrail.org

Sparta Convention and Visitors Bureau
Toll Free (800) 354-2453
Phone (608) 269-2453

Village of West Salem
Phone (608) 786-1858
Fax (608) 786-1988
Email info@westsalemwi.com
Web www.westsalemwi.com

Wildcat Mountain State Park
Phone (608) 337-4775

Onalaska Chamber of Commerce
Toll Free (800) 873-1901
Phone (608) 781-9570
Web www.tourism.onalaska.wi.us

LODGING

Motels/Resorts

La Crosse
Nuttleman's Motor Lodge
N3080 Highway 16
Zip Code 54601
Toll Free (888) 810-9465
Phone (608) 782-0297
Fax (608) 796-0704

Eagle Bluff Motel
2344 Highway 16
Zip Code 54601
Phone (608) 781-7381
Fax (608) 783-2517

Ridgeview Inn
N2052 Bahr Rd
Zip Code 54601
Phone (608) 787-5775

West Salem
AmericInn
125 Buol Rd
Zip Code 54669
Toll Free (800) 634-3444
Phone (608) 786-3340
Fax (608) 786-3340
Email sales@americinnwestsalem.com

Bed and Breakfast

La Crosse
Chateau La Crosse
410 Cass St
Zip Code 54601
Toll Free (800) 442-7969

The Wilson Schoolhouse Inn
W5718 Highway 14-61
Zip Code 54601
Phone (608) 787-1982

Four Gables Inn
W5648 Highway 14-61
Zip Code 54601
Phone (608) 788-7958

West Salem
Wolfway Farm
W2105 County B
Zip Code 54669
Phone (608) 486-2686

Camping

Stoddard
Goose Island Campground
W6488 County GI
Zip Code 54658
Phone (608) 788-7018

West Salem
Neshonoc Lakeside Camp
N5334 Neshonoc Rd, Highway 16
Zip Code 54669
Toll Free (888) 783-0035
Phone (608) 786-1792

Veterans Memorial Campground
N4668 County VP
Zip Code 54669
Phone (608) 786-4011

RESTAURANTS

Bangor
Log Cabin Tavern
Phone (608) 486-4437

Village Inn Restaurant
Phone (608) 486-2741

Chip's Bar
Phone (608) 486-4060

La Crosse
Salsa's Cafe & Cantina
Phone (608) 785-0556

Forest Hills
Phone (608) 784-0566

Onalaska
See Great River Trail

Sparta
See Elroy-Sparta Trail

RESTAURANTS cont'd

West Salem
Westview Inn
Phone (608) 786-1336

GROCERIES

Bangor
Hansen's IGA
(608) 486-2626

Onalaska
See Great River Trail

Rockland
Marnie's Mini Mart
(608) 486-2057

Sparta
See Elroy Sparta Trail

West Salem
Cenex Convenience Store
(608) 786-1108

BIKE RENTAL

LaCrosse
Buzz's Bicycle Shop
Phone (608) 785-2737

Onalaska
See Great River Trail

Sparta
See Elroy Sparta Trail

BIKE REPAIR

LaCrosse
Buzz's Bicycle Shop
Phone (608) 785-2737

Onalaska
See Great River Trail

Sparta
See Elroy-Sparta Trail

BIKE SHUTTLE

Sparta
See Elroy-Sparta Trail

FESTIVALS AND EVENTS

Onalaska
See Great River Trail

Sparta
See Elroy-Sparta Trail

West Salem
June
June Dairy Days
Kickoff breakfast, parade at noon on
Saturday, carnival, softball games, live
music, clowns, magicians, food, dairy
tents, big wheel races, bingo, petting
barn, stagecoach rides and speedway
racing, Village Park, First Weekend
Phone (608) 786-1858

Le Coulee Classique Bike Ride
Organized ride with the option of 35 or
60 miles, sag wagon and rest stops,
part of June Dairy Days, local contact,
Rick Brown, First Weekend
Phone (608) 779-5229

July
LaCrosse Interstate Fair
Rural fair with animals, 4-H projects,
carnival and food booths, local con-
tact, Ronald Hoyer
Phone (608) 786-0428

ALTERNATE ACTIVITIES

Bangor
Bangor City Park
Old fashioned swimming hole in Dutch
Creek, visible from the trail

Onalaska
See Great River Trail

Ontario
Wildcat Mountain State Park
Scenic vistas and great hiking trails
Phone (608) 337-4774

Rockland
Restored Prairie
Along the trail

Sparta
See Elroy-Sparta Trail

West Salem
Wolfway Farm
One of Wisconsin's Century Farms,
registered Holsteins milked twice daily,
reservations required
Phone (608) 486-2686

Historic West Salem
Home of Hamlin Garland, Pulitzer Prize
winning author, also two octagon
homes, Thomas Leonard's colonial
style home, check out Veterans'
Memorial Park

Elroy-Sparta Trail

Vital Information:

Trail Distance: 32 miles

Trail Surface: limestone

Access Points: Sparta, Norwalk, Wilton, Kendall, Elroy

Fees and Passes: Wisconsin State Trail Pass, $3.00 daily fee or $10 for an annual pass. State Trail passes are good on all Wisconsin State Trails

Trail Website:
www.elroy-sparta-trail.org

See Trail Map on page M47

ABOUT THE TRAIL

Developed in 1967, this is the grand-daddy of them all. It shows in the mature trees, full canopy and well-maintained trail surface. The trail rises and drops very slowly as it passes through hilly, scenic, Driftless area. Explore the three tunnels, spend an evening in one of the small trail towns and enjoy the camaraderie of riding with cyclists from around the nation. Three major bike trails converge at Elroy Commons in Elroy. A short stretch of quiet road connects to the eastern end of the LaCrosse River Trail in Sparta. See city maps for details. Weekends and holidays are extremely busy.

TRAIL HIGHLIGHTS

The tunnels are unique. The trail rises slowly and passes through deep road cuts near the tunnel entrances creating a cool, damp microenvironment. Bring flashlights for the tunnels, then get off the bike and walk. Water runs along both sides of the trail in the three-quarter mile long Tunnel #3 and falling water splashes loudly near the center. You'll get dripped on lightly in the tunnel. Note the cool breeze flowing out of the lower, western end.

ABOUT THE ROADS

First timers come for the trail. Repeat visitors explore the roads. Expect grinding climbs, hair-raising descents, horse drawn Amish buggies, virtually no traffic, and pastoral views that belong in picture books. The roads are low traffic and the pavement ranges from smooth to pebbly.

ROAD ROUTE HIGHLIGHTS

The town roads between Kendall and Norwalk offer the most challenging climbs and descents near the trail. On one descent, from east to west, we hit 52 miles per hour. County T, south of Norwalk, follows a creek bed and stays flat. County F branches off and remains relatively flat for several miles, then climbs long and hard to become rolling ridgetop. Check out the church and convent in St. Mary's, then return to Norwalk via County U. Payback comes as County U nears Norwalk. 16th Ave, near Tunnel #3, passes over the tunnel and appears to run right along the top at one point. No markings along here, so you will have to imagine the folks walking in the dark beneath you.

HOW TO GET THERE

Sparta is approximately 25 miles east of LaCrosse on Interstate 94. Take the Highway 27 exit. Go north to Avon Road and follow the city map to the LaCrosse River Trailhead. To go directly to the Elroy-Sparta Trailhead, or to the trail towns, take the Highway 16 exit off Interstate 94. Go west on Highway 16 (toward Sparta) and turn south on Highway 71.

TOURIST INFORMATION

Village of Wilton
Phone (608) 435-6666
Email villageofwilton@centurytel.net
Web www.windingrivers.com/wilton.html

Sparta Area Chamber of Commerce
Toll Free (800) 354-2453
Phone (608) 269-4123

Elroy Commons
Phone (608) 462-2410

Village of Norwalk
Phone (608) 823-7760
Email villageofnorwalk@centurytel.net
Web
www.windingrivers.com/norwalk.html

Kendall Depot
Phone (608) 463-7109
Email kdepot@mwt.net
Web www.elroy-sparta-trail.org

LODGING

Motels/Resorts

Elroy
Valley Inn Motel
1/2 mile South on 80 & 82
Zip Code 53929
Phone (608) 462-8251

Kendall
Country Livin'
29000 Monarch Ave
Zip Code 54638
Phone (608) 463-7135

Sparta
The Country Inn
737 Avon Rd
Zip Code 54656
Toll Free (800) 456-4000
Phone (608) 269-3110

Budget Host-Heritage Motel
704 West Wisconsin St
Zip Code 54656

Toll Free (800) 283-4678
Phone (608) 269-6991

Sandy's Coach House
Highway 16 & South Water St
Zip Code 54656
Phone (608) 269-3138

Best Nights Inn
303 West Wisconsin St
Zip Code 54656
Toll Free (800) 201-0234
Phone (608) 269-3066

Spartan Motel
1900 West Wisconsin St
Zip Code 54656
Phone (608) 269-2770

Sunset Motel
1009 West Wisconsin
Zip Code 54656
Phone (608) 269-9932

Wilton
Mid-Trail Motel
P.O. Box 296
Highway 71
Zip Code 54670
Phone (608) 435-6685

Bed and Breakfast

Elroy
Waarvik's Century Farm
N4621 County H
Zip Code 53929
Phone (608) 462-8595

Sunburst Haus
27751 Nutmeg Rd
Zip Code 53929
Phone (608) 463-8268

Eastview
33620 County P
Zip Code 53929
Phone (608) 463-7564

Rocky Ridge B&B
N3915 Goodhill Rd
Zip Code 53929
Phone (608) 462-5632

Kendall
Dusk to Dawn
625 Medbury St
Zip Code 54638
Phone (608) 463-7547

Cabin at Trails End
23009 Knollwood Rd
Zip Code 54638
Phone (608) 427-3877

Norwalk
Norwalk House
110 North McGary St
Zip Code 54648
Phone (608) 823-8753

Sparta
Just-N-Trails
7452 Kathryn Ave
Zip Code 54656
Toll Free (800) 488-4521
Phone (608) 269-4522
Email justintrails@centurytel.net

Franklin Victorian
220 East Franklin St
Zip Code 54656
Toll Free (800) 845-8767
Phone (608) 269-3894
Email fvbb@centurytel.net

The Strawberry Lace Inn
603 North Water St
Zip Code 54656
Phone (608) 269-7878
Email strawberry@centurytel.net

Cranberry Country B&B
114 Montgomery St
Zip Code 54656
Toll Free (888) 208-4354
Phone (608) 366-1000

LODGING cont'd

Wilton
Dorset Ridge Guest House
22259 King Rd
Zip Code 54670
Phone (608) 463-7375

Rice's Whispering Pines
Rt 2 Box 225
Zip Code 54670
Phone (608) 435-6531

Camping
Camp Douglas
Mill Bluff State Park
Zip Code 54618
Phone (608) 427-6692

Elroy
E.O. Schultz Park
Village Park
Zip Code 53929
Toll Free (888) 606-2453
Phone (608) 462-2410
Web www.elroywi.com

Kendall
Trailside Campground
31833 Highway P
Zip Code 54638
Phone (608) 463-7185
Email wereon@mwt.net

LaFarge
Kickapoo Valley Reserve
505 North Mill St
Zip Code 54639
Phone (608) 625-2960

Norwalk
Village Park
Zip Code 54648
Phone (608) 823-7760

Ontario
Brush Creek Campground
RR1 Box 26 On Highway 33
Zip Code 54651
Phone (608) 337-4344

Wildcat Mountain State Park
PO Box 99
Zip Code 54651
Phone (608) 337-4775
Web www.dnr.state.wi.us

Sparta
Leon Valley Campground
9050 Jancing Ave
Zip Code 54656
Phone (608) 269-6400

Pine View Recreation Area
Fort McCoy
Zip Code 54656
Phone (608) 388-3517

Primitive DNR Trailhead
Zip Code 54656
Web www.dnr.state.wi.us

Wilton
Tunnel Trail Campground
26983 State Highway 71
Zip Code 54670
Phone (608) 435-6829
Email tunneltrail@elroynet.com
Web www.campgrounds.com/waco

Wilton Village Campground
311 Main St
Zip Code 54670
Phone (608) 435-6666
Web
www.windingrivers.com/wilton.html

RESTAURANTS

Elroy
U.S.A Cafe
Phone (608) 462-8990

Kendall
Zirks Bar & Grill
Phone (608) 463-7115

Norwalk
Judy's Trail Cafe
Phone (608) 823-7551

Diamond Lil's
Phone (608) 823-7708

Sparta
Sydney's Rest. & Pub
Phone (608) 269-5010

Dorine's Family Inn
Phone (608) 269-8258

Sparta Grill
Phone (608) 269-0611

The Foxhole Rest. & Bar
Phone (608) 269-6271

Club 16 Pub & Eatery
Phone (608) 269-9983

Slice of Chicago
Phone (608) 269-2181

Wilton
Dorset Valley Rest.& Bakery
Toll Free(800) 775-0698
Phone (608) 435-6525

Gina's Pies are Square
Phone (608) 435-6541

GROCERIES

Kendall
Kendall Food Center
(608) 463-3663

Norwalk
Lehner's Market
(608) 823-7613

Sparta
Beaver Creek Food Co-op
(608) 269-9770

Ray's Supermarket
(608) 269-3135

Wilton
Wilton Fasttrip
(608) 435-6977

BIKE RENTAL

Elroy
Elroy Commons
Toll Free (888) 606-2453
Phone (608) 462-2410
Web www.elroywi.com

Kendall
Kendall Depot
Phone (608) 463-7109
Email kdepot@mwt.net

Norwalk
Sam's Center
Phone (608) 823-7376

Sparta
Speed's Bicycle
Phone (608) 269-2315
Web www.speedsbike.com

Out Spokin' Adventures
Toll Free (800) 493-2453
Phone (608) 269-6087
Email outspokin@centurytel.net
Web www.outspokinadventures.com

Wilton
Margaret's Market
Phone (608) 435-6517

Wilton Tunnel Trail Campground
Phone (608) 435-6829

BIKE REPAIR

Sparta
Speed's Bicycle
Phone (608) 269-2315
Fax (608) 269-3852

BIKE SHUTTLE

Sparta
Wayne Hollingstad
Phone (608) 269-7466

Franklin Victorian
Phone (608) 269-3894

Roger Lewison
Phone (608) 269-3629

Ken Schure
Phone (608) 269-2825

Barb and Pete Witt
Phone (608) 269-2173

Out Spokin' Avdentures
Toll Free (800) 493-2453
Phone (608) 269-6087
Web www.outspokinadventures.com

FESTIVALS AND EVENTS

Elroy
July
Elroy Fair
Carnival, horse pull, livestock judging, tractor pull, demolition derby, 4-H exhibits Fourth Weekend

Kendall
May
Horse & Pony Pull,
Sponsored by Lions Club, Memorial Day Weekend
Phone (608) 463-7197

September
Labor Day Celebration
Volleyball, dance, parade, chicken BBQ, pancake breakfast
Phone (608) 463-7124

October
Polkafest
Community Hall, dance to the music of several bands, Second Weekend
Phone (608) 463-7124

Norwalk
June
Lions Softball Tournament, Fourth Weekend
Phone (608) 823-7760

July
Black Squirrel Family Fest & Softball Tourney
DJ Saturday night, Lioness Pancake Breakfast on Sunday, Second Weekend
Phone (608) 823-7760

August
Lions Club Tractor Pull/Garden Club Flower Show
BBQ chicken, Lioness pie & ice-cream tent, Second Weekend
Phone (608) 823-7760

Sparta
June
Butterfest
Carnival, live entertainment, magic shows, arts and crafts exhibits, music, food booths, quilt show, and classic car show, large parade on Sunday, Second Weekend
Toll Free (800) 354-2453

August
"Bike Me" Tour
Fully supported, 6-day, 5-night, 300-mile tour of west-central Wisconsin.
Toll Free (800) 354-2453
Phone (414) 671-4560

Human Powered Boat & Bike Races
www.wisconsinbicycletour.com
Phone (414) 671-4560

Sparta Bike Daze
Monroe County Challenge Bike Race, citizens and WISSPORT sanctioned race through Monroe County, 35-40 miles, bike rodeo, live music, and kids' events, Memorial Park, Second Weekend
Toll Free (800) 354-2453

Information Elroy-Sparta Trail

Wilton

Pancake breakfast
Sonsored by the Lions Club each
Sunday, Memorial Day through Labor
Day, Wilton Village Park
Phone (608) 435-6430

August

Wood Turtle Days
Fireworks, softball, volleyball, parade,
arts & crafts show, First Sunday
Phone (608) 435-6666

ALTERNATE ACTIVITIES

Ontario

Kickapoo Paddle Inn
Canoe rental on the Kickapoo River
Phone (608) 337-4726

Wildcat Mountain State Park
Beautiful scenery, nature trails and
camping
Phone (608) 337-4775

Drifty's Canoe Rental
Canoe rental on the Kickapoo River
Phone (608) 337-4288

Sparta

Deke Slayton Memorial Space &
Bicycle Museum
Deke Slayton, one of America's original
astronauts, was born in the Sparta
area and raised in Monroe County.
Exhibits from Mercury, Gemini, Apollo
and Space Shuttle missions, also
includes the history of bicycles
Phone (608) 269-0033

Paul and Matilda Wegner Grotto
Locally known as 'The Glass Church',
an example of grassroots art, For more
information contact the Local History
Room at 200 West Main St, Sparta.
Phone (608) 269-8680

Cabin on the Rock
Located on a 365 acre, four generation, working dairy farm, Holstein
cows, calves, and horseback riding
atop Redrock Ridge, cabin overlooks
the farm including 200 acres of woodlands with plenty of hiking trails, 5
miles to Elroy-Sparta Bike Trail
Phone (608) 823-7865

Out Spokin' Adventures
Kayaks, canoe rentals, with shuttle
Toll Free (800) 493-2453
Phone (608) 269-6087
Email outspokin@centuryinter.net
Web www.outspokinadventures.com

Monroe County Local History Museum
& Research Room
The story of Monroe County and its
pioneer history through photographs
and memorabilia, genealogical source
materials including census records,
church, cemetery and school records
Phone (608) 269-8680

Down A Country Road
Take a tour of the Amish community
and get a glimpse of this unique way
of life, then browse the Amish gift
shop, Highway 33 off Highway 27
Phone (608) 654-5318
Email downacountryroad@yahoo.com
Web downacountryroadamish.com

M&M Ranch
Tour the Largest Exotic Animal Ranch
in the Midwest. African Pygmy hedge-
hogs, talking parrots, potbellied pigs,
toucans, emus, ostriches, Erkel the
Camel, etc
Phone (608) 486-2709
Fax (608) 486-4052
Email m1m2ranch@aol.com
Web www.centuryinter.net/mmranch

Vital Information:

Trail Distance: 34 miles

Trail Surface: limestone

Access Points: Omaha, Camp Douglas, Hustler, Elroy, "400"-Elroy, Union Center, Wonewoc, LaValle, Reedsburg

Fees and Passes 400 Trail: Wisconsin State Trail Pass; $3 daily fee or $10 for an annual pass. State Trail passes are good on all Wisconsin State Trails. Omaha Trail: Daily pass $1.00

Trail Website: www.400statetrail.org

ABOUT THE TRAILS

The Omaha Trail is a paved county trail from Camp Douglas to Elroy. Good for a quick break when traveling the Interstate between the Twin Cities and Milwaukee or Chicago. The 400 Trail more or less follows the Baraboo River, although the real scenery is away from the river toward the distant bluffs. Small towns with scenic parks dot the trail. Both trails meet at the Elroy-Sparta Trail in Elroy creating a lot of opportunities for the repeat or long term visitor.

TRAIL HIGHLIGHTS

The southern end of the Omaha Trail passes through some steep walled valleys as it climbs to the tunnel south of Hustler. Pass through the 875 foot tunnel, then take a break at the rest stop with modern bathrooms and a hand pump for water. The trail follows another small valley before the land levels out near Hustler.

Hemlock Park is a pretty little park across a small lake from the 400 Trail. Take Dutch Hollow Road to the park sign and drop down a steep hill to the water's edge. The little park bordering the Baraboo River on the north side of LaValle provides a shaded, restful stopping point. The first two miles from the Reedsburg Depot parallel an active railline. The trail gets better after the active line branches off. Baker's Field and Wonewoc Park provide pleasant breaks near the trail in Wonewoc. Wonewoc Park has an artesian well.

ABOUT THE ROADS

The roads in this area go through the heart of the Driftless Area. If you don't mind lots of hills, these roads are a delight because of their low traffic and rural panoramas. Asphalt surfaces vary from smooth to patchy or pebbly.

ROAD ROUTE HIGHLIGHTS

County H from Camp Douglas to the tunnel on the Omaha Trail is reasonably flat. It offers a good return route after going one way on the trail. The east and west routes between Elroy and Wonewoc are prime roads if you don't mind hills. Stop at Wonewoc Park and refill your water bottle at the artesian well. Dutch Hollow Road has some traffic on weekends and holidays because of the lake cabins around Dutch Hollow Lake. Same story with County V between the trail and Reedsburg. Worth riding if you are comfortable with some traffic.

HOW TO GET THERE

Camp Douglas is on Interstates 90/94 about 10 miles south of the intersection of the two Highways near Tomah. To get to Elroy, stay on the Interstate to Mauston, then take Highway 82 west. To get to Reedsburg, take Interstate 90/94 to Lake Delton, then Highway 23 south to Reedsburg. The Omaha and 400 Trails meet in Elroy, the eastern terminus of the Elroy-Sparta Trail. For more information about getting to the Elroy-Sparta Trail, see previous chapter.

Superior

Menomonie
Eau Claire   Wausau

Green Bay

Tomah Camp Douglas
LaCrosse   Elroy
Reedsburg

Milwaukee

Madison

See Trail Map on page M49

Information Omaha and "400" Trails

Elroy Commons
Toll Free (888) 606-2453
Phone (608) 462-2410
Web www.elroywi.com

"400" Trail Headquarters
Toll Free (800) 844-3507
Phone (608) 524-2850
Web www.400statetrail.org

Wildcat Mountain State Park
Phone (608) 337-4775

Reedsburg Chamber of Commerce
Toll Free (800) 844-3507
Web www.reedsburg.com

LODGING

Motels/Resorts
Camp Douglas
K & K Motel
Highways 12 & 16
Zip Code 54618
Phone (608) 427-3100

Reedsburg
Super 8
1470 East Main St
Zip Code 53959
Toll Free (800) 800-8000
Phone (608) 524-2888

Copper Springs Motel
E7278 Highway 23/33
Zip Code 53959
Phone (608) 524-4312

Comfort Inn
2115 East Main St
Zip Code 53959
Phone (608) 524-8535
Fax (608) 524-6570

Voyageur Inn
200 Viking Dr (Highway H)
Zip Code 53959
Toll Free (800) 444-4493
Phone (608) 524-6431

Parkview B&B
211 North Park St
Zip Code 53959
Phone (608) 524-4333

Bed and Breakfast
Hustler
Sunnyfield Farm
Zip Code 54637
Toll Free (888) 839-0232
Phone (608) 427-3686
Email soltvedt@mwt.net

Camping
Reedsburg
Lighthouse Rock Campground
S2330 County V
Zip Code 53959
Phone (608) 524-4203

Wonewoc
Chapparal Campground
S320 Highway 33
Zip Code 53968
Phone (608) 464-3944

RESTAURANTS
Camp Douglas
Target Bluff Rest. & Cheese
Phone (608) 427-6542

Elroy
See Elroy-Sparta Trail

Hustler
Suzy's Hustle Inn
Phone (608) 427-3424

La Valle
Trail Break Pizza Pies
Phone (608) 985-8464

Reedsburg
Culver's Frozen Custard
Phone (608) 524-2122

Longley's Restaurant
Phone (608) 524-6497

Marty's Steakhouse
Phone (608) 524-6431

GROCERIES
Reedsburg
Viking Foods
(608) 524-6108

Jubilee Foods
(608) 524-4533

BIKE RENTAL
La Valle
Trail Break Pizza Pies
Toll Free
Phone (608) 985-8464

Reedsburg
Baraboo River Bike Shop
Phone (608) 524-0798

BIKE REPAIR
Reedsburg
Baraboo River Bike Shop
Phone (608) 524-0798

FESTIVALS AND EVENTS
Camp Douglas
May
Armed Forces Day Festival
Weekend saluting the armed forces
and nearby Volk Field, home base of
the Air National Guard, Third Weekend
Phone (608) 427-1280

Hustler
August
Hustler Fest

Parade, tractor pull, 3 on 3 basketball, carnival rides, games, music and dancing, three day event, Fourth Weekend
Phone (608) 847-9389

Reedsburg
June
Butter Festival
Parade, carnival rides, tractor and truck pulls, arts and crafts, Butter Run, music and food, Nishan Park, Father's Day weekend
Phone (608) 524-2850

August
Little League Tournament
First Weekend
Toll Free (800) 844-3507
Phone (608) 524-2850

October
Harvest Fest
Downtown Main Street, arts and crafts, contests, music, auto displays, food, First Saturday
Toll Free (800) 844-3507
Phone (608) 524-2850

ALTERNATE ACTIVITIES

Camp Douglas
Wisconsin National Guard Library and Museum
Located at historic Volk Field, museum is housed in an 1896 log lodge that has been restored to its original appearance, exhibits, dioramas, video and slide programs, self guided tour maps available
Phone (608) 427-1280
Web www.volkfield.ang.af.mil

Volk Field
Air National Guard Base, view aircraft, artillery and tanks on static display, then watch modern jet aircraft operate at the Combat Readiness Training Center, open to the public 7:30 am to 4:00 pm, Monday through Saturday
Phone (608) 427-1280
Web www.volkfield.ang.af.mil

Mill Bluff State Park
Primitive camping, picnic shelters, swimming beach, hiking trails, beautiful rock formations
Phone (608) 427-6692

LaValle
Carr Valley Cheese Company
100 years of family cheesemaking, fresh curds daily, self-guided tours, open Mon-Sat
Phone (608) 986-2781

E-Z Roll Riding Stable
Guided trail rides Apr 1-Sept 1 or call for reservations for weekend rides anytime
Phone (608) 985-7722

Ontario
See Elroy Sparta Trail

Reedsburg
Museum of Norman Rockwell Art
Largest collection of Norman Rockwell Art plus Rockwell video, large gift shop
Phone (608) 524-2123

Reedsburg Area Historical Society
Pioneer Log Village, 1890 log homes, church, blacksmith shop and school in settlement, weekend afternoons Memorial Day through Labor Day
Phone (608) 524-2850

Park Lane Model Railroad Museum
3,000 models of trains, farm tractors, fire trucks and cars, operating layouts in 'N', 'Z' and 'HO' scales, open mid May-mid Sept
Phone (608) 254-8050

Military Ridge Trail

Vital Information:

Trail Distance: 37 miles

Trail Surface: limestone

Access Points: Dodgeville, Ridgeway, Barneveld, Blue Mounds, Mount Horeb, Verona

Fees and Passes: Wisconsin State Trail Pass; $3 daily fee or $10 for an annual pass. State Trail passes are good on all Wisconsin State Trails

ABOUT THE TRAIL

Formerly a Chicago and North Western Railway, the trail follows the top of Military Ridge, the divide between the watersheds of the Wisconsin River, to the north, and the Pecatonica and Rock Rivers to the south. It comes off the ridge just east of Mount Horeb and drops nearly 400 feet into the Sugar River Valley. The drop is very gentle, 2% to 5%, and the changing terrain makes the eastern part of the trail quite interesting. Agriculture, woodlands, wetlands and prairies border the trail.

TRAIL HIGHLIGHTS

The Riley Tavern, in Riley, has been a watering hole for bicyclists for at least three decades. Stop in for a laid back slice of life. The most interesting part of the trail runs between Mount Horeb and the trailhead near Verona. The trail climbs slowly from east to west, often along the sides of hills, and passes through a mix of natural and agricultural landscapes. To the west the trail runs near Highway 151/18. The noise and barrenness of the Highway take away much of the pleasure of riding the trail. That's too bad, because the towns of Blue Mounds, Barneveld and Ridgeway are all worth stopping in for a brief visit. Blue Mound State Park offers swimming and scenic overlooks. Governor Dodge State Park has a full range of recreation facilities.

ABOUT THE ROADS

This is the Driftless Area of Wisconsin, ideal for dairy farms, paved lightly traveled roads and big hills. The opportunities for exploring are endless. Try the routes on these maps. If you get hooked on the area, stop in Madison at one of the bike shops and ask for more route information. You'll learn about more miles of good roads than you can possibly ride.

ROAD ROUTE HIGHLIGHTS

The loop near Dodgeville offers everything the trail misses: hills and valleys, scenic vistas, constantly changing terrain and quiet roads. The hills are long; occasionally a mile or more of climbing. For a short, flat, out and back on a quiet road, take the Klevinville-Riley Road to County P. It nestles in among wetland trees and small creeks. The southern loop starts low along the Sugar River Valley, then climbs and rolls mightily as it loops back to the trail.

HOW TO GET THERE

Verona is southwest of Madison on U.S. Highway 151/18. Take the County PB exit and turn right at the end of the ramp. You will be on the west side of the highway and going north on Nesbitt Road. There isn't a sign for Nesbitt, so make sure you are NOT going south on PB towards Paoli. The trailhead is 1.1 miles north. All trail towns can be readily accessed via Highway 151/18. Trail access in Dodgeville is at the intersection of County YZ and Johns Street. Take County YZ 0.2 miles east of Highway 23. See trail map.

Superior
Eau Claire Wausau
Green Bay
Tomah
LaCrosse
Dodgeville Madison
Verona Milwaukee

See Trail Map on page M51

TOURIST INFORMATION

Verona Chamber of Commerce
Phone (608) 845-5777
Fax (608) 845-2519
Email vacc@tds.net
Web veronawi.com

Trail Office at Blue Mound State Park
Phone (608) 437-7393

Mount Horeb Area Chamber of Commerce
Toll Free (888) 765-5929
Phone (608) 437-5914

Dodgeville Chamber of Commerce
Toll Free (877) 863-6343
Phone (608) 935-5993
Fax (608) 935-5324
Email info@dodgeville.com
Web www.dodgeville.com

LODGING

Motels/Resorts
Dodgeville
Pine Ridge Motel
County YZ
Zip Code 53533
Phone (608) 935-3386

Super 8 Motel
1308 Johns St
Zip Code 53533
Toll Free (800) 800-8000
Phone (608) 935-3888

New Concord Inn
3637 Highway 23 North
Zip Code 53533
Toll Free (800) 348-9310
Phone (608) 935-3770

Mt. Horeb
Karakahl Country Inn
1405 Business 18-151
Zip Code 53572
Phone (608) 437-5545
Fax (608) 437-5908

Village Inn Motel
701 Springdale St
Zip Code 53572
Phone (608) 437-3350

Verona
The Grandview Motel
512 West Verona Ave
Zip Code 53593
Phone (608) 845-6633

Bed and Breakfast
Dodgeville
Grand View B & B
4717 Miess Rd
Zip Code 53533
Phone (608) 935-3261

Camping
Blue Mounds
Blue Mound State Park
Box 98
Zip Code 53517
Phone (608) 437-5711
Web www.dnr.state.wi.us

Dodgeville
Blackhawk Lake Rec. Area
County BH
Zip Code 53533
Phone (608) 623-2707

Governor Dodge State Park
4175 State Road 23 N
Zip Code 53533
Phone (608) 935-2315
Web www.dnr.state.wi.us

Tom's Campground
2751 County BB
Zip Code 53533
Phone (608) 935-5446

RESTAURANTS
Barneveld
Betsy's Kitchen
Phone (608) 924-1803

Dodgeville
The Cook's Room
Phone (608) 935-5282

Courthouse Inn
Phone (608) 935-3663

Gordon's Café & Coffee
Phone (608) 935-9362

Thym's Supper Club
Phone (608) 935-3344

Quality Bakery
Phone (608) 935-3812

Mt. Horeb
Schubert's
Phone (608) 437-3393

Mt. Horeb Pub & Brewery
Phone (608) 437-4200

Main Street Pub & Grill
Phone (608) 437-5733

GROCERIES
Dodgeville
Dick's Supermarket
(608) 935-2366

Dodgeville IGA
(608) 935-9315

Mt. Horeb
Blue Mounds Grocery
(608) 437-8027

Kalscheur's Fine Foods
(608) 437-3081

The General Store Co-op
(608) 437-5288

Verona
Miller & Son Supermarket
(608) 845-6478

Information Military Ridge Trail

BIKE REPAIR

Madison
REI
Phone (608) 833-6680
Fax (608) 833-4065

FESTIVALS AND EVENTS

Mt. Horeb

July
Art Fair
Held in conjunction with Sons of Norway Kaffe Stue, 110 artists on "Trollway" plus food, entertainment, Third Weekend
Phone (608) 437-5914

Old Time Fiddlers Convention
Music Jamboree for musicians and music lovers at Grundahl Park, Web www.trollway.com, Second Weekend
Phone (608) 437-5914

August
National Mustard Day
Mustard Games, Mustard tasting, visiting celebrities, refreshments, First Weekend
Phone (608) 437-5914

Norwegian American Fest
Entertainment, costumes, demonstrations and food at the High School, First Weekend
Phone (608) 437-5914

Verona

May
City Wide Garage Sale
Mother's Day Weekend

August
Hometown Days Festival
Midway, family entertainment, concessions, bands, bicycle race, parade at Community Park, runs Thursday-Sunday, Second Weekend
Phone (608) 845-5777

ALTERNATE ACTIVITIES

Blue Mounds
Little Norway
1856 Norwegian Farmstead and 'Stavkirke'
Phone (608) 437-8211
Fax (608) 437-7827
Web www.littlenorway.com

Cave of the Mounds
A registered National Natural Landmark
Phone (608) 437-3038
Fax (608) 437-4181
Web www.caveofthemounds.com

Blue Mound State Park
Camping, observation towers, swimming pool and nature trails
Phone (608) 437-5711
Fax (608) 437-6214
Web www.dnr.state.us

Dodgeville
Governor Dodge State Park
Wisconsin's second largest park, swimming, camping, boating, hiking
Phone (608) 935-2315
Web www.dnr.state.wi.us

Dolby Stables
One & two hour guided rides in Governor Dodge State Park, 45 minute ride on ranch, reservations helpful
Phone (608) 935-2315

Museum of Minerals and Crystals
Displays of rocks, minerals, crystals and flourescents from around the world
Phone (608) 935-5205

Mt. Horeb
Mustard Museum
The world's largest collection of mustard, more than 3100 varieties
Phone (608) 437-3986
Web www.mustardmuseum.com

Mt Horeb Pub and Brewery
Microbrewery located in historic creamery, hand-crafted beers, tours available
Phone (608) 437-4200

Trail Maps

MINNESOTA

Legend

Revisions: Did you find a mistake? Did the trail change? We'd like to hear about it. Send us a photocopy of the map with your changes added, or contact us and we'll send you a copy of the map so you can mark it up. Our address is: Little Transport Press PO Box 8123, Minneapolis, MN 55408.

------- State or Regional Bike Trail

-------- City Bike Trail

_____ Bike Route on Road

▬▬▬ Major Highway

_____ Paved Road

---------- Town Road
(gravel or unknown surface)

◇▪▪▪◇ Mileage Beween Markers *
11.5 mi (State or Regional trails only)

◇____◇ Mileage Between Markers*
6.4 (road routes)

*Cyclometer readings will differ depending on tire pressure, riding style and computer settings. Your mileage may differ slightly from the stated distances.

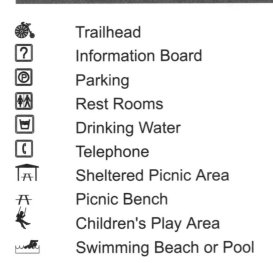

Trailhead	Camping
Information Board	Hiking Trails
Parking	Church
Rest Rooms	Cemetery
Drinking Water	Golf Course
Telephone	Museum
Sheltered Picnic Area	Baseball Diamond
Picnic Bench	Downhill Ski Area
Children's Play Area	Canoe Rental
Swimming Beach or Pool	Boat Launch

N
W — E
S

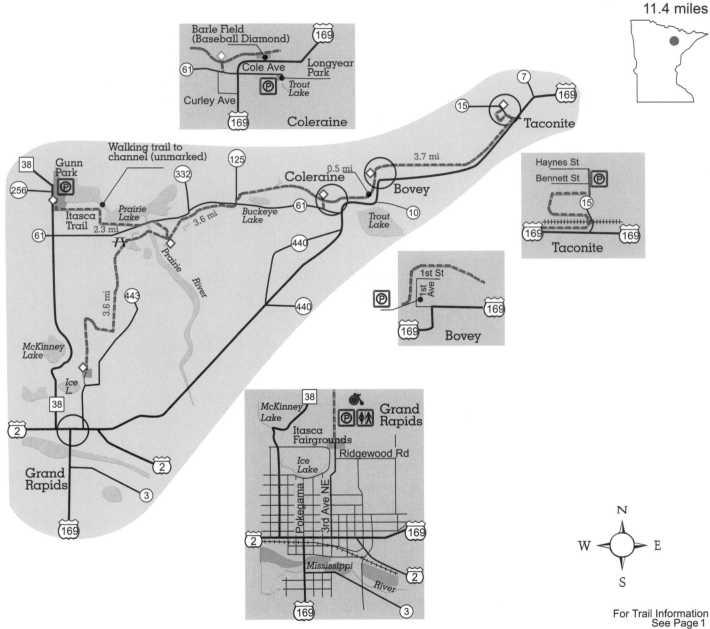

Mesabi Trail

Grand Rapids to Taconite
11.4 miles

Barle Field
(Baseball Diamond)
169
61
Cole Ave
Longyear Park
Curley Ave
Trout Lake
169
Coleraine

Walking trail to channel (unmarked)
38
Gunn Park
256
Itasca Trail
61
2.3 mi
332
125
3.6 mi
Prairie Lake
Buckeye Lake
61
440
Prairie River
440
443
3.6 mi
McKinney Lake
Ice L.
38
2
Grand Rapids
2
3
169

7
169
15
Taconite

3.7 mi
0.5 mi
Coleraine
Bovey
Trout Lake
10

Haynes St
Bennett St
15
169
169
Taconite

1st St
1st Ave
169
169
Bovey

McKinney Lake
38
Grand Rapids
Itasca Fairgrounds
Ice Lake
Ridgewood Rd
Pokegama
3rd Ave NE
2
169
2
Mississippi River
169
3

N
W E
S

For Trail Information
See Page 1

M3

Mesabi Trail

Nashwauk to Kinney
22.8 miles

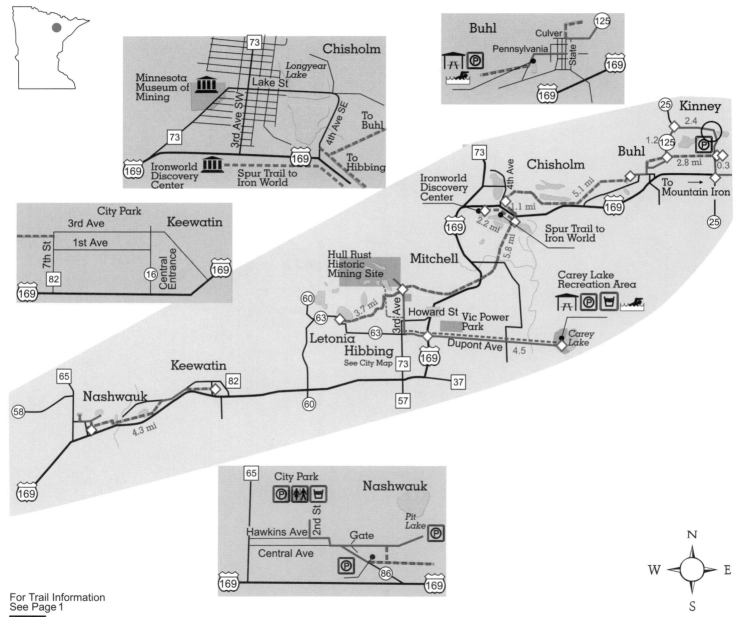

Chisholm (inset)
- 73
- Longyear Lake
- Minnesota Museum of Mining
- Lake St
- 3rd Ave SW
- 4th Ave SE
- To Buhl
- To Hibbing
- 73
- 169
- Ironworld Discovery Center
- Spur Trail to Iron World

Buhl (inset)
- Culver
- 125
- Pennsylvania
- State
- 169
- 169

Keewatin (inset)
- City Park
- 3rd Ave
- 1st Ave
- 7th St
- 82
- 16
- Central Entrance
- 169
- 169

Main map
- 25 Kinney 2.4
- 1.2 125
- Buhl 2.8 mi 0.3
- To Mountain Iron
- 25
- 73
- 4th Ave
- Chisholm
- 5.1 mi
- Ironworld Discovery Center
- 1.1 mi
- 169
- 2.2 mi
- Spur Trail to Iron World
- 5.8 mi
- Carey Lake Recreation Area
- Hull Rust Historic Mining Site
- Mitchell
- 60
- 63
- 3.7 mi
- 3rd Ave
- Howard St
- Vic Power Park
- Dupont Ave
- 4.5
- Carey Lake
- Letonia
- 63
- Hibbing
- See City Map
- 73
- 169
- 37
- 57
- 60
- Keewatin
- 65
- 82
- Nashwauk
- 58
- 4.3 mi
- 169

Nashwauk (inset)
- 65
- City Park
- 2nd St
- Nashwauk
- Hawkins Ave
- Pit Lake
- Gate
- Central Ave
- 169
- 86
- 169

Compass: N, S, E, W

For Trail Information
See Page 1

M4

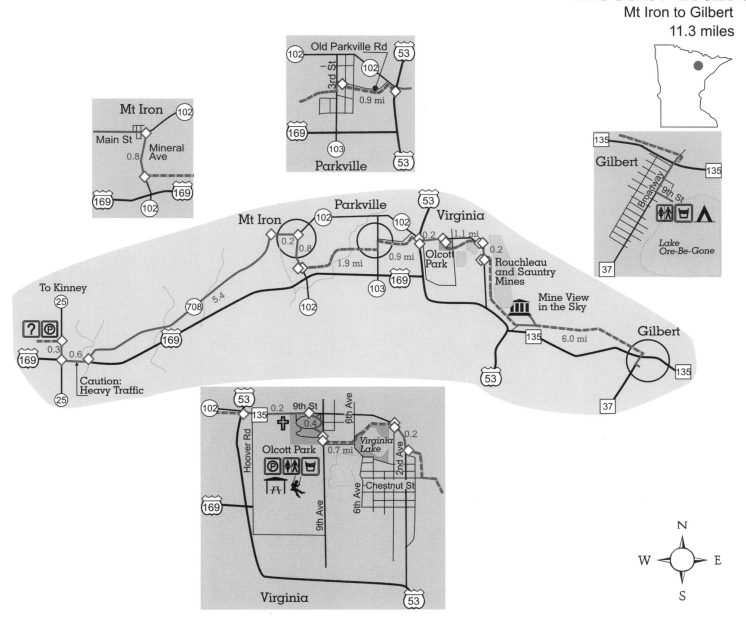

Mesabi Trail
Mt Iron to Gilbert
11.3 miles

Parkville
Old Parkville Rd
102 · 102 · 53
3rd St
0.9 mi
169 · 103 · 53

Mt Iron
102
Main St
Mineral Ave
0.8
169 · 102 · 169

Gilbert
135 · 135
Broadway
9th St
37
Lake Ore-Be-Gone

Mt Iron
102
0.2
0.8

Parkville
102
1.9 mi
0.9 mi
103
102
169

Virginia
53
102
0.2
1.1 mi
Olcott Park
0.2
Rouchleau and Sauntry Mines

Mine View in the Sky

To Kinney
25
? P
169
0.3 0.6
25
Caution: Heavy Traffic

708   5.4
169

135   6.0 mi
53
Gilbert
135
37

Virginia
53
102   135
0.2   9th St
0.4
6th Ave
Hoover Rd
Olcott Park
P
0.7 mi
Virginia Lake
0.2
2nd Ave
9th Ave
6th Ave   Chestnut St
169
9th Ave
Virginia   53

N
W   E
S

For Trail Information
See Page 1

Mesabi Trail

City Maps

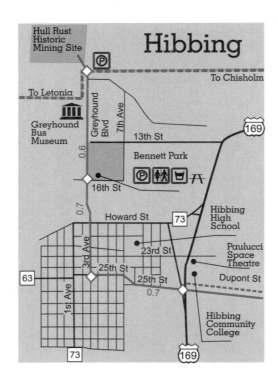

Hull Rust
Historic
Mining Site

Hibbing

To Chisholm

To Letonia

Greyhound
Bus
Museum

Greyhound Blvd

7th Ave

0.6

13th St

Bennett Park

16th St

169

0.7

Howard St

73

Hibbing
High
School

3rd Ave

23rd St

Paulucci
Space
Theatre

25th St

25th St

Dupont St

63

1st Ave

0.7

73

169

Hibbing
Community
College

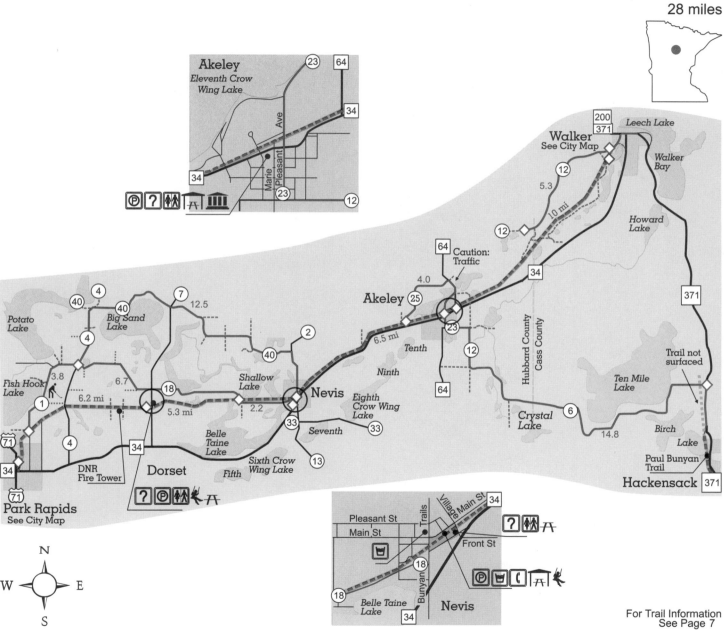

Heartland Trail ■

Park Rapids to Walker
28 miles

Akeley

Eleventh Crow Wing Lake

23 · 64 · 34 · 23 · 12

Walker See City Map

Leech Lake · 200 · 371

Walker Bay · *Howard Lake*

5.3 · 12 · 10 mi · 12 · 34 · 371

64 Caution: Traffic

4.0

Akeley 25 · 23 · 12 · 64

6.5 mi · *Tenth* · *Ninth*

Hubbard County / Cass County

Ten Mile Lake

Trail not surfaced

40 · 4 · 40 · 7 · 12.5

Potato Lake · *Big Sand Lake*

40 · 4 · 2 · 40

Shallow Lake

3.8 · 6.7 · 18 · 5.3 mi · 2.2 · **Nevis**

Fish Hook Lake · 1 · 6.2 mi

Eighth Crow Wing Lake

33 · *Seventh* · 33

Crystal Lake · 6 · 14.8 · *Birch Lake*

4 · 34 · *Belle Taine Lake* · 13 · *Sixth Crow Wing Lake* · *Fifth*

DNR Fire Tower · **Dorset**

? P 👫 🏕

Park Rapids See City Map · 71 · 34 · 71

Paul Bunyan Trail · 371

Hackensack · 371

N / W E / S

Nevis

Pleasant St · *Trails* · *Village Main St* · 34

Main St · *Front St* · ? 👫 🏕

18 · *Bunyan* · P 🍴 (🏕 · **Nevis**

18 · *Belle Taine Lake* · 34

For Trail Information
See Page 7

M7

Heartland Trail

City Maps

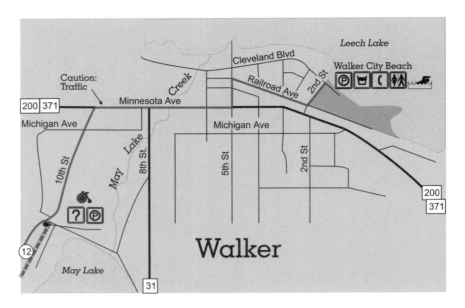

Caution: Traffic

Leech Lake

Cleveland Blvd

Walker City Beach

Railroad Ave

Minnesota Ave

200 371

Michigan Ave

Michigan Ave

10th St

May Lake Creek

8th St.

5th St

2nd St

2nd St

200 371

12

May Lake

Walker

31

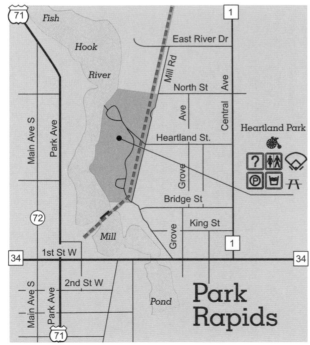

71

Fish

Hook

River

1

East River Dr

Mill Rd

North St

Ave

Central Ave

Heartland Park

Main Ave S

Park Ave

Heartland St.

Grove

Bridge St

72

Mill

Grove

King St

1

34

1st St W

34

Main Ave S

Park Ave

2nd St W

Pond

Park Rapids

71

For Trail Information
See Page 7

M8

N

W E

S

Paul Bunyan Trail

Baxter to Pequot Lakes
21 miles

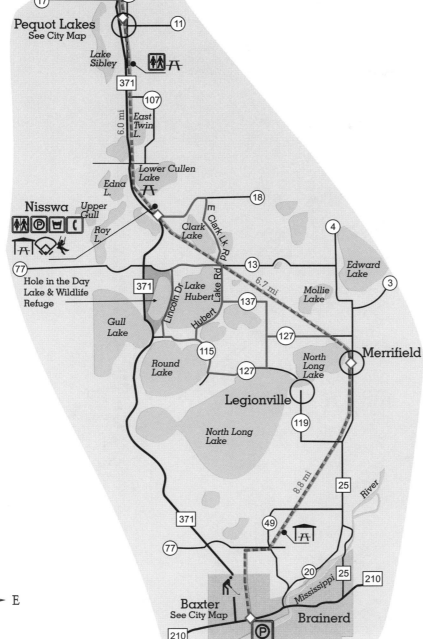

To Jenkins
17
112
Pequot Lakes
See City Map
11
Lake Sibley
371
107
6.0 mi
East Twin L.
Lower Cullen Lake
Edna L.
Nisswa
Upper Gull
18
Clark Lake
E Clark Lk Rd
Roy L.
4
77
Hole in the Day Lake & Wildlife Refuge
13
Edward Lake
3
371
Lincoln Dr
Lake Hubert
Lake Rd
6.7 mi
Mollie Lake
137
Gull Lake
Hubert
127
Round Lake
115
North Long Lake
Merrifield
127
Legionville
119
North Long Lake
8.8 mi
25
River
371
49
77
25
20
25
210
Baxter
See City Map
Mississippi
Brainerd
210

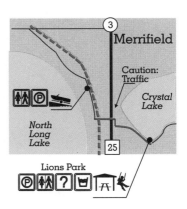

3
Merrifield
Caution: Traffic
Crystal Lake
North Long Lake
25
Lions Park

N
W   E
S

For Trail Information
See Page 12

M9

Paul Bunyan Trail

Pequot Lakes to Hackensack
26 miles

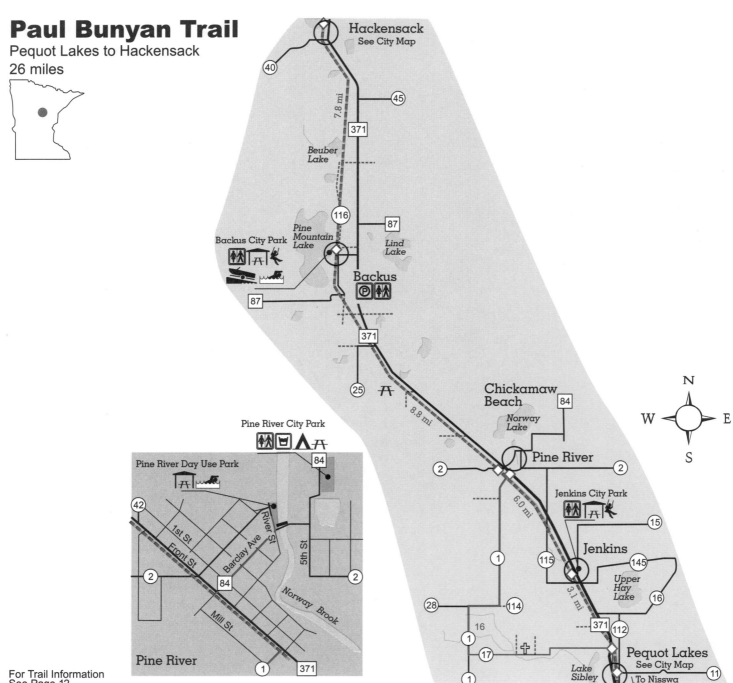

Hackensack
See City Map

40

45

371

7.8 mi

Beuber Lake

116

87

Pine Mountain Lake

Backus City Park

Lind Lake

Backus

87

371

25

8.8 mi

Chickamaw Beach

84

Norway Lake

Pine River

2

2

Jenkins City Park

15

6.0 mi

1

115

Jenkins

145

Upper Hay Lake

16

28

114

3.1 mi

371

112

16

1

371

Pequot Lakes
See City Map

17

11

1

Lake Sibley

↓ To Nisswa

Pine River City Park

Pine River Day Use Park

84

42

1st St

River St

5th St

2

Barclay Ave

2

84

Mill St

Norway Brook

1

371

Pine River

Front St

For Trail Information
See Page 12

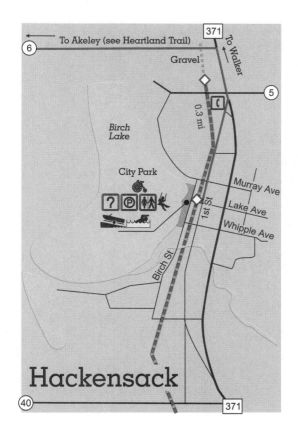

To Akeley (see Heartland Trail) ←

6

371 To Walker

Gravel

5

0.3 mi

Birch Lake

City Park

Murray Ave

Lake Ave

1st St

Whipple Ave

Birch St

Hackensack

40

371

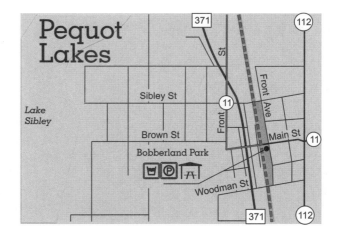

Pequot Lakes

371 · 112

Lake Sibley

St

Sibley St

Front

Front Ave

Brown St

11

Main St

11

Bobberland Park

Woodman St

371 · 112

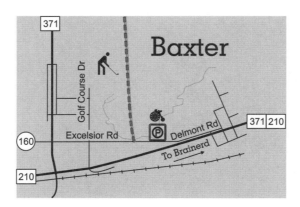

371

Baxter

Golf Course Dr

160

Excelsior Rd

Delmont Rd

371 | 210

To Brainerd

210

N
W · E
S

For Trail Information
See Page 12

Willard Munger Trail

Hinckley to Sturgeon Lake

27 miles

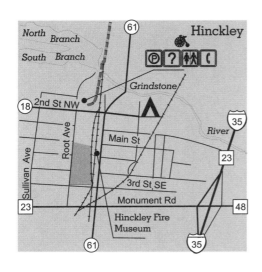

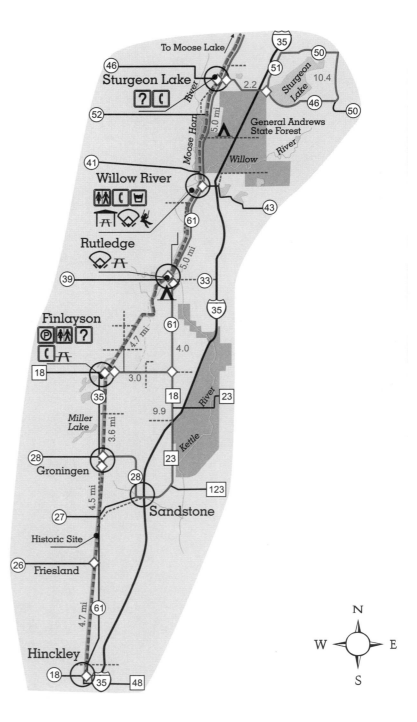

For Trail Information
See Page 19

M12

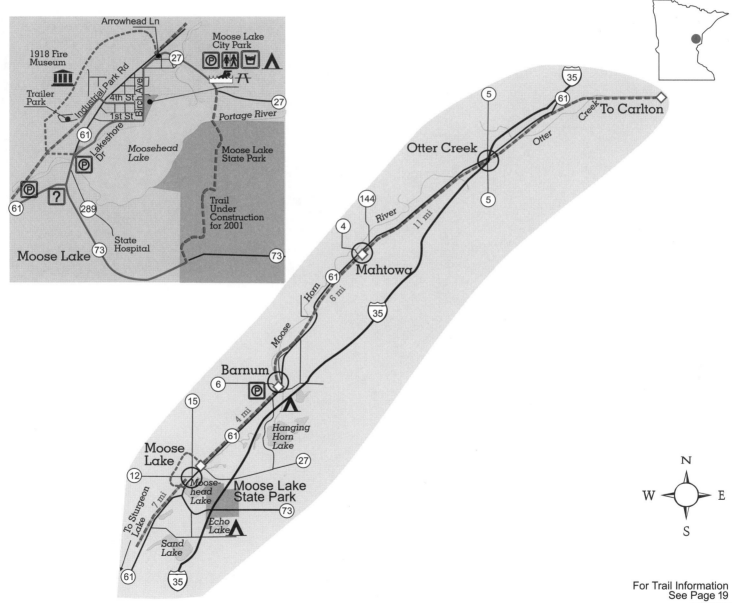

Willard Munger Trail

Moose Lake to Carlton
28 miles

Inset map (Moose Lake):

Arrowhead Ln
Moose Lake City Park
1918 Fire Museum
Trailer Park
Industrial Park Rd
4th St
1st St
Birch Ave
Lakeshore Dr
27
61
Moosehead Lake
Portage River
Moose Lake State Park
Trail Under Construction for 2001
289
State Hospital
73
73
Moose Lake

Main map:

35
61
To Carlton
5
Otter Creek
Creek
Otter
144
River
11 mi
4
Mahtowa
61
6 mi
35
Moose
Horn
Barnum
6
4 mi
15
61
Hanging Horn Lake
27
Moose Lake
12
Moosehead Lake
7 mi
Moose Lake State Park
73
Echo Lake
To Sturgeon Lake
Sand Lake
61
35

N
W · E
S

For Trail Information
See Page 19

M13

Willard Munger Trail

Carlton to Duluth
15 miles

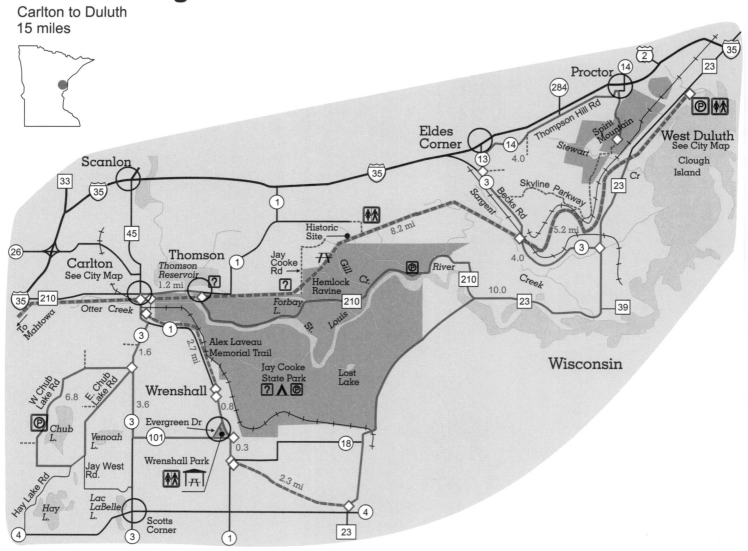

Scanlon

Thomson
Thomson Reservoir
1.2 mi

Carlton
See City Map

Jay Cooke Rd →

Historic Site

Hemlock Ravine

Forbay L.

Gill Cr.

St. Louis

Eldes Corner

Proctor

Thompson Hill Rd

Spirit Mountain

Stewart

Skyline Parkway

Becks Rd

Sargent

West Duluth
See City Map

Clough Island

River

8.2 mi

5.2 mi

4.0

4.0

10.0

To Mahtowa

Otter Creek

Alex Laveau Memorial Trail

2.7 mi

1.6

Jay Cooke State Park

Wrenshall

3.6

0.8

Evergreen Dr

0.3

Lost Lake

W Chub Lake Rd

E. Chub Lake Rd

6.8

Chub L.

Venoah L.

Jay West Rd.

Wrenshall Park

Hay Lake Rd

Hay L.

Lac LaBelle L.

Scotts Corner

2.3 mi

Wisconsin

N
W — E
S

For Trail Information
See Page 19

M14

Willard Munger Trail

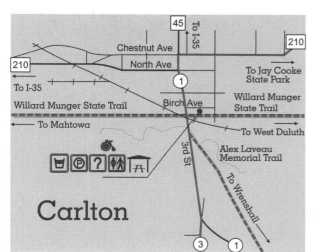

Carlton

45
To I-35
210
Chestnut Ave
North Ave
210
To I-35
1
To Jay Cooke State Park
Willard Munger State Trail
Willard Munger State Trail
Birch Ave
To Mahtowa
To West Duluth
Alex Laveau Memorial Trail
3rd St
To Wrenshall
3
1

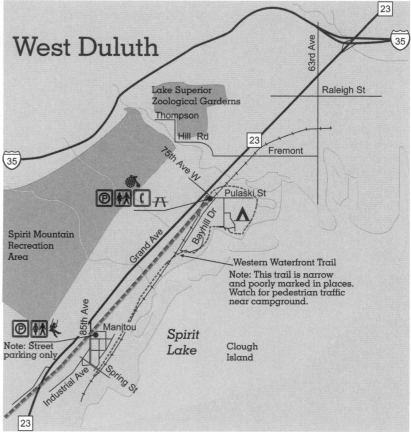

West Duluth

23
63rd Ave
35
Raleigh St
Lake Superior Zoological Gardens
Thompson
Hill Rd
23
Fremont
35
75th Ave W
Pulaski St
Grand Ave
Bayhill Dr
Spirit Mountain Recreation Area
Western Waterfront Trail
Note: This trail is narrow and poorly marked in places. Watch for pedestrian traffic near campground.
85th Ave
Manitou
Spirit Lake
Clough Island
Note: Street parking only
Industrial Ave
Spring St
23

N
W — E
S

For Trail Information
See page 19

M15

Lake Wobegon Trail

Avon to Sauk Centre
22.1 miles

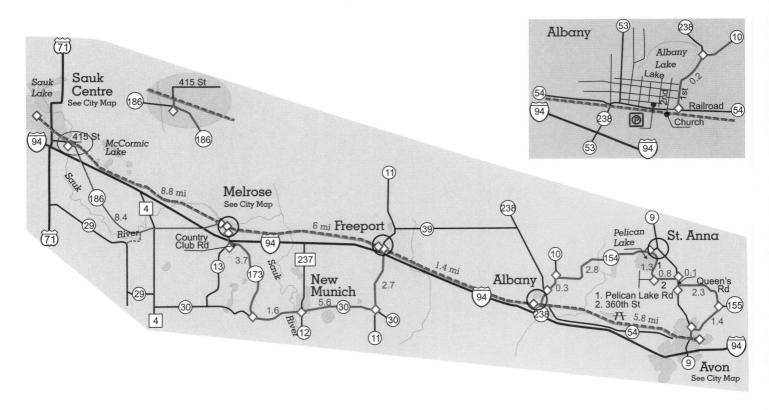

Lake Wobegon Trail

City Maps

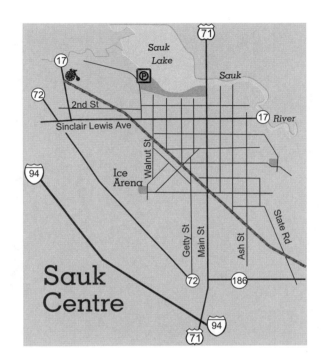

Sauk Centre

- 71
- 17
- Sauk Lake
- Sauk
- 72
- 2nd St
- 17 River
- Sinclair Lewis Ave
- Walnut St
- 94
- Ice Arena
- Getty St
- Main St
- Ash St
- State Rd
- 72
- 186
- 72
- 94
- 71

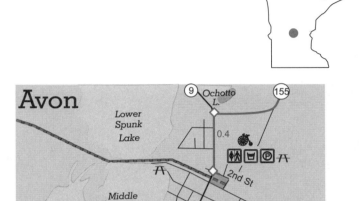

Avon

- 9
- Ochotto L.
- 155
- Lower Spunk Lake
- 0.4
- 2nd St
- Middle Spunk Lake
- Avon Ave
- 94
- 94
- 9
- Linneman Lake

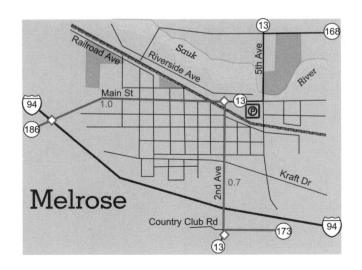

Melrose

- 13
- 168
- Railroad Ave
- Sauk
- Riverside Ave
- 5th Ave
- River
- Main St
- 1.0
- 94
- 13
- 13
- 186
- 2nd Ave
- 0.7
- Kraft Dr
- Country Club Rd
- 173
- 94
- 13

N
W • E
S

For Trail Information
See Page 25

Luce Line Trail

Plymouth to Watertown

21 miles

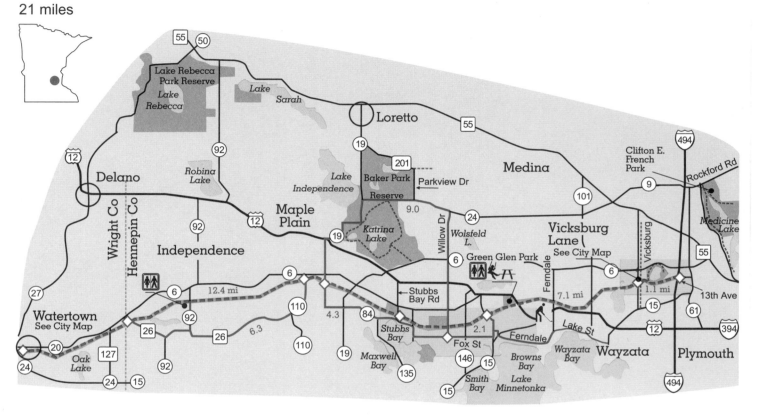

For Trail Information
See Page 29

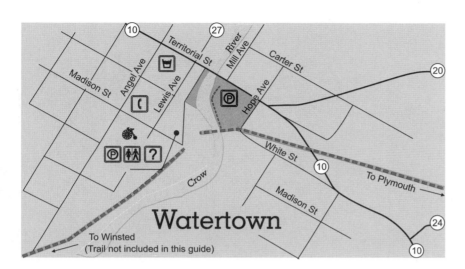

10 · Territorial St · 27 · River · Mill Ave · Carter St · 20

Madison St · Angel Ave · Lewis Ave · Hope Ave

White St · 10 · To Plymouth

Crow

Madison St

Watertown

24

10

To Winsted
(Trail not included in this guide)

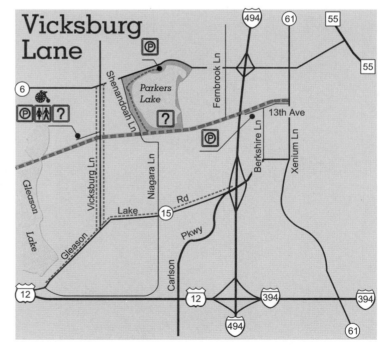

Vicksburg Lane

494 · 61 · 55

Parkers Lake

Fembrook Ln · 55

6 · 13th Ave

Shenandoah Ln · Berkshire Ln · Xenium Ln

Gleason Lake

Vicksburg Ln · Niagara Ln · Lake · Rd · 15 · Carlson · Pkwy

Gleason

12 · 12 · 394 · 394

494 · 61

N
W · E
S

For Trail Information
See Page 29

M19

SW Regional LRT Trails

North: Hopkins to Victoria 16 miles
South: Hopkins to Chanhassen 12 miles

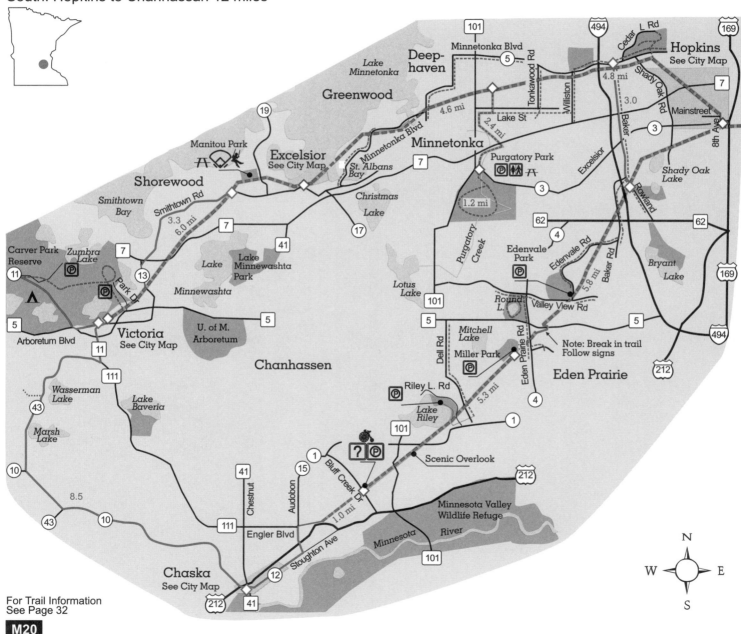

For Trail Information
See Page 32

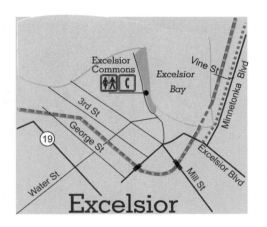

Excelsior Commons
Excelsior Bay
Vine St
Minnetonka Blvd
3rd St
George St
Excelsior Blvd
Mill St
Water St
19
Excelsior

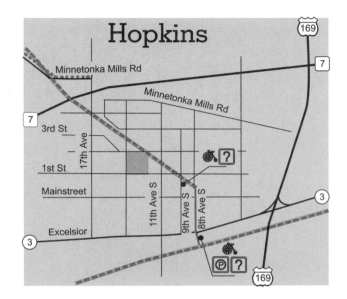

Hopkins
169
Minnetonka Mills Rd
Minnetonka Mills Rd
7
7
3rd St
17th Ave
1st St
Mainstreet
11th Ave S
9th Ave S
8th Ave S
Excelsior
3
3
169

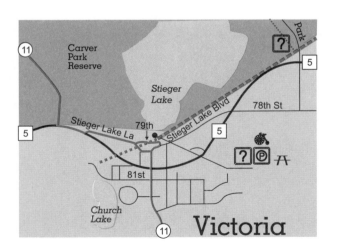

11
Carver Park Reserve
Stieger Lake
Park
5
78th St
Stieger Lake Blvd
79th
Stieger Lake La
5
5
81st
Church Lake
11
Victoria

N
W — E
S

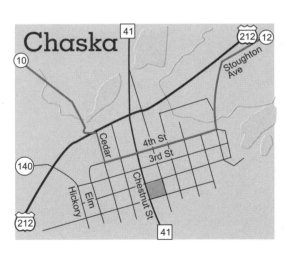

Chaska
41
212 **12**
10
Stoughton Ave
Cedar
4th St
3rd St
140
Chestnut St
Hickory
Elm
212
41

Gateway Trail
St. Paul to Pine Point Park
17 miles

Square Lake Park (55)

Oldfield

Square Lake (59)

Norrel

Lake Tr

4.3

Square

Big Carnelian L.

(7)

(55)

(15)

Withrow

(8A)

120th St N

Pine Point Park

Julianne

7.8

(9)

(68)

Loon L.

Myron

Norrel Ave N

110th

Juliet

110th St

Silver L.

105th St

Norrel Rd

96

(9)

6.3 mi

(15)

(55)

White Bear Lake

Jamaica

96

96

(95)

St. Croix River

Willernie

Trail

(12)

75th St N

Stillwater

(5)

(36)

35E

61

Jasmine

Hilton

Manning Tr N

36

(5)

694

Beam

White Bear Ave

McKnight

55th

Demontreville Loop
and Trail Access
See City Map

Jamaica

Jane

Edgerton St

Keller L.

36

Maplewood

Co Rd B

Oakdale

7.5 mi

L. Jane

45th

(15)

35E

Phalen Keller Park

Frost

Prosperity St

Geneva

Ideal Ave

Jamaica

(5)

(5)

Larpenteur

(5)

L. Phalen

White Bear Ave

(5)

694

St. Paul
See City Map

Arcade St

E 7th St

Century Ave

Stillwater Blvd

Minnehaha Ave

(5)

For Trail Information
See Page 36

(94)

(94)

N
W · E
S

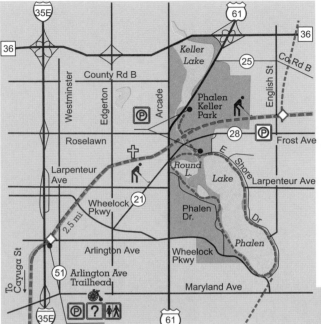

St. Paul
Arlington Ave Trailhead/
Lake Phalen Area

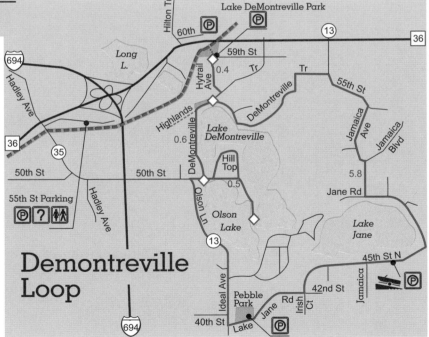

Demontreville
Loop

N
W — E
S

Cannon Valley Trail

Cannon Falls to Red Wing

20 miles

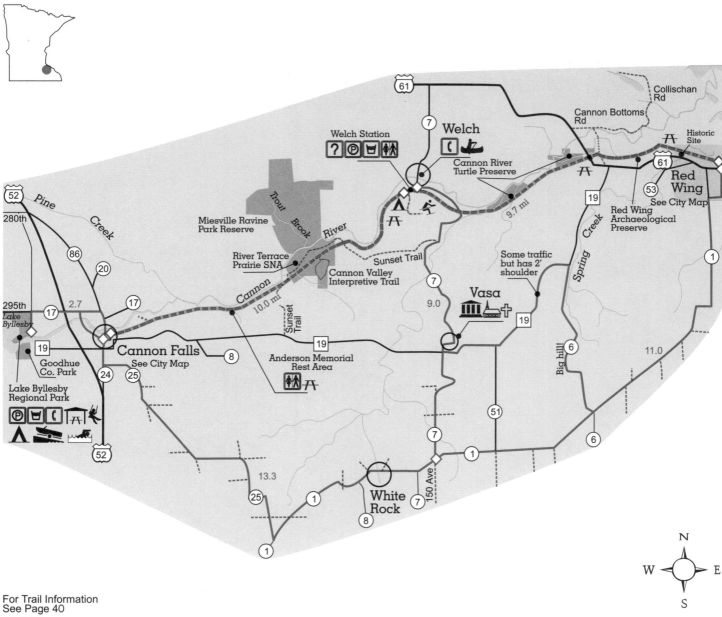

For Trail Information
See Page 40

M24

Cannon Valley Trail

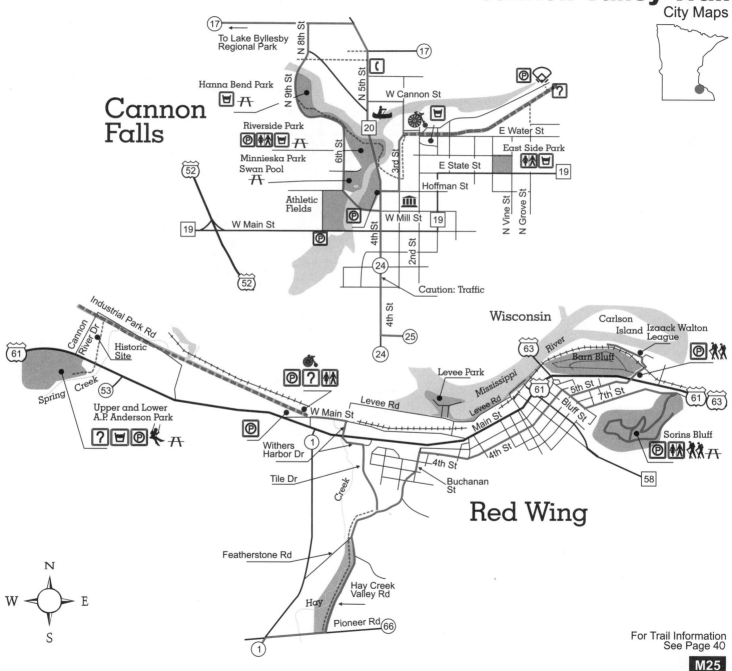

Cannon Falls

To Lake Byllesby Regional Park

17

N 8th St
N 5th St

17

Hanna Bend Park

W Cannon St

20

N 9th St

Riverside Park

6th St

3rd St

E Water St

East Side Park

Minnieska Park
Swan Pool

E State St

19

52

Hoffman St

N Vine St
N Grove St

19

Athletic
Fields

W Mill St

19

W Main St

19

4th St

2nd St

52

24

4th St

Caution: Traffic

25

24

Wisconsin

Carlson
Island

Izaack Walton
League

Industrial Park Rd

63

River

Barn Bluff

61

Cannon River Dr

Historic
Site

Levee Park

Mississippi

5th St

7th St

61

63

53

Spring Creek

Levee Rd

Levee Rd

Bluff St

Main St

Upper and Lower
A.P. Anderson Park

W Main St

4th St

4th St

Sorins Bluff

58

Withers
Harbor Dr

1

Red Wing

Tile Dr

Buchanan
St

Creek

Featherstone Rd

Hay Creek
Valley Rd

Hay

N
W   E
S

Pioneer Rd 66

1

Glacial Lakes Trail

Willmar to New London

11.6 miles

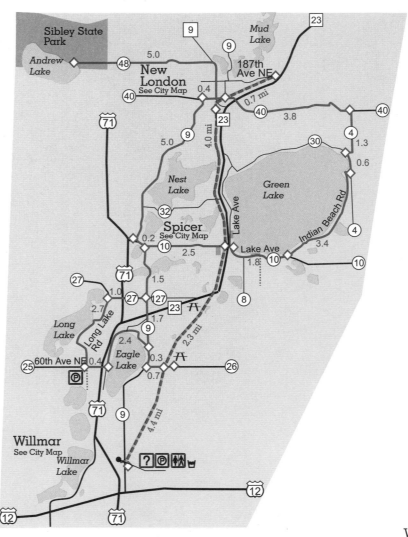

For Trail Information
See Page 45

Glacial Lakes Trail ■

City Maps

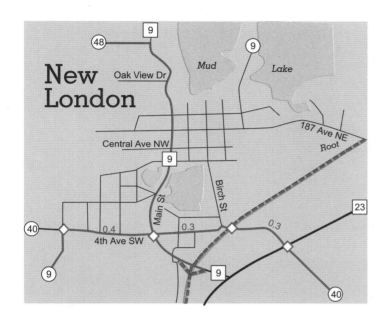

New London

Oak View Dr

Mud   Lake

187 Ave NE

Root

Central Ave NW

Main St   Birch St

0.4   0.3   0.3

4th Ave SW

9   48   9   9   40   40   23   9   40

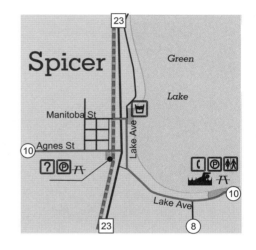

Spicer

Green Lake

Manitoba St

Agnes St

Lake Ave

Lake Ave

23   10   23   8   10

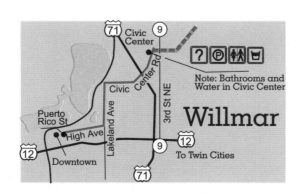

Civic Center

Note: Bathrooms and Water in Civic Center

Civic

Puerto Rico St

High Ave

Willmar

Center Rd   3rd St NE   Lakeland Ave

Downtown

To Twin Cities

71   9   12   9   12   71

N
W   E
S

For Trail Information
See Page 45

M27

Sakatah Singing Hills Trail

Faribault to Mankato

38 miles

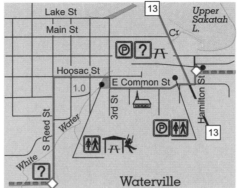

Waterville (inset map)

Lake St
Main St
13
Upper Sakatah L.
Cr
Hoosac St
E Common St
3rd St
1.0
S Reed St
Water
White
Hamilton St
13

Waterville

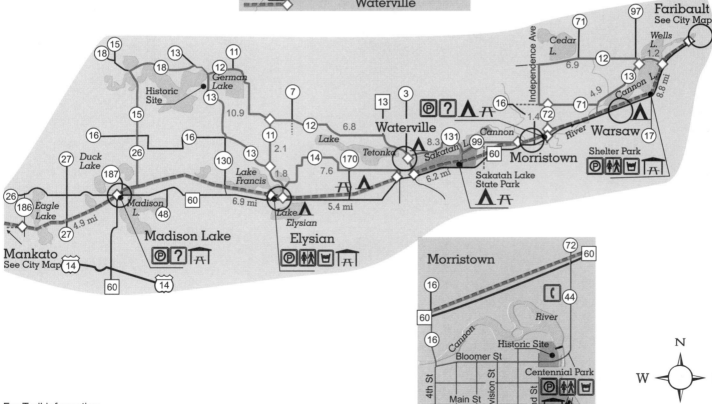

15
18
13
11
18
12 German Lake
Historic Site
13
15
16
26
16
130
13
27 Duck Lake
187
26
186 Eagle Lake
27
4.9 mi
Madison L.
48
60
10.9
11
2.1
1.8
Lake Francis
6.9 mi
7
12
6.8
Lake Tetonka
14
170
7.6
6.2 mi
5.4 mi
Lake Elysian
13
3
Waterville
8.3
131
Sakatah L.
99
60
Cannon
Morristown
1.4
72
71
16
Independence Ave
Cedar L.
6.9
12
71
4.9
13
Cannon L.
8.8 mi
97
71
Faribault
See City Map
Wells L.
1.2
Warsaw
17
Shelter Park
Sakatah Lake State Park
River

Madison Lake

Elysian

Mankato
See City Map
14
60
14

Morristown (inset map)

Morristown
72
60
16
60
16
Cannon
Bloomer St
4th St
Main St
Division St
2nd St
River
44
Historic Site
Centennial Park

N
W — E
S

For Trail Information
See Page 50

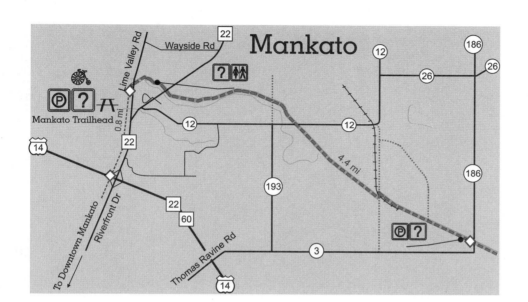

Mankato

22	Wayside Rd

Lime Valley Rd

Mankato Trailhead
0.8 mi
22
14
22
60
To Downtown Mankato
Riverfront Dr
Thomas Ravine Rd
14
12
193
4.4 mi
3
12
12
26
26
186
186

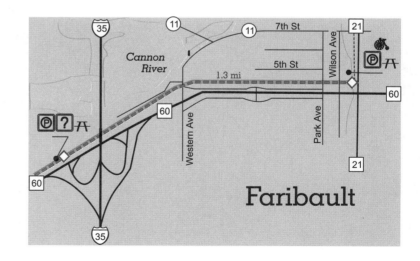

Cannon River
35
11
11
7th St
5th St
Wilson Ave
21
60
Western Ave
Park Ave
1.3 mi
60
60
21
35

Faribault

N
W — E
S

Douglas Trail

Pine Island to Rochester
13 miles

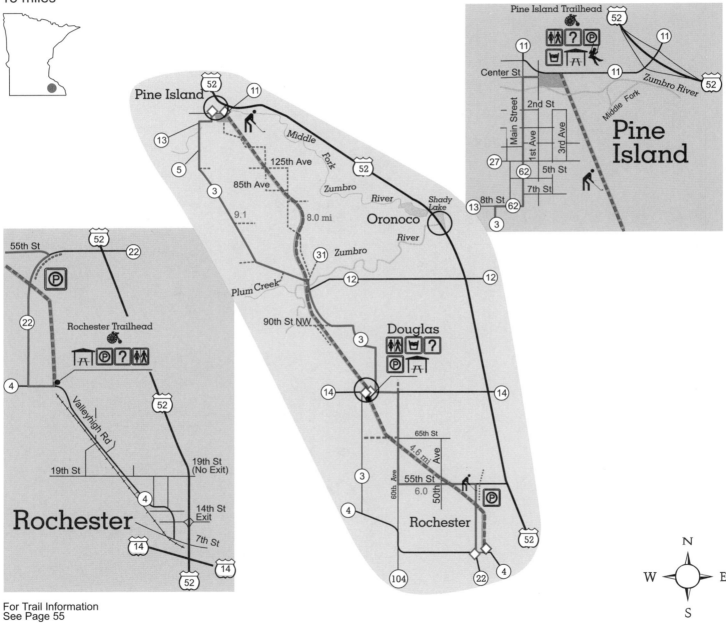

Pine Island Trailhead

Center St

Main Street
2nd St
1st Ave
3rd Ave
27
62
1st Ave
5th St
7th St
8th St
13
62
3

Middle Fork

Zumbro River

Pine Island

Pine Island
52
11
13
5
3

Middle Fork

Zumbro River

125th Ave
85th Ave
9.1
8.0 mi

Shady Lake

52

Oronoco

River

55th St
52
22
22
4
52

Rochester Trailhead

Valleyhigh Rd

19th St
19th St (No Exit)

14th St Exit
7th St

Rochester

14
14
52

31
Zumbro
Plum Creek
90th St NW
3
12
12

Douglas

14
14
3

65th St
4.6 mi
60th Ave
50th Ave
55th St
6.0
3
4

Rochester

104
22
4
52

For Trail Information
See Page 55

W ← → E
N
S

Root River Trail

Fountain to Houston
43 miles

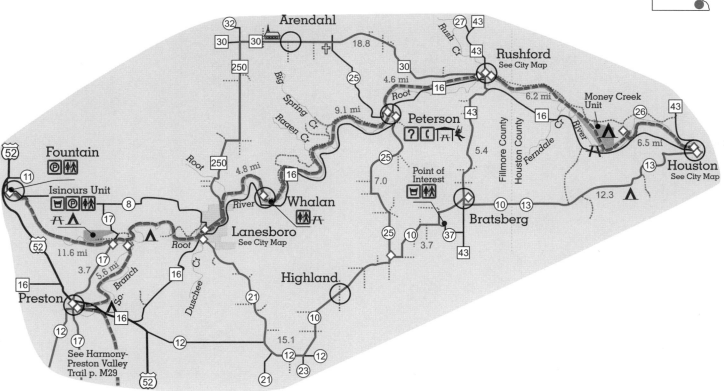

Arendahl

32
30 30
250

Root

250

Big Spring Cr

Rogen Cr

18.8

25

9.1 mi

27 43

Rush Cr

43

Rushford
See City Map

30
4.6 mi
Root 16

6.2 mi

16

Money Creek
Unit

26 43

6.5 mi

Houston
See City Map

52
11
Fountain

Isinours Unit

8

17

11.6 mi

17
3.7

5.6 mi

Branch

So.

52

Whalan

River

Lanesboro
See City Map

Root

16

Duschee Cr

River 16

4.8 mi

Peterson

? (⋔

25

7.0

Point of
Interest
⛺ ⋔

5.4

Fillmore County

Houston County

Ferndale

13

10 13

12.3

Bratsberg

25

10

37

3.7

43

13
⋔

16
Preston

12 17

See Harmony-
Preston Valley
Trail p. M29

16

12

Highland

21

10

15.1

12 12
21 23

52

Root River Trail

City Maps

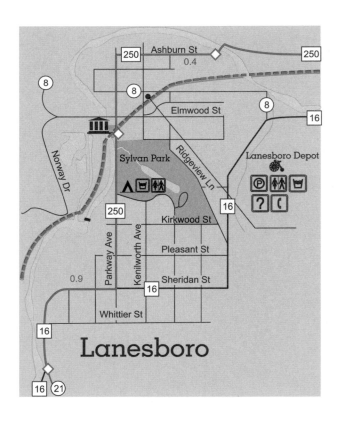

Lanesboro

250   Ashburn St   0.4   250

8   8

Elmwood St

8   16

Norway Dr

Sylvan Park

Ridgeview Ln

Lanesboro Depot

250

Kirkwood St

Parkway Ave   Kenilworth Ave

Pleasant St

0.9   Sheridan St

16

Whittier St

16

16   21

16

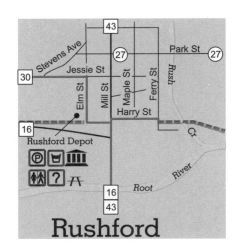

Rushford

43

Stevens Ave   27   Park St   27

30   Jessie St

Elm St   Mill St   Maple St   Ferry St   Rush

Harry St

16

Rushford Depot

16   Root   River   Cr

43

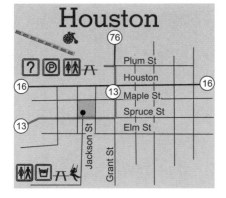

Houston

76

Plum St

16   Houston   16

13   Maple St.

Spruce St

13   Elm St

Jackson St   Grant St

N
W   E
S

Harmony-Preston Valley Trail

Isinours Unit to Harmony
17.6 miles

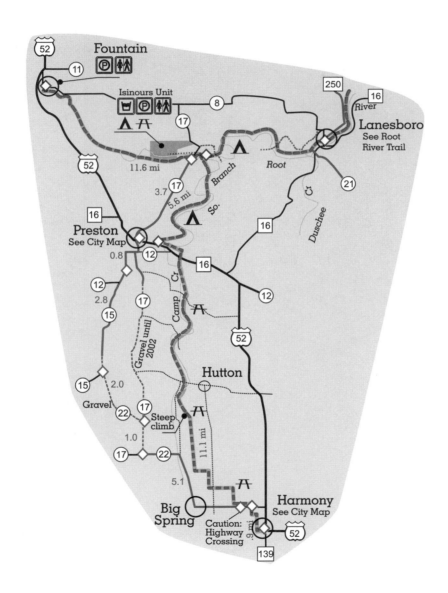

Fountain

Isinours Unit

52 — 11

8

250 — 16

River

Lanesboro
See Root
River Trail

52

17

11.6 mi

Branch

Root

52

17

3.7

5.6 mi

So.

21

16

Ct

Preston
See City Map

16

0.8 — 12

16

12

Duschee

12

2.8

15

17

16

Camp Cr

52

15 — 2.0

Gravel until 2002

Hutton

Gravel

22 — 17

Steep climb

11.1 mi

1.0

17 — 22

5.1

Big Spring

Caution:
Highway
Crossing

Harmony
See City Map

52

139

N
W — E
S

For Trail Information
See Page 62

M33

Harmony-Preston Valley Trail

City Maps

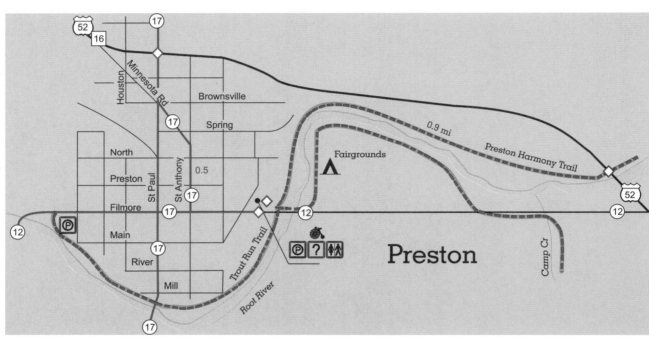

Preston

Minnesota Rd · Houston · Brownsville · Spring · North · Preston · Filmore · Main · River · Mill · St Paul · St Anthony · 0.5 · Trout Run Trail · Root River · Fairgrounds · 0.9 mi · Preston Harmony Trail · Camp Cr

52 · 16 · 17 · 12

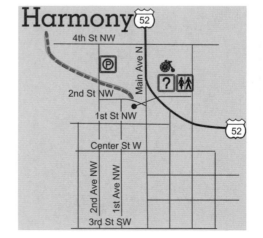

Harmony

4th St NW · 2nd St NW · 1st St NW · Center St W · 3rd St SW · Main Ave N · 2nd Ave NW · 1st Ave NW

52

N
W · E
S

For Trail Information
See Page 62

M34

Trail Maps

WISCONSIN

Legend

▪▪▪▪▪▪	State or Regional Bike Trail
- - - - -	City Bike Trail
―――――	Bike Route on Road
▬▬▬▬	Major Highway
―――――	Paved Road
···········	Town Road (gravel or unknown surface)

 ◇▬▬▬◇ Mileage Beween Markers *
11.5 mi (State or Regional trails only)

 ◇―――◇ Mileage Between Markers*
6.4 (road routes)

*Cyclometer readings will differ depending on tire pressure, riding style and computer settings. Your mileage may differ slightly from the stated distances.

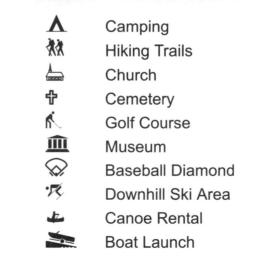

🚲	Trailhead	⛺	Camping
?	Information Board	🚶	Hiking Trails
P	Parking	⛪	Church
👫	Rest Rooms	✝	Cemetery
🚰	Drinking Water	🏌	Golf Course
☎	Telephone	🏛	Museum
🏕	Sheltered Picnic Area	⚾	Baseball Diamond
🪑	Picnic Bench	⛷	Downhill Ski Area
🤸	Children's Play Area	🛶	Canoe Rental
🏊	Swimming Beach or Pool	🚤	Boat Launch

N
W ✦ E
S

Gandy Dancer Trail

St. Croix Falls to Lewis
27 miles

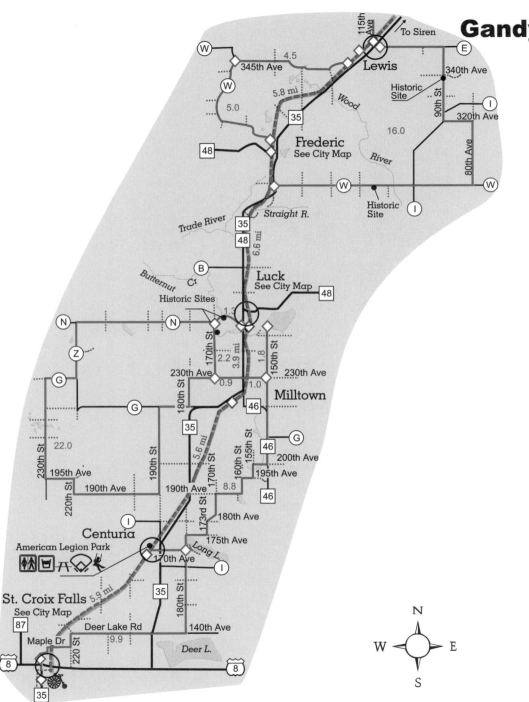

To Siren

115th Ave

Lewis

W

345th Ave — 4.5

W — 5.8 mi

5.0

35

Wood

Historic Site

340th Ave

E

90th St

320th Ave

I

80th Ave

Frederic
See City Map

48

River

16.0

W

W

Historic Site

I

Trade River

Straight R.

35

48

6.6 mi

B

Butternut Cr

Luck
See City Map

48

N

N

Historic Sites

170th St

1.3

2.2 mi

3.9 mi

150th St

1.8

230th Ave

230th Ave

Z

G

180th St

0.9

1.0

Milltown

46

G

46

35

5.6 mi

160th St

155th St

200th Ave

195th Ave

46

230th St

22.0

190th St

170th St

173rd St

190th Ave

8.8

195th Ave

190th Ave

220th St

180th Ave

I

Centuria

American Legion Park

170th Ave

175th Ave

Long L.

I

St. Croix Falls
See City Map

5.9 mi

35

180th St

87

Maple Dr

220 St

Deer Lake Rd

140th Ave

9.9

Deer L.

8

8

35

N
W — E
S

For Trail Information
See Page 66

M35

Gandy Dancer Trail

Siren to Danbury

18 miles

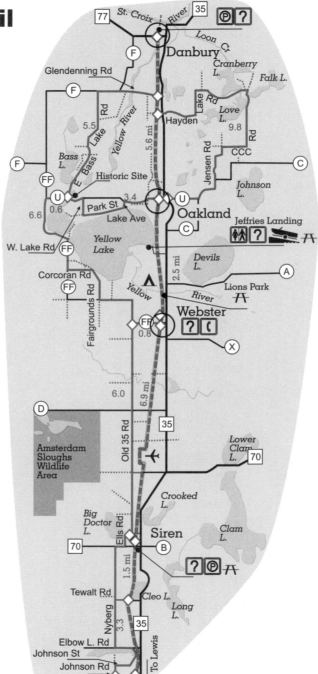

For Trail Information
See Page 66

M36

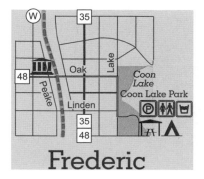

Frederic

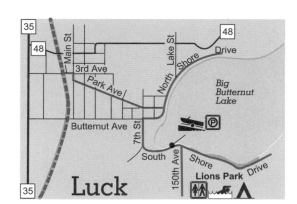

Luck

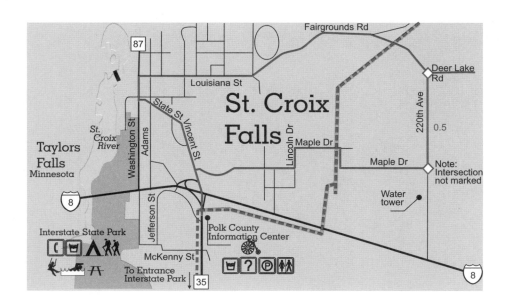

N
W — E
S

For Trail Information
See Page 66

M37

Old Abe Trail

Chippewa Falls to Cornell

18 miles

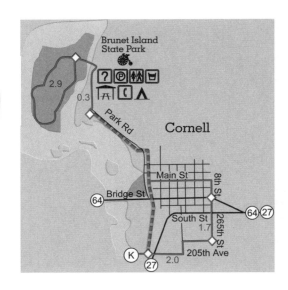

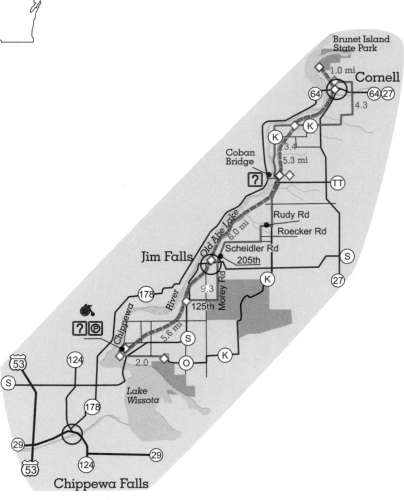

Brunet Island State Park

1.0 mi

Cornell

64 · 64 27

4.3

K

3.4

K · 5.3 mi

Coban Bridge

?

TT

Rudy Rd

Roecker Rd

Jim Falls

Scheidler Rd · 205th

6.0 mi

K · S

Old Abe Lake

9.3

178

River · 125th · Morey Rd

S · 27

Chippewa

5.6 mi

S

53

124

S · 2.0 · O · K

Lake Wissota

178

29

53

29

124

Chippewa Falls

Cornell inset:

Brunet Island State Park

2.9

0.3

Park Rd

Cornell

Main St · 8th St

64 · Bridge St

South St · 265th St

64 27

1.7 · 205th Ave

K · 27 · 2.0

Compass: N · W · E · S

For Trail Information
See Page 71

M38

Red Cedar Trail

Menomonie to Chippewa River Trail

14 miles

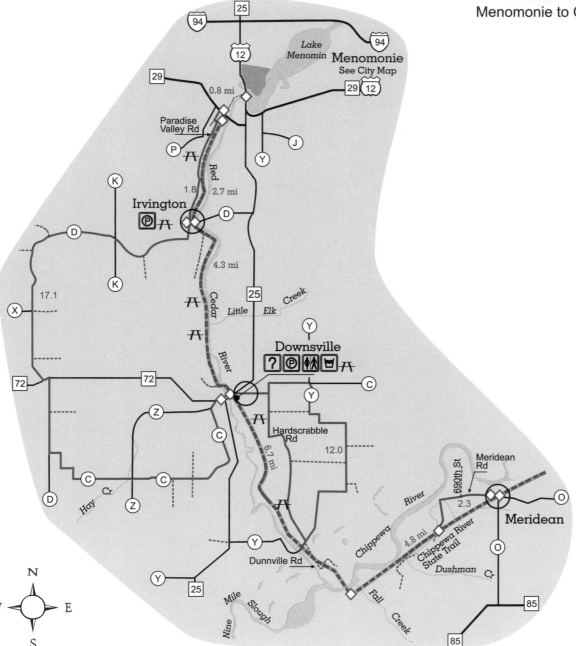

Lake Menomin

Menomonie
See City Map

94
25
12
29

29 12

0.8 mi

Paradise Valley Rd

P

J

Y

Red

1.8   2.7 mi

K

Irvington

P

D

D

4.3 mi

17.1

X

Cedar

Little Elk Creek

25

K

72

72

Z

Downsville

? P

C

Y

C

Hardscrabble Rd

Z

C

River

6.7 mi

12.0

C

C

Meridean Rd

690th St

Chippewa River

2.3

O

Meridean

Hay Cr

Z

D

Y

4.8 mi

Chippewa River State Trail

O

Dunnville Rd

Chippewa

Dushman Cr

Y

Y

25

Nine Mile Slough

Fall Creek

85

85

For Trail Information
See Page 75

M39

N
W   E
S

Red Cedar Trail

City Maps

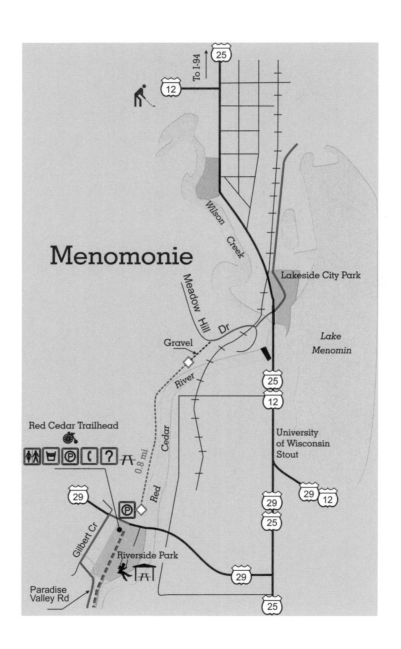

Menomonie

To I-94

Wilson Creek

Meadow Hill Dr

Gravel

River

Red Cedar River

Red Cedar Trailhead

0.8 mi

Lakeside City Park

Lake Menomin

University of Wisconsin Stout

Riverside Park

Gilbert Cr

Paradise Valley Rd

N
W — E
S

For Trail Information
See Page 75

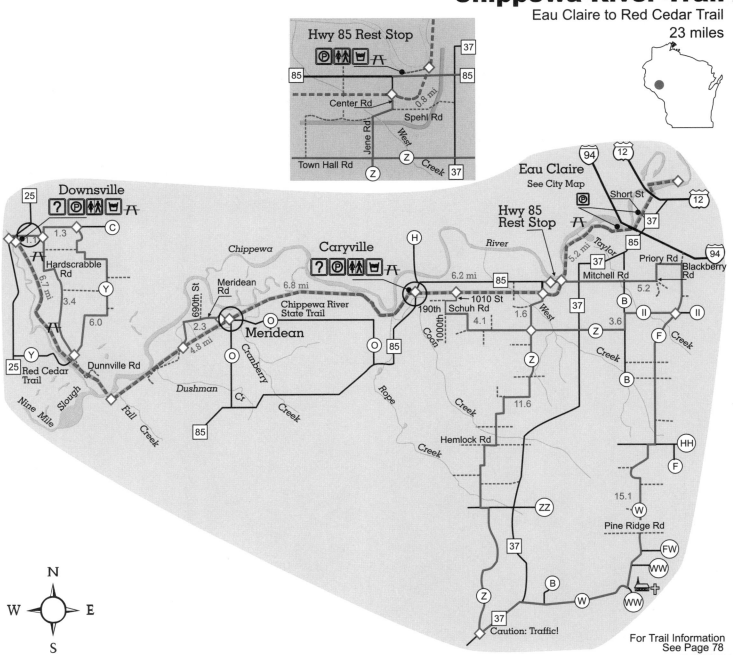

Chippewa River Trail

Eau Claire to Red Cedar Trail

23 miles

Hwy 85 Rest Stop

85 — Center Rd — 85 — 37

0.3 mi

Spehl Rd

Jene Rd — West — Creek

Town Hall Rd — Z — 37

25 — Downsville

? P 👥 🗑 🏕

C

1.1 — 1.3

Hardscrabble Rd — Y

3.4

6.0

6.7 mi

Y

25 — Red Cedar Trail

Dunnville Rd

Nine Mile Slough

Fall Creek

Chippewa

Meridean Rd

690th St

Chippewa River State Trail

6.8 mi

2.3

4.8 mi

Meridean — O — O

Dushman — Cranberry Cr — Creek

85

Caryville

? P 👥 🗑 🏕

H

River

Hwy 85 Rest Stop 🏕

5.2 mi — Taylor

Eau Claire
See City Map

P — Short St

94 — 12

37

12

85

94

Priory Rd — Blackberry Rd

Mitchell Rd — 5.2

6.2 mi — 85

1010 St — Schuh Rd

190th

4.1

1000th — Coon

West — 1.6

37 — B — II — II

Z — 3.6

F — Creek

Z

11.6

Creek

B

Rope

O — 85

Hemlock Rd

Creek

HH — F

15.1 — W

Pine Ridge Rd

ZZ

37

Z — B — W — WW ⛪

FW

WW

37 — Caution: Traffic!

N
W — E
S

For Trail Information
See Page 78

M41

Chippewa River Trail

City Maps

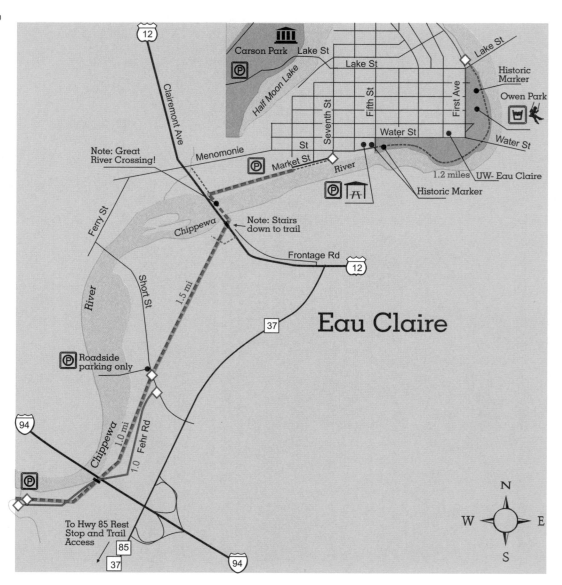

Carson Park

Lake St

Lake St

Lake St

Historic Marker

Owen Park

Half Moon Lake

Seventh St

Fifth St

First Av

St

Water St

Water St

Clairemont Ave

Note: Great River Crossing!

Menomonie

Market St

River

1.2 miles

UW- Eau Claire

Historic Marker

Ferry St

Chippewa

Note: Stairs down to trail

Frontage Rd

12

River

Short St

1.5 mi

37

Eau Claire

Roadside parking only

94

Chippewa

1.0 mi

1.0 Fehr Rd

To Hwy 85 Rest Stop and Trail Access

85

37

94

N

W   E

S

For Trail Information
See Page 78

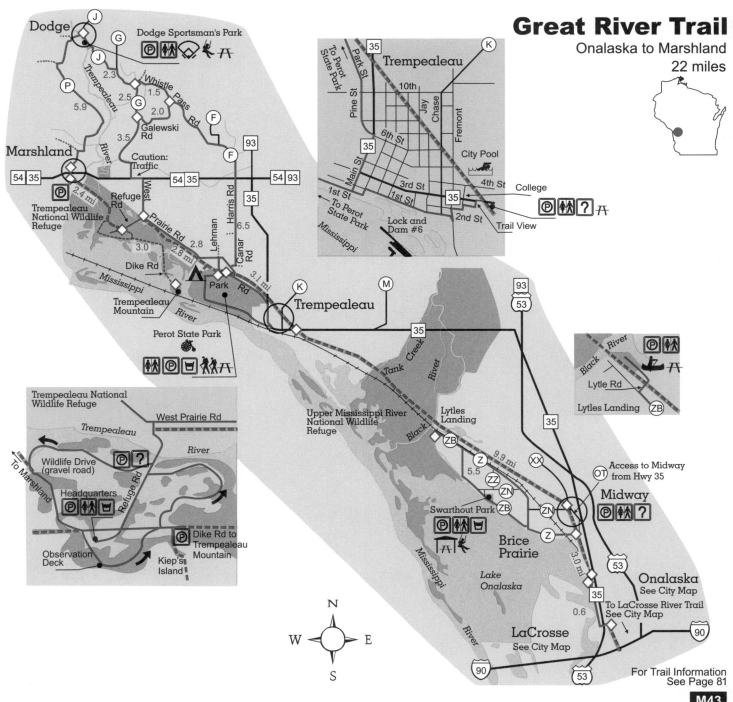

Great River Trail

Onalaska to Marshland
22 miles

Dodge
J
G Dodge Sportsman's Park
J
2.3
P Whistle 1.5
5.9 Trempealeau 2.5 G
2.0
Galewski F
Rd
3.5 F
93
Marshland
54 35
54 35 Caution: Traffic 54 35 54 93
P 2.4 mi West 35
Refuge Rd Prairie Rd 2.8 Lehman Harris Rd 6.5
Trempealeau National Wildlife Refuge 3.0 2.8 mi Canar Rd 35
Dike Rd Park Rd 3.1 mi
Mississippi River
Trempealeau Mountain
Perot State Park

Trempealeau
To Perot State Park Park St 35 K
10th
Pine St Jay Chase Fremont
6th St City Pool
35
Main St 3rd St College
1st St 35
To Perot State Park 1st St 2nd St Trail View
Mississippi Lock and Dam #6
P ? ⚦ ⛺

K Trempealeau M
35

Tank Creek River

Upper Mississippi River National Wildlife Refuge

Lytles Landing
Black ZB
Z 9.9 mi XX
5.5
ZZ ZN
ZB ZN Z

Swarthout Park
P ⚦ ⛺

Brice Prairie
Lake Onalaska

Mississippi River

Trempealeau National Wildlife Refuge
West Prairie Rd
Trempealeau
River
To Marshland Wildlife Drive (gravel road) P ?
Headquarters P ⚦ ⛺
Refuge Rd
P Dike Rd to Trempealeau Mountain
Observation Deck Kiep's Island

93 53
35
Black River P ⚦
Lytle Rd
Lytles Landing ZB

OT Access to Midway from Hwy 35
Midway P ⚦ ?
ZN
Z 3.0 mi 53
Onalaska See City Map
35 To LaCrosse River Trail See City Map
0.6
LaCrosse See City Map
90 53 90

N
W E
S

For Trail Information
See Page 81

M43

Great River Trail

City Maps

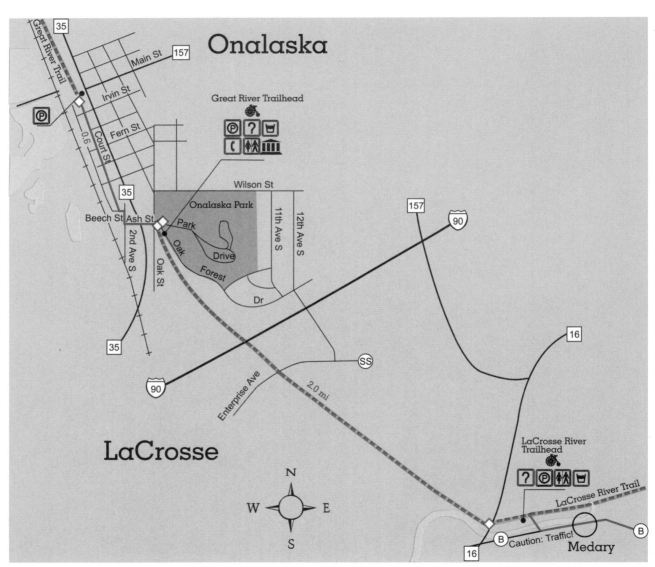

Onalaska

35

Great River Trail

Main St 157

Irvin St

P

Fern St

Court St

0.6

Great River Trailhead

P ? 🛍️
📞 🚶 🏛️

Wilson St

35

Beech St Ash St.

Onalaska Park

Park

2nd Ave S

Oak St

Oak

Drive

Forest

11th Ave S

12th Ave S

157

90

35

Dr

90

SS

16

LaCrosse

Enterprise Ave

2.0 mi

N

W ⊕ E

S

LaCrosse River Trailhead

? P 🚶 🛍️

LaCrosse River Trail

B Caution: Traffic!

16

Medary

B

For Trail Information
See Page 81

LaCrosse River Trail

Medary to Sparta
21 miles

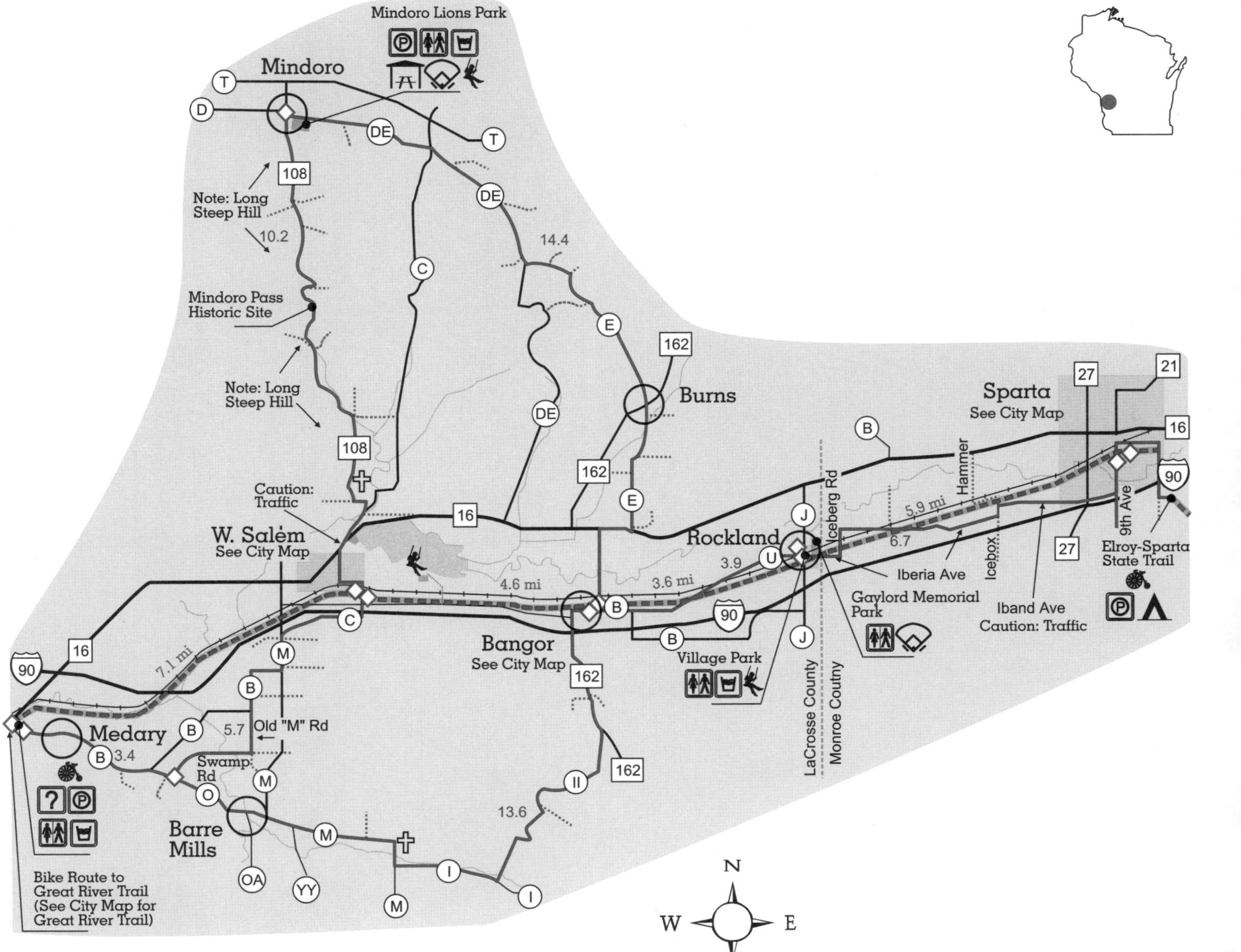

Mindoro Lions Park

Mindoro

Note: Long Steep Hill
10.2

Mindoro Pass Historic Site

Note: Long Steep Hill

108

108

14.4

162

Burns

162

E

Caution: Traffic

16

W. Salem
See City Map

4.6 mi

3.6 mi

Rockland

3.9

Iceberg Rd

B

Sparta
See City Map

Hammer

5.9 mi

27

21

16

90

Icebox

6.7

Iband Ave
Caution: Traffic

9th Ave

Elroy-Sparta
State Trail

27

J

U

Iberia Ave

Gaylord Memorial
Park

Bangor
See City Map

162

B

7.1 mi

C

M

B

Medary

B 3.4

5.7 Old "M" Rd

Swamp Rd

O

M

Barre Mills

OA

YY

M

M

I

I

13.6

II

162

90

B

Village Park

J

LaCrosse County
Monroe County

Bike Route to
Great River Trail
(See City Map for
Great River Trail)

N
W   E
S

LaCrosse River Trail

City Maps

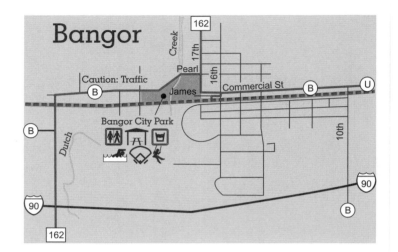

Bangor

Creek

162

17th

Caution: Traffic

Pearl

16th

James

Commercial St

B

U

B

B

Dutch

Bangor City Park

10th

90

90

B

162

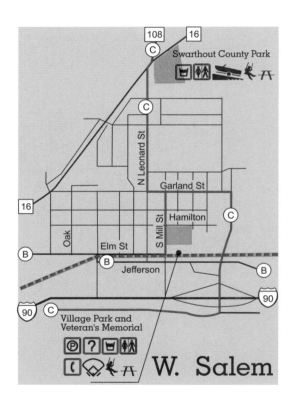

108   16

C

Swarthout County Park

C

N Leonard St

Garland St

16

S Mill St   Hamilton

C

Oak

Elm St

B

B

Jefferson

B

90   C

90

Village Park and
Veteran's Memorial

W. Salem

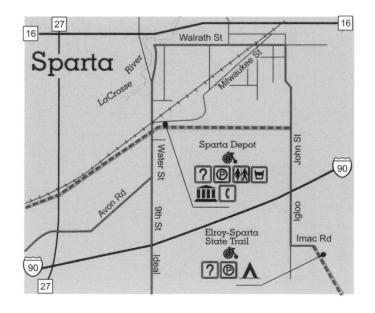

27   16

16

Walrath St

Sparta

River

LaCrosse

Milwaukee St

Water St

John St

Sparta Depot

90

Avon Rd

9th St

Igloo

Imac Rd

Elroy-Sparta
State Trail

90

Ideal

27

For Trail Information
See Page 85

N
W   E
S

Elroy-Sparta Trail

Elroy to Sparta

32 miles

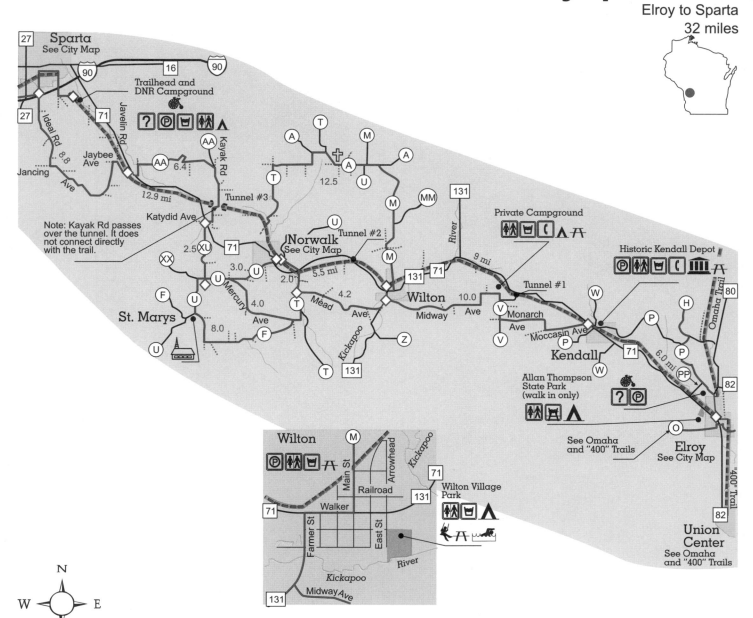

Sparta
See City Map

Trailhead and
DNR Campground

Jaybee Ave

Jancing Ave

Ideal Rd 8.8

Javelin Rd

12.9 mi

Kayak Rd

Tunnel #3

Katydid Ave

Note: Kayak Rd passes
over the tunnel. It does
not connect directly
with the trail.

6.4

12.5

Norwalk
See City Map

Tunnel #2

2.5

3.0

2.0

5.5 mi

4.2

Mercury Ave

Mead Ave

Kickapoo

St. Marys

4.0

8.0

River

Private Campground

Historic Kendall Depot

Omaha Trail

9 mi

Wilton

10.0

Midway Ave

Monarch Ave

Moccasin Ave

Kendall

Allan Thompson
State Park
(walk in only)

See Omaha
and "400" Trails

Elroy
See City Map

6.0 mi

Union
Center
See Omaha
and "400" Trails

Wilton

Main St

Railroad

Arrowhead

Kickapoo

Walker

Wilton Village
Park

Farmer St

East St

River

Kickapoo

Midway Ave

N
W — E
S

See Page 88

M47

Elroy-Sparta Trail
City Maps

N
W · E
S

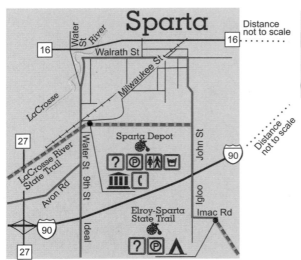

Sparta

Distance not to scale

Water St River
16
Walrath St
Milwaukee St
LaCrosse
27
LaCrosse River State Trail
Water St
9th St
Sparta Depot
Avon Rd
Ideal
90
27
John St
Igloo
Imac Rd
Elroy-Sparta State Trail
16
90
Distance not to scale

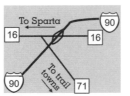

To Sparta
90
16
16
90
To trail towns
71

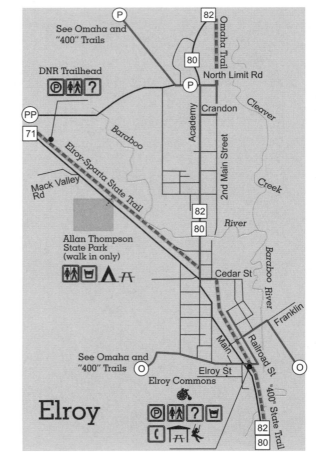

P
See Omaha and "400" Trails
82
Omaha Trail
80
P
North Limit Rd
DNR Trailhead
Academy
Crandon
Cleaver
PP
Baraboo
71
Elroy-Sparta State Trail
2nd Main Street
Creek
Mack Valley Rd
82
80
River
Allan Thompson State Park (walk in only)
Cedar St
Baraboo River
Franklin
Main
Railroad St
See Omaha and "400" Trails
O
"400" State Trail
O
Elroy St
Elroy Commons

Elroy

82
80

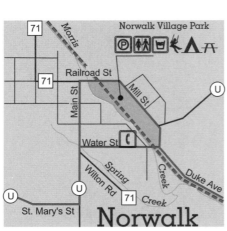

71
Morris
Norwalk Village Park
71
Railroad St
Main St
Mill St
U
Water St
Spring Creek
Wilton Rd
Duke Ave
U
U
71
St. Mary's St

Norwalk

For Trail Information
See Page 88

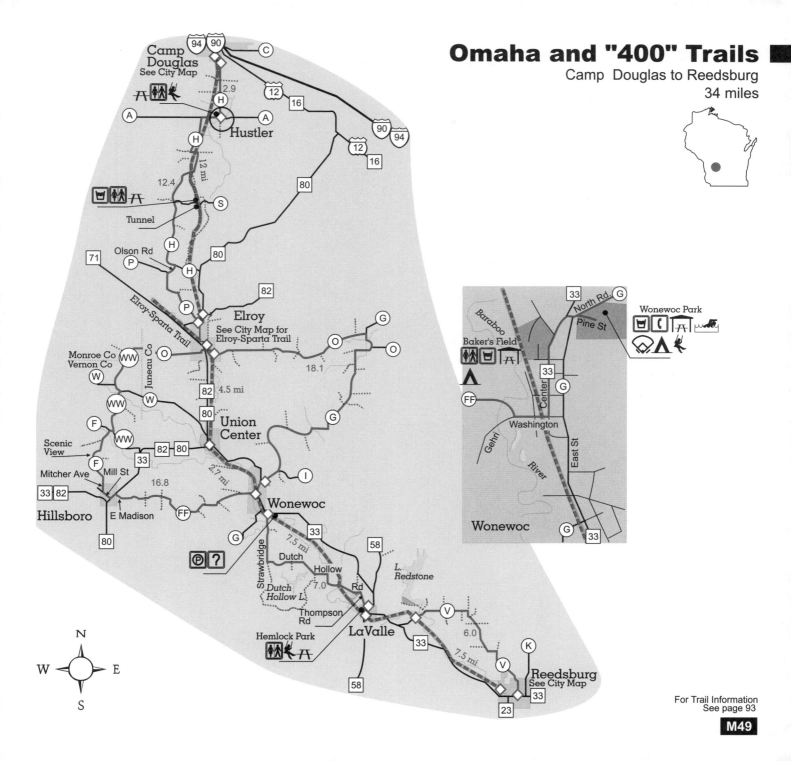

Omaha and "400" Trails
Camp Douglas to Reedsburg
34 miles

Camp Douglas See City Map

Hustler

2.9

12 mi

12.4

Tunnel

Olson Rd

71

Elroy
See City Map for
Elroy-Sparta Trail

Elroy-Sparta Trail

Monroe Co
Vernon Co

Juneau Co

Scenic View

Mitcher Ave

Mill St

E Madison

33 82

Hillsboro

82 80

4.5 mi

Union Center

16.8

2.7 mi

Wonewoc

18.1

Strawbridge

7.5 mi

Dutch
Hollow

7.0

Rd

L. Redstone

Dutch Hollow L.

Thompson Rd

Hemlock Park

LaValle

33

6.0

7.5 mi

Reedsburg
See City Map

23

Wonewoc Park

Baraboo

North Rd.

Pine St

Baker's Field

Washington

Gehri

River

East St

Wonewoc

N
W E
S

For Trail Information
See page 93

M49

Omaha and "400" Trails

City Maps

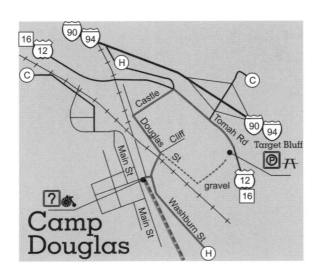

Camp Douglas

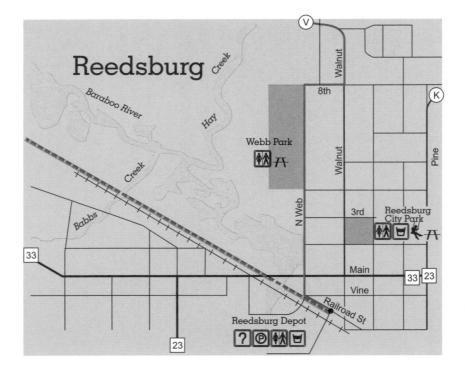

Reedsburg

For Trail Information
See Page 93

M50

Military Ridge Trail

Dodgeville to Blue Mound

18.5 miles

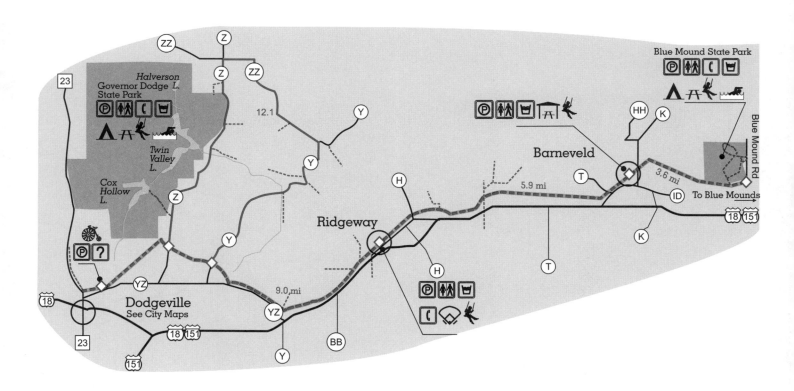

For Trail Information
See Page 96

M51

Military Ridge Trail

Blue Mound to Verona

18.7 miles

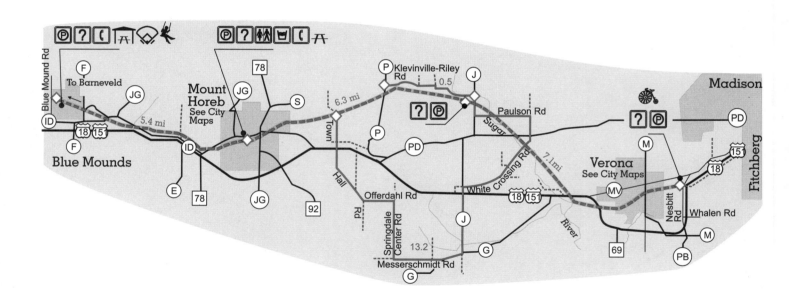

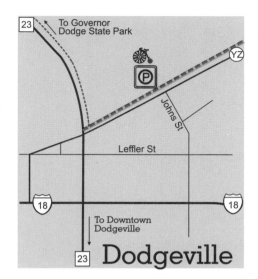

Dodgeville

- 23 To Governor Dodge State Park
- YZ
- Johns St
- Leffler St
- 18
- 18
- To Downtown Dodgeville
- 23

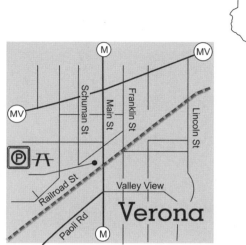

Verona

- M
- MV
- MV
- Schuman St
- Main St
- Franklin St
- Lincoln St
- Railroad St
- Valley View
- Paoli Rd
- M

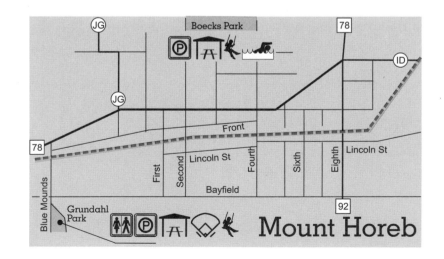

Mount Horeb

- JG
- Boecks Park
- 78
- ID
- JG
- Front
- 78
- First
- Second
- Lincoln St
- Fourth
- Sixth
- Eighth
- Lincoln St
- Bayfield
- Blue Mounds
- Grundahl Park
- 92

N
W · E
S

For Trail Information
See Page 96

M53

Order Blank
Little Transport Press

Bicycle Vacation Guide: Order extras for friends

Twin Cities' Bike Map: The most popular bicycle map in the Twin Cities. Seven counties worth of bicycle friendly roads and trails in the Twin Cities' Area.

	Quantity	Price	Extended
Bicycle Vacation Guide		$16.95	
Twin Cities' Bike Map		$7.95	
		Subtract 10%	
Little Transport Press		Sales tax 6.5% Mn residents	
PO Box 8123 Minneapolis, MN 55408 (Please allow 2 weeks for delivery.)		Shipping: First item $3.50 Additional items $1.00 each	
		Total	

Name _____

Address _____

City _____State _____ Zip_____